Leadership in the Context of a Constitutional Government

Leadership in the Context of a Constitutional Government

Cases and Commentary for the Federal Manager and Students of Public Administration

First Edition

Written By Mark J. Maxin, Esq.

American University

cognella

SAN DIEGO

Bassim Hamadeh, CEO and Publisher
Peaches diPierro, Acquisitions Editor
Skyler Brant, Project Editor
Susana Christie, Senior Developmental Editor
Abbey Hastings, Senior Production Editor
Monica O'Keefe, Editorial Associate
Jessica Delia, Graphic Design Associate
Karisa Kampbell, Licensing Coordinator
Natalie Piccotti, Director of Marketing
Kassie Graves, Senior Vice President, Editorial
Alia Bales, Director, Project Editorial and Production

Printed in the United States of America.

For my wife, Estelle Berman, the love of my life and my heart's constitution.

In memory of my parents, Adele Maxin and William J. Maxin, who always believed in me.

In memory of Joseph V. Kaplan, an outstanding lawyer, professor and advocate for federal employees, whose scholarly insight and passion for the Constitution inspired this book.

Contents

Introduction

There are approximately 2.1 million federal civilian employees.[1] These employees fill positions that are classified into 867 detailed occupations.[2] Federal employees serve in over 600 government departments and agencies[3] and impact almost every aspect of daily living and the common defense and security of American citizens. Despite their extraordinary and diverse work, not to mention the dramatically different missions of their respective agencies, there is one thing all federal employees have in common: every federal employee must take an oath to "support and defend the Constitution of the United States." This oath is so important that it is codified into law.[4] In fact, it is even expressly required in Article VI of the U.S. Constitution.[5] Despite the importance of the oath, however, little attention is given as to what it means. How does a federal employee support and defend the Constitution if the employee does not fully understand its requirements, expectations, and prohibitions? How can a federal supervisor manage their staff and support and defend the Constitution if the supervisor does not understand how the Constitution impacts them as manager?

This book serves as a reminder of the following:

1. *See* Congressional Research Service, Federal Workforce Statistics Sources: OPM and OMB, (2020).
2. *See* U.S. Bureau of Labor Statistics, *2018 Standard Occupational Series*, https://www.bls.gov/soc/.
3. *See* Administrative Conference of the United States, Sourcebook of Executive Agencies 12 (2d ed. 2018) (hereinafter Sourcebook) (citing *U.S. General Services Administration, A–Z Index of U.S. Government Departments and Agencies,* https://www.usa.gov/federal-agencies/a (last visited Oct. 30, 2017), as "the most inclusive list" of Federal government departments and agencies. (Interestingly, ACUS explains that "since what constitutes an agency under the APA is governed on a case-by-case basis through litigation, there is no authoritative list of government agencies.")
4. Oath of Office, 5 U.S.C. § 3331 ("Any individual, except the President, elected or appointed to an office of honor or profit in the civil service or uniformed services, shall take the following oath: 'I, (Name), do solemnly swear (or affirm) that I will support and defend the Constitution of the United States against all enemies, foreign and domestic; that I will bear true faith and allegiance to the same; that I take this obligation freely, without any mental reservation or purpose of evasion; and that I will well and faithfully discharge the duties of the office on which I am about to enter. So help me God.'").
5. U.S. Const. art. VI., § 3 ("The Senators and Representatives before mentioned, and the members of the several State Legislatures, *and all executive and judicial Officers*, both of the United States and of the several states, *shall be bound by Oath and Affirmation, to support this Constitution*; but no religious Test shall ever be required as Qualifications to any Office or public Trust under the United States.") (emphasis added).

- Article II of the Constitution covers the Executive Branch, which includes all federal employees.[6] Every federal employee is, therefore, unique because they are a representative of a limited government that separates powers and creates checks and balances between the federal government and the Legislative Branch[7] and Judicial Branch.[8]
- Every federal employee is also part of the fabric of Federalism, wherein the powers not granted to the federal government by enumerated authorities in Article II remain with the states pursuant to the Tenth Amendment but where federal law takes precedence over state laws under the Supremacy Clause.[9]
- All federal employees have rights and obligations protected by the Bill of Rights, including, but not limited to, the First Amendment right of free speech, including a citizen's right to criticize the government; the First Amendment's Establishment Clause and its prohibition of federal government action that endorses a religion; the Fourth Amendment's prohibition against unreasonable searches and seizures; the Fifth Amendment's guarantee that life, liberty, and property cannot be taken without due process of law and the entitlement of equal protection under the law.
- The federal manager must be mindful that the employees they supervise have the foregoing constitutional rights as well and must be careful not to retaliate because of the exercise of such rights.

This book should also be a reminder of the dramatic impact the Constitution plays on government, including employment law for federal, state, and local governments as compared to private sector employment law. While the federal government, as an employer, must abide by the constitutional rights of its employees, private sector employers do not have a similar obligation because the Constitution only limits government action. For example, if retaliated against by their employer or team because of their speech, neither an employee from Walmart nor a football player in the National Football League is protected by the First Amendment because the Constitution only limits government action. Of course, the employee may be protected by an employment contract, collective bargaining agreement, or state or federal statute. For example, an employee who is removed by a private sector employer because of their race, national origin, gender, or other protected category can bring a complaint of discrimination pursuant to the 1964 Civil Rights Act before the Equal Employment Opportunity Commission. However, a private sector employee may not raise a constitutional argument against their private sector employer because, as previously stated, the Constitution only covers government action.

This revelation that the federal government and its employees must abide by the Constitution, whereas private sector businesses and other nongovernmental entities and their employees do not have similar limitations, raises extraordinary issues about which every federal employee and manager should give careful thought.

First, every federal employee should take great pride that everything they do is bound up in the

6. U.S. Const. art. II.
7. U.S. Const. art. I.
8. U.S. Const. art. III.
9. U.S. Const. art. VI, para. 2.

Constitution. All federal employees help implement federal law and, in doing so, "take care" that the laws are faithfully executed, in accordance with Article II, Section 3 of the Constitution. Further, they must implement the law in a manner that does not violate the Bill of Rights and may not act beyond the authority provided to them by federal statute. While the limitations imposed on federal employees can be deemed significant and confusing, it is a "delicious burden," wherein every action of a federal employee comes with the responsibility to act in accordance with the will of our forefathers.

Second, if a federal employee violates a clearly established constitutional right, they could be sued in their individual capacity. This is generally referred to as a Bivens action.[10] While recent legal developments have made such a lawsuit unlikely to prevail,[11] especially where the remedy for the wrong is covered by federal statute,[12] a federal employee should be aware of the constitutional limitations imposed upon them to avoid being embroiled in such litigation in the first place.

Third, while federal employees do have rights under the Constitution, these rights often provide less protection than when the government infringes on the rights of private citizens. For example, a private citizen's free speech rights regarding protesting government action are only limited by the "imminent lawless action" test of *Brandenburg v. Ohio*,[13] whereas the free speech rights of government employees apply a more management-friendly balancing test between the speech, expressing a matter of public concern, and the disruption it causes in the workplace, in accordance with *Pickering v. Board of Education*.[14]

Fourth, a federal manager must always be mindful that their actions must be in accordance with the Constitution while managing their staff. Federal managers rarely receive training on the Constitution. As a federal sector management employment attorney for over 40 years, I am certain that few managers question whether their management decisions comply with the Constitution. This book provides particular focus on this issue so that a federal manager does not act in a manner that violates the Constitution.

This book is entitled *Leadership in the Context of a Constitutional Government* because it is critical for a leader in the federal government to understand the rights, limits, and authorities that may impact government decision-making under the Constitution. Leading without knowing is like driving without seeing—even if you understand exactly where you are going as a leader and how to get there, without sufficient knowledge, you are bound to crash. Knowledge, along with inspiration, helps one see and understand and serves as a guiding light that allows the leader to arrive at their destination safely.

This book is intended to shed light on the Constitution, so the federal manager can avoid unconstitutional roadblocks on their leadership journey and arrive at their destination safely and in accordance with the will of the Founding Fathers. It is designed to raise the manager's consciousness about how the Constitution affects their daily lives at work and otherwise. It is not intended to transform the federal manager into a constitutional expert but to help the manager examine the federal workplace

10. *Bivens v. Six Unknown Named Agents*, 403 U.S. 388 (1971).
11. *Egbert v. Boule*, 142 S. Ct. 1793 (2022).
12. *Liff v. Office of Inspector General for the U.S. Department of Labor*, 881 F.3d 912 (D.C. Cir. 2018) (denying a constitutional cause of action where the Privacy Act covered the wrongdoing).
13. *Brandenburg v. Ohio*, 399 U.S. 444 (1969).
14. *Pickering v. Board of Education*, 391 U.S. 563 (1968).

through a constitutional lens as part of their decision-making process, spot issues and concerns that may implicate the Constitution, and seek legal counsel before they act.

Each chapter includes important cases interpreting the Constitution, with probing questions to enhance class discussion and a section focused on how a leader in the federal government is impacted by the constitutional right or obligation covered in the chapter. The outline of the book is as follows:

Chapter 1: A Brief History and Overview of the U.S. Constitution. This chapter provides a brief history of the Constitution and focuses on separation of powers, checks and balances, and federalism.

Chapter 2: The Limited Power of Congress. This chapter focuses on the Commerce Clause and other enumerated authorities.

Chapter 3: Due Process. This chapter addresses due process generally and focuses on due process and disciplinary actions in the federal government.

Chapter 4: Free Speech and the First Amendment. This chapter addresses the right to free speech generally and focuses on the free speech rights of federal employees.

Chapter 5: Whistleblowing of the President and Federal Employees. This chapter focuses on the rights of federal employees under the Whistleblower Protection Enhancement Act.

Chapter 6: The Fourth Amendment. This chapter focuses on protections against unreasonable searches and seizures generally and in the federal government workplace.

Chapter 7: Religious Expression and the First Amendment. This chapter focuses on the rights of federal employees under the Free Exercise Clause and the Establishment Clause.

Chapter 8: Sovereign, Absolute, and Qualified Immunity for the President and Government Employees. This chapter focuses on when the President and federal employees can be sued or criminally prosecuted in their individual capacity.

Chapter 9: Nexus, Appropriate Penalty Analysis, and the Federal Disciplinary Action Process as Distinguished from the Unacceptable Performance Action Process. This chapter focuses on rendering reasoned decisions when disciplining federal employees and taking performance based actions.

Chapter 10: The Limited Power of the President and Article II Enumerated Authorities. This chapter focuses on Article II enumerated authorities of the President and employees of the executive branch.

Chapter 11: Investigatory Interviews and the Constitution: *Miranda*, *Kalkines*, *Garrity* Warnings and *Weingarten* Rights. This chapter focuses on the rights of federal employees under investigation for misconduct.

Chapter 12: An Overview of Administrative Law. This chapter focuses on rulemaking, the prohibition of arbitrary and capricious government decision-making, and a discussion on recent Supreme Court caselaw that ends deference to an agency's interpretation of a law it administers.

Chapter 13: An Overview of the Equal Protection Clause and Civil Rights Laws. This chapter focuses on a practical discussion of the Equal Protection Clause and discrimination in the private sector and federal government workplace.

Chapter 14: An Overview of Substantive Due Process. This chapter focuses on the meaning of substantive due process and the impact the decision *Dobbs v. Jackson Women's Health Organization* had on limiting the right to an abortion and potentially other substantive due process rights.

Finally, this book is designed to help the federal employee appreciate the unique nature of their job. The constitutional oath separates the federal employee from the private sector employee, and it is my hope that after reading this book, the oath's promise—to "support and defend the Constitution"—will gain new meaning for the federal employee, who can return to their place of work with a renewed pride in their job as well as wisdom and vision imparted by the Founding Fathers.

Chapter 1

A Brief History and Overview of the U.S. Constitution

Introduction

This chapter provides a brief history of the creation of the Constitution, from the Articles of Confederation, through the Constitutional Convention including the debates over slavery, representational rights of large vs small states, whether to include a list of individual rights upon which the government could not violate, and the eventual adoption of a Bill of Rights. This chapter also briefly summarizes core doctrines upon which the Constitution relies, Separation of Powers, Checks and Balances, Federalism, and the central goal of our Forefathers, to create a workable national government that does not invade the fundamental rights of its citizens. This will be followed by a section on Leadership in the Content of a Constitutional Government, which focuses on how the Constitution fundamentally influences the rights and obligations of a manager in the Federal government. Finally, the Chapter includes links to the landmark Supreme Court decisions *Marbury vs. Madison*[1], and *Immigration and Naturalization Service v. Chadha*,[2] followed by probing questions about these cases to stimulate the thought of Federal managers and students of public administration.

1. 5 U.S. 137 (1803)
2. 462 U.S. 919, 959 (1983).

A Brief History of the Constitution[3]

On September 3, 1783, the Revolutionary War ended, and Great Britain formally recognized the independence of the United States in the Treaty of Paris. The United States was a free nation, and its first constitution was the Articles of Confederation. The Articles were in effect from 1781 to 1789 and were a strong reaction by the 13 states to a powerful British King and Parliament that minimized state independence and authority. The Articles of Confederation created a "league of friendship" between 13 strong independent sovereign states and a very weak and ineffective Congress with insufficient power to regulate commerce between the states or to tax the citizens of the new nation. It had no authority to enforce any legislation it passed and could only ask the states for funding. Thus, Congress could not effectively protect the United States against foreign invasion, nor function with a depleted treasury. It had little power to resolve disputes amongst the states over territory, navigational rights, or trade which "threatened to tear the country apart."[4]

1. In May of 1787, the Constitutional Convention assembled in Philadelphia to revise the Articles of Confederation. Seventy-four delegates were appointed to the convention, of which 55 attended sessions. James Madison proposed the creation of a strong national government, with three branches: the legislative, executive, and judicial, but with each branch designed to check and balance the powers of the others. The proposal included a legislature divided into a Senate and House of Representatives, and representation in both houses to be determined by each state's population. This system of government, which favored large states over smaller populated states, was referred to as the "Virginia Plan." A major feature of the Virginia Plan created a national veto over state laws, "meant to prevent tyranny in the states."[5]
2. William Paterson, a New Jersey delegate, proposed a one body legislature that gave equal representation regardless of the population of the state. This system of government, which favored smaller states, was referred to as the "New Jersey Plan."
3. Ultimately the delegates adopted the "Connecticut Compromise," which created a bicameral (two house) legislature, with equal state representation in the Senate regardless of population, and proportional state representation in the House of Representatives, based on the population of individual states. The Virginia Plan's national veto over state laws was not adopted.[6]
4. State representation in the House of Representation, and direct taxation, would be determined by the number of free white persons and three-fifths of "all other persons," meaning the slaves. It was understood that without this compromise the convention would have been unable to reach

3. The History of the Constitution set forth in this chapter is gleaned from the National Archives: "Constitution of the United States—A History," https://www.archives.gov/founding-docs/more-perfect-union. For a more detailed account, the reader is encouraged to read the entire version set forth in this link. There are also marvelous documents and videos at the National Constitution Center available if you require additional information related to the history of the Constitution or any subject matter related to the Constitution. https://constitutioncenter.org/.
4. https://www.archives.gov/milestone-documents/articles-of-confederation
5. https://www.senate.gov/civics/common/generic/Virginia_Plan_item.htm
6. https://www.senate.gov/civics/common/generic/Virginia_Plan_item.htm

agreement on the Constitution.[7] See Article I, Section 2 of the Constitution:

> Representatives and direct Taxes shall be apportioned among the several States which may be included within this Union, according to their respective Numbers, which shall be determined by adding to the whole Number of free Persons, including those bound to Service for a Term of Years, and *excluding Indians not taxed, three fifths of all other Persons.* (Emphasis added)

5. Another issue arose regarding whether to stop or continue unlimited slave importation. A compromise was reached. In exchange for limiting continued slave importation for 20 years, until 1808, slaves were permitted to be sold within the borders of the United States without limitation.[8] See Article I, Section 9, Clause 1 of the Constitution:

   > The Migration or Importation of such Persons as any of the States now existing shall think proper to admit, shall not be prohibited by the Congress prior to the Year one thousand eight hundred and eight, but a Tax or duty may be imposed on such Importation, not exceeding ten dollars for each Person.

6. Further, the Constitution prohibited the foregoing clause from being amended. See Article V:

   > Provided that no Amendment which may be made prior to the Year One thousand eight hundred and eight shall in any Manner affect the first and fourth Clauses in the Ninth Section of the first Article.

7. The Constitution also contains a "fugitive slave clause"[9] which required slaves that escaped to free states be returned to their owner. See Article IV Section 2 Clause 3:

   > No Person held to Service or Labour in one State, under the Laws thereof, escaping into another, shall, in Consequence of any Law or Regulation therein, be discharged from such Service or Labour, but shall be delivered up on Claim of the Party to whom such Service or Labour may be due.

8. The fugitive slave clause was ultimately nullified in 1865 by the 13th Amendment's abolition of slavery:

   > Neither slavery nor involuntary servitude, except as a punishment for crime whereof the party shall have been duly convicted, shall exist within the United States, or any place subject to their jurisdiction.

7. https://www.archives.gov/founding-docs/more-perfect-union, p.7
8. https://www.archives.gov/education/lessons/slave-trade.html#toc-the-act-prohibiting-the-importation-of-slaves-1808-2
9. https://constitution.congress.gov/browse/essay/artIV-S2-C3-1/ALDE_00013571/%5b%27clause%27%5d

a. It took a civil war and between 600,00 and 800,000 deaths before this amendment was ratified.[10]
b. Another difficult issue that arose involved the method of electing the President. The United States National Archives describes how our Forefathers arrived at a compromise to create the Electoral College, set forth in Article II.
c. A number of proposals including direct election by the people, by state legislatures, by state governors, and by the national legislature were considered. The result was the electoral college, a master stoke of compromise ... The large states got proportional strength in the number of delegates, the state legislatures got the right of selecting delegates, and the House the right to choose the President in the event no candidate received a majority of electoral votes.[11]

9. Our Forefathers also had to decide whether the Constitution should include a list of fundamental rights upon which the government could not violate. On September 12, 1787, George Mason proposed a Bill of Rights. This was rejected, in part, because of concern that continuing extended debate might endanger passage of the Constitution itself. Further, as discussed in more detail below, James Madison at that time did not think it was necessary to include such a list of rights. He eventually strongly embraced including a Bill of Rights.[12]
10. The Constitution was signed by 38 of the 41 delegates present on September 17, 1787.[13] George Mason (Virginia), Elbridge Gerry (Massachusetts), and Edmond Randolph (Virginia) refused to sign because the Constitution did not include a Bill of Rights.[14] They were referred to as "Anti-Federalists." Other Anti-Federalists were opposed to the Constitution for various reasons such as the fear of losing power, expressing a general revulsion against taxation and suspicion that a centralized government would be insensitive to local interests. The "Federalists," like George Washington, James Madison, Alexander Hamilton, and John Jay, supported the Constitution and set out to ratify it.[15]
11. The Constitution required nine of thirteen states to ratify it. By January 9, 1788, five of the nine states required for ratification had approved the Constitution–Delaware, Pennsylvania, New Jersey, Georgia, and Connecticut. But the eventual outcome remained uncertain in pivotal states such as Massachusetts, New York, and Virginia. On February 6, 1988, with Federalists agreeing to recommend a list of amendments amounting to a Bill of Rights, Massachusetts ratified the Constitution. This paved the way for final ratification of the Constitution. On July 2, 1788, New Hampshire became the 9th state needed to ratify the Constitution. All states eventually ratified

10. https://www.history.com/news/american-civil-war-deaths
11. https://www.archives.gov/founding-docs/more-perfect-union, p.9
12. https://www.archives.gov/founding-docs/bill-of-rights/how-did-it-happen
13. https://www.history.com/this-day-in-history/u-s-constitution-ratified#:~:text=On%20September%2017%2C%201787%2C%20after%20three%20months%20of,delegates%20present%20at%20the%20conclusion%20of%20the%20convention.
14. https://www.archives.gov/founding-docs/more-perfect-union, p.12
15. Id at p. 12.

the Constitution. Rhode Island, which had rejected the Constitution in March 1788, approved it on May 29, 1790.[16]

The Bill of Rights

The Bill of Rights, written by James Madison, refers to the first 10 amendments of the Constitution and includes some of our most cherished liberties and were eventually ratified by the States and went into effect on December 15, 1791. The Bill of Rights initially applied only to the National Government, not the States. However, the 14th Amendment, passed by Congress on June 13, 1866, and ratified on July 9, 1868, extended the Bill of Rights to the States, and ensured that those fundamental rights also applied to formerly enslaved people.[17] The history of the Bill of Rights is as follows:

1. Many Americans, persuaded by a pamphlet written by George Mason, opposed the Constitution. As previously discussed, Mason, along with Elbridge Gerry and Edmond Randolph, were present on the final day of the convention and refused to sign the Constitution because it lacked a declaration of fundamental individual rights upon which the government could not trample.
2. James Madison initially argued that a Bill of Rights was unnecessary because "the government can only exert the powers specified by the Constitution." But he eventually agreed when ratification was in danger in the key state of Massachusetts. James Madison, once the most vocal opponent of the Bill of Rights, eventually saw the wisdom in it and introduced a list of amendments to the Constitution on June 8, 1789. Madison had come to appreciate the importance voters attached to these protections, the role that enshrining them in the Constitution could have in educating people about their rights, and the chance that adding them might prevent its opponents from making more drastic changes to it.[18]
3. The House passed a joint resolution containing 17 amendments based on Madison's proposal. The Senate changed the joint resolution to consist of 12 amendments. A joint House and Senate Conference Committee settled remaining disagreements in September. On October 2, 1789, President Washington sent copies of the 12 amendments adopted by Congress to the states. By December 15, 1791, three-fourths of the states had ratified 10 of these, now known as the "Bill of Rights."[19]
4. The first two amendments of the 12 that Congress proposed to the states were rejected: The first dealt with apportioning representation in the House of Representatives; the second prevented members of Congress from voting to change their pay until the next session of Congress. This original "Second Amendment" was finally added to the Constitution as the 27th Amendment, more than 200 years later.[20] As previously stated, the Bill of Rights did not initially apply to the states until the 14th Amendment was ratified in 1868. [21]

16. https://www.archives.gov/founding-docs/more-perfect-union, p.12
17. The 14th Amendment to the Constitution: Civil Rights 1968, National Archives; https://www.archives.gov/milestone-documents/14th-amendment
18. The Bill of Rights: How Did it Happen, National Archives; https://www.archives.gov/founding-docs/bill-of-rights/how-did-it-happen
19. The Bill of Rights: How Did it Happen, National Archives; https://www.archives.gov/founding-docs/bill-of-rights/how-did-it-happen

a. The Bill of Rights identifies certain fundamental guaranteed individual rights and liberties that the government may not violate. This includes such rights as: freedom of religion, speech, press, the right to assemble and petition the government and a prohibition against the government establishing a religion (1st Amendment); the right to keep and bear arms (second amendment); a prohibition against the government forcing homeowners to allow soldiers to use their homes (3rd Amendment); a prohibition against unreasonable searches and seizures of private property (4th Amendment); a protection against self-incrimination in a criminal case, prohibition against being tried twice for the same offense (double jeopardy), a promise that life liberty or property cannot be taken away without due process of law and that private property cannot be taken without just compensation (5th Amendment); a promise that people accused of crimes, are entitled to a speedy and public trial by an impartial jury, are informed of criminal charges, that the accused must face their accusers, and that the accused are allowed to present his or her own witnesses and to be represented by a lawyer (6th Amendment); the right to a jury trial was extended to Federal civil cases (7th Amendment); a prohibition against excessive bail and cruel and unusual punishment (8th Amendment); clarifying that listing specific rights in the Constitution does not mean that people do not have other rights that have not been spelled out (9th Amendment) and that the Federal Government only has those powers delegated in the Constitution and all other powers belongs to the states or to the people (10th Amendment).[22]

5. After the Constitution, the Bill of Rights, and a civil war, the 13 Amendment was ratified on December 6, 1865, which, as previously discussed, abolished slavery.
6. On July 9, 1868, the 14th Amendment was ratified and extended the Bill of Rights to the states. A major provision of the 14th Amendment was to grant citizenship to "All persons born or naturalized in the United States," thereby granting citizenship to formerly enslaved people. Another equally important provision was the statement that "nor shall any state deprive any person of life, liberty, or property, without due process of law; nor deny to any person within its jurisdiction the equal protection of the laws." The right to due process of law and equal protection of the law now applied to both the federal and state governments.[23]

Important Constitutional Doctrines

The Constitution was designed to create a national government strong enough to function effectively, yet

20. Eight Basic Facts about the Bill of Rights, National Constitution Center; https://constitutioncenter.org/interactive-constitution/blog/everything-you-ever-wanted-to-know-about-the-bill-of-rights-2
21. The 14th Amendment to the Constitution: Civil Rights 1968, National Archives; https://www.archives.gov/milestone-documents/14th-amendment
22. Eight Basic Facts about the Bill of Rights, National Constitution Center; https://constitutioncenter.org/interactive-constitution/blog/everything-you-ever-wanted-to-know-about-the-bill-of-rights-2
23. The 14th Amendment to the Constitution: Civil Rights 1968, National Archives; https://www.archives.gov/milestone-documents/14th-amendment

not so powerful as to trample on the rights and liberties of those they govern. In this vein, our Forefathers valued freedom over efficiency[24] in the context of a "workable government."[25] This tension between a workable government that preserves the freedom of its citizens is accomplished, not only by the Bill of Rights, but also by diffusing, checking, balancing, and limiting the power of government in various ways. Thus we will address the meaning and effect of Separation of Powers, Checks and Balances, Creation of a Bicameral Legislative Branch, Creation of a Limited National Government Acting in Accordance with Enumerated Authorities, State Governments Limited by the Supremacy Clause, and Federalism.

The Constitution and Separation of Powers

Our forefathers intended to create a strong national government that could control itself. James Madison described the challenge this way:

> But what is government itself but the greatest of all reflections on human nature? If angels were to govern men, neither external nor internal controls on government would be necessary. In framing a government which is to be administered by men over men, the great difficulty lies in this: You must first enable the government to control the governed; and in the next place, oblige it to control itself.

See Federalist No. 51.[26] To enable the national government to control itself our forefathers believed that "Ambition must be made to counteract ambition." Id. Thus, they created a government wherein ambition in one branch of government is counteracted by ambition in another branch. Power would not be concentrated in a king, or single branch of government, but would be diffused. As James Madison wrote:

> "[t]he accumulation of all powers, legislative, executive, and judiciary, in the same hands, whether of one, a few, or many, and whether hereditary, self-appointed, or elective, may justly be pronounced the very definition of tyranny."
>
> James Madison, Federalist No. 47.[27]

The concept of diffusing power within different branches of the national government, is referred to as "Separation of Powers." Our Constitution separates the power of government between three separate branches: Article I, the Legislative Branch (Congress) responsible for enacting laws and, among other things, appropriating the funds necessary for the government to operate; Article II, the Executive Branch, headed by a single President of the United States, and which currently includes approximately 2.1 million Federal workers, who, among other things, "takes care" that the laws passed by Congress are implemented and properly administered; and Article III, the Judicial Branch, headed by a single Supreme Court and a system of Federal courts created by Congress, that interprets the Constitution and laws and applies their

24. *Immigration and Naturalization Service v. Chada*, 462 U.S. 919, 959 (1983)
25. *Youngstown Sheet & Tube Co. v. Sawyer*, 343 U.S. 579, 635 (1952) (Jackson, J., concurring).
26. Federalist No. 51; https://founders.archives.gov/documents/Hamilton/01-04-02-0199
27. Federalist No. 47; https://founders.archives.gov/documents/Madison/01-10-02-0266

interpretations to controversies brought before it. The Supreme Court's interpretation of the Constitution and the law is final.

By diffusing power amongst the three independent branches, with no one branch more powerful than another, the Framers envisioned a workable government that would create both "separateness and interdependence, autonomy but reciprocity" within the national government even as it secured liberty amongst its citizens. The Supreme Court in *Youngstown Sheet & Tube Co. v. Sawyer* explained:

> While the Constitution diffuses power the better to secure liberty, it also contemplates that practice will integrate the dispersed powers into a workable government. It enjoins upon its branches separateness but interdependence, autonomy but reciprocity.[28]

The Supreme Court in *Bond v. United States,* further emphasized:

> Separation-of-powers principles are intended, in part, to protect each branch of government from incursion by the others. Yet the dynamic between and among the branches is not the only object of the Constitution's concern. The structural principles secured by the separation of powers protect the individual as well.[29]

Finally, the Supreme Court in *Immigration and Naturalization Service v. Chadha* explained:

> ... the Framers ranked other values higher than efficiency ... The choices we discern as having been made in the Constitutional Convention impose burdens on governmental processes that often seem clumsy, inefficient, even unworkable, but those hard choices were consciously made by men who had lived under a form of government that permitted arbitrary governmental acts to go unchecked. There is no support in the Constitution or decisions of this Court for the proposition that the cumbersomeness and delays often encountered in complying with explicit constitutional standards may be avoided, either by the Congress or by the President. (Citation omitted). With all the obvious flaws of delay, untidiness, and potential for abuse, we have not yet found a better way to preserve freedom than by making the exercise of power subject to the carefully crafted restraints spelled out in the Constitution.[30]

The Separation of Powers doctrine may be violated in two ways:

1. One branch may interfere impermissibly with the other's performance of its constitutionally assigned function. Alternatively, the doctrine may be violated when one branch assumes a function that more properly is entrusted to another.[31]
2. More than two centuries after the ratification of the Constitution, separation of power questions remain amongst the most vexing and complicated issues before the Supreme Court today.[32]

28. *Youngstown Sheet & Tube Co. v. Sawyer,* 343 U.S. 579, 635 (1952) (Jackson, J., concurring)
29. *Bond v. United States*, 564 U.S. 211, 222 (2011)
30. *462 U.S. 919*, (1983).
31. *INS v. Chadha*, 462 U.S. 919, 963 (1983).

The Constitution and a System of Checks and Balances

In addition to separating powers amongst the branches, our Forefathers believed: "The structure of the Government must furnish the proper checks and balances between the different departments." James Madison, Federalist No. 51. The concept of creating within each branch of government specific authorities to limit the abuse of another is commonly referred to as a "system of checks and balances."

Examples of checks and balances include but are not limited to the following: Congress has the power to pass a law, but the President has the power to veto it and Congress can override the veto with two thirds vote by both houses of Congress and the Supreme Court can overturn that law if a case is brought before it and the law is found to be either unconstitutional or otherwise illegal. The President can negotiate a treaty, but it does not become a formal treaty of the United States unless two thirds of the Senate ratifies the treaty. Again, the Supreme Court can overturn a treaty in a case brought before it if it has jurisdiction and it determines the treaty illegal. The President may wish to go to war, but cannot do so absent persuading Congress, because only Congress has the Power to declare war, yet Congress relies on the President to implement it, even as the President relies on Congress to appropriate funds to prosecute the war. The President can nominate certain high-level officials in the Federal government or Supreme Court Justices, but the nominee is only appointed after the advice and consent of Senate. The House of Representatives can impeach a President and the Senate convict the President for high crimes and misdemeanors. Federal Judges can also be removed by Congress via impeachment. These are just a few of the many checks and balances created in the Constitution.

The Constitution Further Diffuses Power Within the Legislative Branch and Balances Power Between the Large and Small States.

Under Article I, power is diffused within Congress because a law cannot be passed absent agreement of both the House of Representatives and the Senate. Further, as previously discussed, our Forefathers sought to design a legislative branch that balanced the power and representational rights of both the large and small states. Under Article I, the Legislative branch is comprised of a bicameral House of Representatives and a Senate which together form the Congress. The number of representatives in the House of Representatives, 435, is apportioned based upon each state's population The number of senators, 100, is evenly distributed (2 senators per state) regardless of each state's population. California currently has 53 members of the House of representatives, whereas states with the smallest population: Alaska, Delaware, Montana, North Dakota, South Dakota, Vermont, and Wyoming only have 1 representative. In the Senate, however, there are 2 senators per state, regardless of state population. Accordingly, in the Senate, California has the same number of representatives, 2, as the smallest population states referenced above.[33] Some scholars have asserted this permits domination by the minority. James

32. *West Virginia v. U.S. Environmental Protection Agency, 597* U.S. (2022)
33. https://www.house.gov/representatives

Madison "bitterly opposed" equal representation for every state in the Senate[34] as did Alexander Hamilton.[35] It has been postulated that "By 2040, if population trends continue, 70% of Americans will be represented by just 30 senators, and 30% of Americans by 70 senators."[36]

The Constitution, Enumerated Authorities, and Limited Government

To create a limited national government, the Constitution permits each branch to act (with few exceptions) only in accordance with enumerated authorities set forth in the Constitution. Enumerated authorities are powers identified in the Constitution for each branch of the National government. Thus, the Constitution serves as a guardrail to prevent an overzealous branch from acting beyond the scope intended by our Forefathers. Thus, President Truman could not authorize seizing a steel mill in a time of war where the Constitution did not provide him with the authority to do so.[37] Enumerated authorities, like the power of Congress to lay and Collect taxes or regulate interstate commerce, are required for Congress to Act. Congress also has implied power under the necessary and proper clause under the Constitution, where those impowers are otherwise related to an enumerated authority. This will be discussed at length in Chapter 2 of this book.

The Constitution and Federalism: The Interaction Between the National and State Governments

The Framers sought to further diffuse power between the national government and the states. Federalism is a system of government that divides power between the national government and the state governments. Whereas the national government may only act pursuant to enumerated authorities set forth in the Constitution, "State legislatures, exercising their plenary police powers, are not limited to Congress's enumerated powers ..."[38] Thus, the Constitution imposes far fewer limitations on the state government to act. For example, in *US. v. Lopez,*[39] Congress could not pass the Gun Free School Zone Act, which prohibited carrying a gun within 1,000 feet of a school, because no enumerated authorities in the Constitution authorized Congress to pass such a law. However, a state legislature, not limited by the enumerated authorities under the Federal Constitution, could pass such a state law in accordance with its plenary police powers, so long as it did not violate its own state Constitution in the process. Moreover, the broad authority of the states to act is further supported by the 10th Amendment to the Constitution which provides:

34. See *Small States are getting a much bigger say in who gets on the Supreme Court* by Ronald Brownstein, CNN (July 10, 2018)
35. See *Alexander Hamilton Speaks Out III: Two Senators per State Regardless of Population,* by Hendrik Hertzberg, The New Yorker (January 8, 2011)
36. *Democrats Increasing Say American Democracy is Sliding Toward Minority Rule* by Mara Liasson NPR (June 9, 2021)
37. *Youngstown Sheet & Tube Co. v. Sawyer,* 343 U.S. 579 (1952
38. *Torres v. Lynch*, 578 U.S. 452, 457–58, (2016).
39. *US. v. Lopez,* 514 U.S. 549 (1995).

The powers not delegated to the United States by the Constitution, nor prohibited by it to the states, are reserved to the states respectively, or to the people.

Federalism and the Limitations Imposed on the States by the Supremacy Clause and Other Constitutional Provisions

The Constitution does impose some limitations on the states. A major check on state power is the Supremacy Clause. Article VI clause 2. The Supremacy Clause provides a clear rule that federal law "shall be the supreme Law of the Land ... any Thing in the Constitution or Laws of any state to the Contrary notwithstanding."[40] Put simply, federal law preempts contrary state law.[41]

Federal law may preempt state law under the Supremacy Clause in three ways—by "express preemption," by "field preemption," or by "conflict preemption." Express preemption occurs when federal law explicitly preempts state law. Field preemption applies where Congress has legislated comprehensively to occupy an entire field of regulation, leaving no room for the states to supplement federal law and conflict preemption arises where state law "conflicts with federal law." These three types of preemption are forms of "ordinary preemption" that serve as federal defenses to a state law claim.[42] For example, the state of Arizona immigration law was unconstitutional because it was preempted by Federal immigration law.[43]

Other limitations on the states in the Constitution are set forth in Article I, Section 10:

> Section 10: No State shall enter into any Treaty, Alliance, or Confederation; grant Letters of Marque and Reprisal; coin Money; emit Bills of Credit; make any Thing but gold and silver Coin a Tender in Payment of Debts; pass any Bill of Attainder, ex post facto Law, or Law impairing the Obligation of Contracts, or grant any Title of Nobility.
>
> No State shall, without the Consent of the Congress, lay any Imposts or Duties on Imports or Exports, except what may be absolutely necessary for executing its inspection Laws: and the net Produce of all Duties and Imposts, laid by any State on Imports or Exports, shall be for the Use of the Treasury of the United States; and all such Laws shall be subject to the Revision and Controul of the Congress.
>
> No State shall, without the Consent of Congress, lay any Duty of Tonnage, keep Troops, or Ships of War in time of Peace, enter into any Agreement or Compact with another State, or with a foreign Power, or engage in War, unless actually invaded, or in such imminent Danger as will not admit of delay.

The states are further limited by Article IV Section 2 of the Constitution which provides in part that "The Citizens of each State shall be entitled to all Privileges and Immunities of Citizens in the several

40. *Arizona v. United States*, 567 U.S. 387, 399, (2012).
41. *Hughes v. Talen Energy Mktg., LLC,* 578 U.S. 150, 162 (2016).
42. *Richards v. New Rez, LLC,* No. CV ELH-20-1282, 2022 WL 657568, at *21 (D. Md. Mar. 4, 2022) (case cites referenced herein omitted).
43. *U.S. v. Arizona, supra.*

States." For example, the Privileges and Immunities Clause has enjoyed a long association with protecting individual rights to travel and migrate interstate.[44]

Upon the ratification of the 14th Amendment, states were bound and limited by the Bill of Rights as well.[45]

In conclusion, by creating government that separates and diffuses power with checks and balances between the branches, and between the national government and the states, the Constitution creates an intricate and complex limited government, which must work together to accomplish its goals and in doing so preserves the freedom of its citizenry.

Leadership in the Context of a Constitution Government

Some of the leadership lessons learned from our forefathers include be courageous, inventive, be adaptive and learn on the job and learn to function as a team.[46] Other important lesson learned from the drafting of the Constitution, is the importance of communicating and compromising with those having differing views. Whether the issue involved the right of small states versus big states, whether to have a strong central government or one that defers more to the states, whether to include a Bill of Rights in the Constitution or address it later, the leadership lesson is to listen respectfully to all views, not let the perfect be the enemy of the good and to compromise and work together to the extent possible to achieve a common good. However, the Constitution did not initially irradicate slavery. Slavery was not abolished until well after the Constitution was ratified, until after a civil war was waged and until after the 13th Amendment. The delegates to the convention would not have been able to reach agreement, if the Constitution, as originally drafted, required the abolition of slavery. Did the delegates that opposed slavery compromise too much by permitting slavery to continue under the Constitution? How would you have voted if you were a delegate at the Constitutional convention?

Cases and Review Questions

Directions: Use the links provided to access each case. Then, provide complete and detailed responses to the questions and prompts about each case.

Marbury v. Madison, 5 USC 137 (1803)

https://supreme.justia.com/cases/federal/us/5/137/

1. What is the significance of *Marbury v. Madison*?
2. In accordance with *Marbury v. Madison*, what role does the Constitution play in our government and who is the final decisionmaker on what the Constitution says and means?

44. *Zobel v. Williams*, 457 U.S. 55, 78-79 (1982).
45. *Gitlow. New York*, 268 U.S. 652 (1925)
46. See "Four Leadership Lessons from Our Founding Fathers" by Geoff Loftus, Forbes Magazine, (2015)

3. What import did the case have on the status of the Supreme Court?
4. What import did the case have on the appointment authority of the president?
5. How did the Court arrive at its decision to support President Jefferson as a defendant, when it ruled that Marbury should have been entitled to a magistrate position?
6. What would you have done differently, if you were representing Marbury, to ensure his success in this lawsuit?
7. What if Justice Marshall ruled against President Jefferson and President Jefferson decided not to honor the decision? What impact would that have had on our Judicial branch?

Immigration and Naturalization Service v. Chadha, 462 U.S. 919 (1983)

https://supreme.justia.com/cases/federal/us/462/919/

1. What is meant by Bicameralism in Chadha?
2. According to Chadha, what is the highest "value" the Framers reflected in the Constitution?
3. To what extent is efficiency in government sacrificed to benefit other values under our Constitution?
4. Did the Framers err by separating and diffusing power amongst the branches so much that it is difficult for the government to get anything done?
5. In what way if any, would you have changed the Constitution to make our government more efficient?

National Treasury Employees Union v. Reagan

https://openjurist.org/663/f2d/239/national-treasury-employees-union-v-w-reagan-m-boutilier

1. How did *Marbury v. Madison* impact the analysis of whether the plaintiffs were formally appointed to their jobs in the context of the 1981 President Reagan federal hiring freeze case?
2. What determines whether you are appointed to the Federal government?
3. Who can withdraw an offer of appointment in the Federal government and describe the circumstances under which an appointment to a position in the Federal government can be formally withdrawn.
4. What does it say about our legal system that a 1981 freeze decision was impacted by an 1803 Supreme Court decision?

Chapter 2

The Limited Power of Congress: The Commerce Clause and Other Enumerated Authorities

Introduction

This chapter addresses the limitation on Congress to pass laws only in accordance with enumerated authorities in the Constitution, whereas states do not need to comport with this requirement. This chapter focuses on the Commerce Clause as an important enumerated authority behind a significant amount of congressional legislation followed by a discussion of those cases that expand the reach of the Commerce Clause and those that limit its applicability.

This chapter also discusses the Tax and Spend Clause, the Necessary and Proper Clause, the Appropriations Clause, and the Anti-Commandeering restrictions on Congressional authority. There is also discussion of what the courts have called the "Dormant Commerce Clause" and its limitation on state laws designed to unduly interfere with interstate commerce. The chapter concludes with a section on leadership in the context of a limited government and a list of cases with questions for class discussion.

Congress Can Only Pass Laws Pursuant to an Enumerated Authority in the Constitution

Congress has not been given plenary power by the Constitution to pass any law it wants, even if it is clearly in the interest of the public. Rather, the Founding Fathers created a limited government, which only permits Congress to act if authorized by the Constitution, pursuant to "enumerated authorities" set forth therein. If Congress passes a law unrelated to such authorities, it is unenforceable. Thus, a defendant can avoid liability for violating a federal law, by showing that the law itself is unenforceable because there is no authority that would permit Congress to pass it in the first instance.[1] Most enumerated authorities relied upon by Congress are set forth in Article I, Section 8 of the Constitution, which includes but is not limited to the power to lay and collect taxes; borrow money; coin money; establish rules of naturalization and bankruptcy; protect patents and copyrights; establish lower courts; declare war; and raise and support an Army and Navy.[2] Another very important authority, discussed later in this chapter, is the power to regulate interstate commerce.

The States Have Authority to Pass Laws Affecting Local Concerns Pursuant to Their General Police Powers

The states do not have to satisfy the enumerated authority requirement under the U.S. Constitution. Rather, as explained by the Supreme Court in *Lewis v. BT Inv. Managers Inc.*: "In the absence of conflicting federal legislation, the States retain authority under their general police powers to regulate matters of legitimate local concern, even though interstate commerce may be affected."[3] Further, "state police powers are broad in permitting state decisions that relate to public health, safety, and welfare."[4] State laws may not, however, violate the Supremacy Clause, Article VI, Clause 2[5] or their own state constitution. States are also empowered by the Tenth Amendment, which provides: "The powers not delegated to the United States by the Constitution, nor prohibited by it to the states, are reserved to the states respectively, or to the people."[6]

The Commerce Clause

The Commerce Clause is an enumerated authority frequently relied upon by Congress to pass laws. Specifically, Article I, Section 8, Clause 3 provides, "The Congress shall have Power ... To regulate Commerce with foreign Nations, *and among the several States,* and with the Indian Tribes."[7] The reference to commerce "among the several states" is commonly referred to as the "Interstate Commerce Clause." There are more than 700 federal statutes based on either "interstate" or "foreign" commerce."[8] The Commerce Clause has been used to justify an extraordinarily broad array of federal laws, including but not limited to the following:

1. *See U.S. v. Lopez,* 514 U.S. 549 (1995).
2. U.S. Const. art. I, § 8; *see* The Tenth Amendment Center, Thirty Enumerated Powers, https://tenthamendmentcenter.com/historical-documents/united-states-constitution/thirty-enumerated-powers/ (a complete list of 35 enumerated authorities of Congress).
3. *Lewis v. BT Inv. Managers, Inc.*, 447 U.S. 27, 36, (1980)
4. *Velasquez-Rios v. Wilkinson*, 988 F.3d 1081, 1088 (9th Cir. 2021)
5. See U.S. Const. art. I, § 8 (makes federal law the supreme law of the land).
6. See *Murphy v. National Collegiate Athletic Association*, 138 S. Ct. 1461 (2018) ("The legislative powers granted to Congress are sizable, but they are not unlimited. The Constitution confers on Congress not plenary legislative power but only certain enumerated powers. Therefore, all other legislative power is reserved for the States, as the Tenth Amendment confirms.").
7. U.S. Const. art. I, § 8, cl. 3 (emphasis added).
8. Congressional Research Service, The Power to Regulate Commerce: Limits on Congressional Power, Report No. RL8244 (May 16, 2014) https://www.everycrsreport.com/reports/RL32844.html.

> laws relating to agriculture, banking, antitrust, securities, business regulation, energy regulation, hazardous substances, consumer credit, sports regulation, the Internet, endangered species, civil rights, child support, child pornography abortion, criminal law, controlled substances, food, firearms control, terrorism, obscenity, gambling devices, labor, industrial safety, pensions, environmental law, fish and wildlife, medical products, water pollution, atomic energy, shipping, motor vehicle safety, airplanes, and tort litigation.[9]

There are three categories of laws covered by the Interstate Commerce Clause. Specifically, the clause covers laws that (1) regulate the use of *channels* of interstate commerce (e.g., roads, waterways, and airways); (2) regulate and protect the *instrumentalities* of interstate commerce (e.g., cars, trucks, trains, and planes); and (3) regulate activities that *substantially affect* interstate commerce.[10] The Commerce Clause has provided Congress with the authority to pass numerous laws, some of which are described below:

> As *Lopez* acknowledged, the Supreme Court has "upheld a wide variety of congressional Acts regulating intrastate economic activity," based on its conclusion "that the activity substantially affected interstate commerce." *Lopez,* 514 U.S. at 559, 115 S. Ct. 1624. Among the approved objects of regulation are intrastate coal mining, *see Hodel v. Va. Surface Mining & Reclamation Ass'n, Inc.,* 452 U.S. 264, 101 S.Ct. 2352, 69 L.Ed.2d 1 (1981), intrastate extortionate credit transactions, *see Perez v. United States,* 402 U.S. 146, 91 S.Ct. 1357, 28 L.Ed.2d 686 (1971), restaurants utilizing interstate supplies, *see Katzenbach v. McClung,* 379 U.S. 294, 85 S.Ct. 377, 13 L.Ed.2d 290 (1964), inns and hotels accommodating interstate guests, *see Heart of Atlanta Motel, Inc. v. United States,* 379 U.S. 241, 85 S.Ct. 348, 13 L.Ed.2d 258 (1964), and the cultivation of wheat for home consumption, *see Wickard v. Filburn,* 317 U.S. 111, 63 S.Ct. 82, 87 L. Ed. 122 (1942). This list, *Lopez* observed, "is by no means exhaustive, but the pattern is clear": "Where economic activity substantially affects interstate commerce, legislation regulating that activity will be sustained." *Lopez,* 514 U.S. at 560, 115 S. Ct. 1624.[11]

A statute passes constitutional scrutiny under the Commerce Clause if there is a rational basis for concluding that the law substantially affects interstate commerce by applying these four factors:

1. whether the statute relates to an activity that has something to do with "'commerce' or any sort of economic enterprise, however broadly one might define those terms."
2. whether the statute contains an "express jurisdictional element which might limit its reach" to activities having "an explicit connection with or effect on interstate commerce."
3. whether congressional findings in the statute or its legislative history support the judgment that the activity in question has a "substantial effect on interstate commerce"; and whether the link between the activity and a substantial effect on interstate commerce is attenuated.[12]

9. *Id.*
10. *United States v. Lopez, 514 U.S. 549* (1995).
11. *United States v. Peters,* 403 F.3d 1263, 1273 (11th Cir. 2005)

4. If the law does not involve some sort of economic activity, it is not authorized under the Commerce Clause.[13] If the law's connection to "economic activity" is too "attenuated," it is also not covered under the Commerce Clause.[14]

Cases That Broaden the Application of the Commerce Clause

In *Wickard v. Filburn*, the Court upheld a law that imposed a small penalty on an Ohio farmer for growing wheat on 12 or more acres for his personal consumption, under the Agricultural Adjustment Act.[15] The law was sustained under the Commerce Clause because the effect of the law on the price of wheat, *taken cumulatively*, had a substantial effect on interstate commerce.

Similarly, in *Gonzales v. Raich*, the Court upheld the power of Congress to authorize the seizure of doctor-prescribed marijuana, including that grown by the individual in this case for his own use, which was allowed under state law but prohibited under a federal statute: the Controlled Substances Act (CSA).[16] The Supreme Court broadly interpreted commerce as economic activity that substantially affects interstate commerce, and economic activity included "the production, distribution, and consumption of commodities."[17] It held that Marijuana was a "fungible commodity for which there is an established, albeit illegal, interstate market" and that the CSA represented a legislative attempt to comprehensively regulate that market across state lines.[18] By characterizing the CSA as "economic" in nature, the Court was able to apply the cumulative effects principle utilized in *Wickard v. Filburn*[19] and held that the use of medical marijuana had a *cumulative effect* on the black market for marijuana and therefore substantially related to interstate commerce.[20]

The Commerce Clause has played a critical role in authorizing civil rights law in our country. In one of the most prominent examples, the Supreme Court found that the Commerce Clause authorized Congress to pass the 1964 Civil Rights Act.[21]

Cases That Limit the Application of the Commerce Clause

In *U.S. v. Lopez*, the Supreme Court—for the first time in more than fifty years—invalidated a federal law on

12. *See United States v. Gilbert,* 677 F.3d 613, 624 (4th Cir. 2012) (citing U.S. v. *Morrison,* 529 U.S. at 610–13 (2000)).
13. *National Federation of Independent Businesses v. Sebelius* (NFIB), 567 U.S. 519 (2012); *U.S. v. Morrison*, 529 U.S. 598 (2000).
14. *Id.*
15. *Wickard v. Filburn*, 317 U.S. 111 (1942).
16. *Gonzales v. Raich*, 545 U.S. 1, (2005); Controlled Substances Act, 84 Stat. 1236.
17. *Id.*
18. *Id.*
19. *Wickard v. Filburn*, 317 U.S. 111 (1942)
20. *Id.*
21. *See* Heart of Atlanta vs U.S., 379 U.S. 241 (1964) (upholding 1964 Civil Rights Act that required the 216-room Heart of Atlanta Motel to rent its rooms to persons regardless of race); *Katzenbach v. McClung*, 379 U.S. 294 (1964) (upholding the 1964 Civil Rights Act prohibiting racial discrimination at small restaurants, such as Ollie's Bar-B-Q in Birmingham, AL).

the ground that it was outside the scope of the Commerce Clause.[22] The Court found unconstitutional a provision of the Gun-Free School Zone Act that made it a federal crime to possess a gun within a thousand feet of a school. The Court held that the impact of the law did not regulate the purchase of a gun, only where a citizen could carry a gun. Such a law did not regulate economic activity, and while it could be issued by a state under its police powers, the law had an insignificant effect on interstate commerce, failed to meet the "substantially affects" test, and was unenforceable.[23]

In *U.S. v. Morrison,* a student of Virginia Tech alleged she was raped by two university football players,[24] which, if proven true, would have violated the Violence Against Women Act (VAWA). This Act allowed victims of gender-motivated violence to bring federal civil suits for damages.[25] The players and university argued the Act was outside the scope of the Commerce Clause, and the Supreme Court agreed. The Court found that the VAWA had little to do with commerce and was too attenuated, even though Congress made specific findings that gender-motivated violence deterred interstate travel, diminished national productivity, and increased medical costs when it passed the statute.[26] The Court concluded that upholding VAWA under the Commerce Clause would lead to the federalization of virtually all serious crime, which should be handled through the police power of the states. The Court emphasized that Congress must distinguish between "what is truly national and what is truly local."[27] The Commerce Clause reaches only commerce that is truly national, that is, substantially affects interstate commerce.

In *National Federation of Independent Business v. Sebelius*, the Supreme Court considered whether the Affordable Care Act of 2010 was constitutional.[28] The Court, in a five to four vote, found that the individual mandate provision of the Act, which required all persons to buy health insurance or pay a penalty, was not within Congress' powers under the Commerce Clause but was upheld because it was passed pursuant to Congress' enumerated power to tax. Specifically, Chief Justice Roberts concluded that the Commerce Clause gave Congress no power to regulate *inactivity* (the decision of an individual not to buy health insurance). To allow such a power, Roberts argued, would give almost limitless power to Congress because there are "an infinite number" of things people do not do every day.[29] The Court reasoned that Congress, for example, could not order people to buy broccoli if they did not want to purchase it. The Commerce Cause covers commerce, not a decision by an individual not to participate in commerce. Ultimately, the individual mandate was upheld, not under the Commerce Clause but under a different enumerated authority: the Taxing clause. Chief Justice Roberts concluded that the "penalty" levied against anyone who did not purchase health insurance was, in effect, a federal tax, which Congress had the authority to issue. On a separate matter, the Court found that a significant expansion of Medicaid was not a valid exercise of Congress' spending power, since it would improperly coerce states to either accept the expansion or risk losing existing Medicaid funding.

22. *U.S. v. Lopez*, 514 U.S. 549 (1995).

23. *Id.*

24. *U.S. v. Morrison*, 529 U.S. 598 (2000).

25. *See* Violence Against Women Act of 1993, 42 U.S.C. ch. 136.

26. *Id.*

27. *Id.*

28. *National Federation of Independent Business v. Sebelius*, 567 U.S. 519 (2012).

29. *Id.*

The Tax and Spend Clause

Article I, Section 8, Clause 1 of the U.S. Constitution provides, "The Congress shall have the Power ... To lay and collect Taxes, Duties, Imposts, and Excises, to pay the Debts and provide for the common Defence and general Welfare of the United States ... ."[30] In other words, "Congress may tax and spend."[31] Under the "Spending Clause," Congress may attach conditions on the receipt of federal funds and exercise the spending power "to further broad policy objectives by conditioning receipt of federal moneys *upon* compliance by the recipient with federal statutory and administrative directives."[32] Although Congress may use the spending power to persuade the states, it may not unduly coerce or compel the states to act. As clarified in *National Federation of Independent Business v. Sebelius*, "[W]hen pressure turns into compulsion, ... the legislation runs contrary to our system of federalism."[33]

The Necessary and Proper Clause

Article I, Section 8, Clause 18 of the U.S. Constitution provides, "The Congress shall have Power ... To make all Laws which shall be necessary and proper for carrying into Execution the foregoing Powers, and all other Powers vested by this Constitution in the Government of the United States, or in any Department or Officer thereof."[34] The "Necessary and Proper Clause" is the last of the 18 enumerated authorities under Article I. It permits Congress to "legislate on that vast mass of incidental powers which must be involved in the constitution."[35] These incidental powers may only be exercised if they are "rationally related" to the implementation of other enumerated authorities.[36]

In *U.S. v. Comstock*, the Supreme Court explained that while the Constitution does not, for example, expressly address any federal crimes beyond those related to counterfeiting, treason, piracies, and felonies committed on the high seas or against the law of nations, Congress routinely exercises its authority, under the Necessary and Proper Clause to enact criminal laws in furtherance of other enumerated powers to regulate interstate and foreign commerce, enforce civil rights, spend funds for the general welfare, establish federal courts, establish post offices, regulate bankruptcy, and regulate naturalization—just to name a few of its authorities.[37] Further, the Necessary and Proper Clause permits Congress to help ensure the enforcement of these federal criminal laws, to pass laws that establish a federal prison, and to pass laws that require the safe and responsible administration of the prison because these laws are rationally related

30. U.S. Const. art. I, § 8, cl. 1.
31. *National Federation of Independent Business v. Sebelius*, 567 U.S. 519 at 537 (2018) (NFIB).
32. *South Dakota v. Dole*, 483 U.S. 203, 207 (1987).
33. *Supra* note 28 at 577–578 (internal marks omitted) (Affordable Care Act provision involving a significant expansion of Medicaid was not a valid exercise of Congress's spending power, since it would improperly coerce states to either accept the expansion or risk losing existing Medicaid funding altogether.).
34. U.S. Const. art. I, § 8, cl. 18.
35. *Supra* note 28.
36. *U.S. v. Comstock*, 560 U.S. 126, 134 (2010).
37. *Id.* at 136.

to an existing enumerated authority in the Constitution.[38] However, the Necessary and Proper Clause does not, in and of itself, grant Congress the independent authority to legislate unrelated to other enumerated authorities.

Although the Clause gives Congress authority to "legislate on that vast mass of incidental powers which must be involved in the constitution," it does not license the exercise of any "great substantive and independent power[s]" beyond those specifically enumerated.[39] Instead, the Clause is "'merely a declaration, for the removal of all uncertainty, that the means of carrying into execution those powers otherwise granted are included in the grant.'"[40] Thus, the Supreme Court continues to require this Clause to always be read in connection with other existing enumerated powers.

The Appropriations Clause

Article I, Section 9, Clause 7 of the U.S. Constitution provides, "No Money shall be drawn from the Treasury, but in Consequence of Appropriations made by Law; and a regular Statement and Account of the Receipts and Expenditures of all public Money shall be published from time to time."[41] The Office of the General Counsel, In 2013, the United States General Accountability Office published *Principles of Federal Appropriations Law* (4th ed.), which is the best regarded resource of federal appropriation law and is often referred to as the "Red Book."[42] The Red Book clarifies, in simplest terms, that a federal agency or employee cannot expend government funds, unless they are authorized to do so in an agency appropriation or other federal statute. Specifically, in chapter 1, it explains the following:

> The framers vested Congress with the power of the purse by providing in the Constitution that "no Money shall be drawn from the Treasury, but in Consequence of Appropriations made by Law." 3 U.S. Const., art. I, § 9, cl. 7. Time and again, the Supreme Court has reaffirmed that this clause means exactly what its straightforward language suggests: "no money can be paid out of the Treasury unless it has been appropriated by an act of Congress." 4 *Cincinnati Soap Co. v. United States*, 301 U.S. 308, 321 (1937). This principle, when stated differently, reveals a tenet that is of critical importance to every agency, every officer, every employee of the federal government: "The established rule is that the expenditure of public funds is proper only when authorized by Congress, not that public funds may be expended unless prohibited by Congress … ."[43]

So unless it has been expressly authorized in an agency appropriation or other federal statute, a

38. *Id.* at 137.

39. *Id.* at 411, 421.

40. *Kinsella v. United States ex rel.* Singleton, 361 U.S. 234, 247, 80 S. Ct. 297, 4 L.Ed.2d 268 (1960) (quoting James Madison, *The Writings* Vol. VI 383 (G. Hunt ed., 1906)).

41. U.S. Const. art. I, § 9, cl. 7.

42. Government Accountability Office Principles of Federal Appropriations Law (4th ed., 2019).

43. *See* Introduction to the Principles of Federal Appropriations Law 5 (4th ed.) (citations omitted), https://www.gao.gov/assets/2019-11/675699.pdf.

federal agency or employee cannot access government funds. An agency would be best advised to refer to GAO and the Red Book for information about any appropriation law questions.[44]

The Anti-commandeering Restrictions on Congressional Authority

The Constitution recognizes dual sovereignty between the federal government and the states. Under this principal, Congress, as a sovereign, cannot pass a law that commands a state, as a sovereign, to address or not address a particular matter or command a state officer to enforce a federal law that the federal government can require or prohibit. Moreover, Article I does not authorize Congress to issue direct orders to the states, and the Tenth Amendment reserves all unenumerated powers for the states:

> The Constitution confers on Congress not plenary legislative power but only certain enumerated powers. Therefore, all other legislative power is reserved for the States, as the Tenth Amendment confirms. And conspicuously absent from the list of powers given to Congress is the power to issue direct orders to the governments of the States. The anticommandeering doctrine simply represents the recognition of this limit on congressional authority.[45]

Although Congress itself can require or prohibit certain acts, it cannot compel states to require or prohibit such acts.[46]

In *Printz v. United States*, the Supreme Court overturned a provision of a federal statute, the Brady Handgun Violence Protection Act (BHVPA) because it "commandeered" state and local officers to serve as the "chief law enforcement officer" (CLEO) for their state and conduct background checks before issuing a gun license.[47] The law could have been enforceable if it required federal employees to serve as the CLEO or if the federal government authorized spending to states that voluntarily agreed to enforce the federal statute. However, the BHVPA improperly ordered state officials to implement this federal statute. In *Murphy v. NCAA*, the Supreme Court invalidated the Professional and Amateur Sports Protection Act (PASPA) because it "commandeered" state legislatures to pass laws prohibiting sports betting.[48] The law was unconstitutional because it directed the states to legislate anti-gambling laws. In other words, "Congress can regulate sports gambling directly, but if it elects not to do so, each State is free to act on its own."[49]

The Dormant Commerce Clause

Although states are given broad authority to regulate local matters pursuant to their police powers,

44. *See also Maine Community Health Options v. United States*, 140 S. Ct. 1308, 1321–22, (2020).

45. *See Murphy v. National Collegiate Athletic Association*, 138 S. Ct. 1461, 1476 (2018).

46. *See New York v. United States,* 505 U.S. 144, 166 (1992).

47. *Printz v. United States*, 521 U.S. 898 (1997).

48. Supra note 42.

49. *Murphy v. National Collegiate Athletic Association*, 138 S. Ct. 1461, 1484–85 (2018).

the Courts have found, imbedded in the Commerce Clause, a state prohibition against passing laws that excessively burden interstate commerce. This prohibition is referred to as the "Dormant Commerce Clause." and is driven by concern about "economic protectionism—that is, regulatory measures designed to benefit in-state economic interests by burdening out-of-state competitors ... ." [50] The Dormant Commerce Clause is intended "to effectuate the Framers' purpose to prevent a State from retreating into the economic isolation ... that had plagued relations among the Colonies and later among the States under the Articles of Confederation."[51] State laws that regulate "even-handedly to effectuate a legitimate local public interest ... will be upheld unless the burden imposed on such commerce is clearly excessive in relation to the putative local benefits."[52]

Leadership in the Context of a Limited Government

A major challenge for any government employee serving under the U.S. Constitution is learning to lead within a system designed to limit the breadth and scope of government authority and power. Congress cannot pass a law that exceeds the limits on its enumerated powers under Article I. The President cannot act in a manner that exceeds the limits on enumerated powers under Article II or a statute passed by Congress authorizing the exercise of executive power. A federal employee cannot spend the government's money without an express appropriation or Congressional statute permitting such spending. The states, while having the police power to handle a wide range of local matters, may be prohibited by the Supremacy Clause to act contrary to federal legislation and have further limitations under the Dormant Commerce Clause, preventing them from making decisions that promote economic protectionism in their respective states. Further, the Legislative and Executive Branches are, of course, also limited by the Judicial Branch. The Judicial Branch, however, receives their budget from Congress, and Congress can create, eliminate, and alter the jurisdiction of the Courts. The Judicial Branch is also limited by the enumerated authorities in Article III. Finally, no form of government within the United States can act contrary to the U.S. Constitution itself—the law of the land, with its checks and balances and a Bill of rights, with subsequent amendments, that protects many fundamental rights of all American citizens.

To lead effectively and with integrity within a government designed to limit power requires an ability to respect and defer to the roles and responsibilities of others as well as understand your role and the limitations imposed on your power. It requires patience, planning, deference, intelligence, perseverance, and commitment to the rule of law and the citizens you serve. It also requires a deeper understanding that:

> the Framers ranked other values higher than efficiency. ... With all the obvious flaws of delay, untidiness, and potential for abuse, we have not yet found a better way to preserve freedom than by making the exercise of power subject to the carefully crafted restraints spelled out in the Constitution.[53]

50. *Department of Revenue of Kentucky v. Davis*, 553 U.S. 328, 329 (2008) (citations omitted).

51. *Id.*

52. *See South Dakota v. Wayfair*, 138 S. Ct. 2080, 2090–91 (2018) (citations omitted).

53. *Immigration and Naturalization Service v. Chadha*, 462 U.S. 919, 959 (1983) (citations omitted).

The effective U.S. government employee should embrace these words of wisdom, understanding that each of us, as leaders, play an important role in carrying forth the vision of the Founding Fathers to preserve the liberty of U.S. citizens and preserve the rule of law, as set forth in the Constitution.

Cases and Review Questions

Directions: Use the provided links to access each noteworthy case. Then, provide complete and detailed responses to the questions and prompts about each case.

Heart of Atlanta Motel v. United States, 379 U.S. 241 (1964)

https://www.law.cornell.edu/supremecourt/text/379/241

1. How does the Supreme Court explain why the 1964 Civil Rights Act, prohibiting discrimination in housing, is authorized under Commerce Clause?
2. What does this case mean for the passage of other civil rights law and the breadth and scope of the Commerce Clause as an enumerated authority?
3. How would you rely on this case in passing future legislation under the Commerce Clause?

U.S. v. Lopez, 514 U.S. 549 (1995)

https://www.law.cornell.edu/supct/html/93-1260.ZO.html

1. Why can't Congress pass a law stating where a citizen can carry a gun?
2. How will this case impact future legislation Congress wishes to pass under the Commerce Clause?
3. How could the government have redrafted the language of the statute to make it enforceable under the Commerce Clause?
4. How does this impact the ability of Congress to pass future legislation?

U.S. v. Morrison, 529 U.S. 598 (2000)

https://www.law.cornell.edu/supct/html/99-5.ZO.html

1. Why was Congress prohibited from passing the Violence Against Women Act?
2. Why couldn't Congress pass such a law when it was clearly in the interest of the public?
3. What are police powers, and why is a state authorized to pass this statute but not Congress?
4. What are the criteria to consider, pursuant to this case, when crafting a statute under the Commerce Clause?
5. How would you rely on this case when drafting future legislation?

National Federation of Independent Business v. Sebelius, 567 U.S 519 (2012)

https://supreme.justia.com/cases/federal/us/567/519/

1. Why was the individual mandate under the Affordable Care Act not authorized under the Commerce Clause?
2. Why was the individual mandate authorized under the taxing power of Congress granted by Article I of the Constitution?
3. How will this case impact future legislation Congress wishes to pass?
4. What types of legislation would you like Congress to pass that it cannot because of this case?

Printz v. United States (1997)

https://www.law.cornell.edu/supct/html/95-1478.ZO.html

1. What is the anti-commandeering doctrine referenced in this case and its relationship to the states and the 10th Amendment?
2. Why was Congress prohibited from requiring state employees from conducting a firearms background check under a federal law?
3. Can Congress permit states to volunteer to carry out responsibilities under a federal statute authorized under the spending clause of the constitution?

Murphy v. National College Athletic Association, 138 S. Ct 1361 (2018)

https://www.supremecourt.gov/opinions/17pdf/16-476_dbfi.pdf

1. How did the anti-commandeering doctrine impact Congress to direct states to pass state law related to sports betting?
2. How has this case affected you?
3. What do you think the future of sports betting will be, considering this Supreme Court case?

C&A Carbone, Inc. v. Town of Clarkstown, New York, 511 U.S. 383 (1994)

https://supreme.justia.com/cases/federal/us/511/383/

1. What is the dormant commerce clause?
2. How does it restrict the authority of the states?
3. How important is this case to preserving the competitive commerce between the states?
4. How did it restrict the authority of the town of Clarkstown in this case?

Chapter 3

Due Process

Introduction

This chapter addresses the general principles of procedural due process. This is followed by a discussion of due process and federal employment, including what process is due when disciplining a federal employee, circumstances in which due process issues emerge, how *ex parte* communications can violate the due process clause and a discussion of due process and security clearances. The chapter concludes with a section on leadership in the context of a constitutional government and a list of cases with questions for class discussion.

General Principals of Procedural Due Process

The Due Process Clause of the Fifth Amendment provides, in pertinent part, that "no person shall ... be deprived of life, liberty or property without due process of law." The Fifth Amendment is applicable to the federal government. Similar due process requirements, expressly set forth in the Fourteenth Amendment, are applicable to the states.[1]

An individual may not be deprived by the government, including federal, state, and local government, of a property interest without procedural due process. Property interests are not created by the Constitution itself, but from existing rules or understandings that stem from an independent source, such as a federal or state law.[2]

Property interests protected by procedural due process extend well beyond ownership of real estate, personal property, or money.[3] Property may also include a benefit. A benefit becomes a property interest if the individual has "a legitimate claim of entitlement" to the benefit, as opposed to just an abstract need, desire, or unilateral expectation to the benefit.[4]

1. *Bolling v. Sharpe*, 347 U.S. 497, 500 (1954).
2. *Board of Regents v. Roth*, 408 U.S. 564, 576-78 (1972).
3. *Id.* at 571–72.
4. *Id.* at 577.

For example, in *Goldberg v. Kelly*, the Supreme Court held that a state could not terminate a recipient's welfare benefits, without first providing pretermination due process rights.[5]

What procedural process is due varies, depending upon a balancing test that weighs the following factors: "first, the private interest that will be affected by the official action; second, the risk of an erroneous deprivation of such interest through the procedures used, and the probable value, if any, of additional or substitute procedural safeguards; and, finally, the Government's interest, including the function involved and the fiscal and administrative burdens that the additional or substitute procedural requirement would entail."[6] In *Goldberg v. Kelly*, twenty state welfare recipients were entitled to a full formal evidentiary hearing, prior to terminating their benefits because without these welfare benefits, the recipients could be deprived of the very means necessary to survive while waiting for redress by the government bureaucracy.[7] In *Mathews v. Eldridge*, however, a recipient denied Social Security disability benefits was entitled to less rigorous pretermination due process procedures in the form of only advance written notice, a written opportunity to respond, and a decision before terminating disability benefits, where the benefits were not based on financial need and the recipient could still apply for welfare benefits if necessary.[8] In that case, a post-disability benefits termination hearing with full retroactive benefits was sufficient. The Supreme Court also held that disability benefits decisions often turn on routine and uncomplicated evidence, where government error is unlikely and the costs associated with a pretermination hearing are high.

Accordingly, a federal employee who administers benefits to the public or other federal employees must comply with constitutional due process requirements, usually set forth in statutes and/or governmentwide rules before reducing or taking away a benefit. Moreover, once a federal employee legally qualifies for a government benefit, that benefit is considered property and cannot be taken away without providing due process.

Due Process and Federal Employment

This section addresses whether federal employees have a due process property interest in their job, what process is due employees who have a property interest, circumstances in which due process issues typically arise in disciplinary and unacceptable performance actions, ex parte communications that can cause due process concerns.

Does the Federal Employee Have a Property Interest in Their Job?

The Fifth Amendment's protection that no person shall be deprived of property without due process of law

5. *Goldberg v. Kelly*, 397 U.S. 254 (1970).
6. *Mathews v. Eldridge*, 424, U.S. 319, 335 (1976).
7. *Goldberg v. Kelly*, 397 U.S. 254 (1970).
8. *Mathews v. Eldridge*, 424 U.S. 319 (1976).

extends to federal employment.[9] A non-probationary federal employee has a due process property interest in their job.

Property rights are not created by the Constitution but by an independent source, such as a statute. Once those rights are created, however, they cannot be deprived without due process of law. In *Cleveland Bd. of Educ. v. Loudermill*, the Supreme Court clarified:

> The right to due process is conferred, not by legislative grace, but by constitutional guarantee. While the legislature may elect not to confer a property interest in public employment, it may not constitutionally authorize the deprivation of such an interest, once conferred, without appropriate procedural safeguards.[10]

In *Lachance v. Erickson*, the Supreme Court held that a due process property right to notice and a meaningful opportunity to respond, prior to a decision to remove, as set forth in *Loudermill*, applies to non-probationary employees in federal civil service.[11] The Court emphasized, however, that the Fifth Amendment did not preclude an agency from disciplining an employee for making false statements during that response.

Due process applies if an employee can only be removed for cause.[12] In *Stone v. Federal Deposit Insurance Corporation*, the Court carefully examined the statutory scheme by which most federal employees are employed.[13] The Civil Service Reform Act of 1978 provides that a non-probationary federal employee can only be removed "for such cause would promote the efficiency of the Service"[14] or for "unacceptable performance." Accordingly, these federal employees have a property right in their job and cannot be removed absent adequate due process procedures.[15]

9. The Fifth Amendment applies to the federal government, whereas the Fourteenth Amendment applies to the states. Accordingly, neither the federal government nor the states can "deprive any person of life, liberty, or property, without due process of law." U.S. Const. amend. V. Further, the Supreme Court has applied the same due process standards for public employees in the federal government as well as employees in state and local governments. Accordingly, cases like *Loudermill, Cleveland Board of Education v. Loudermill*, 470 U.S. 532 (1985), which is a state employee case, serve as applicable precedent for federal employees.
10. *Cleveland Board of Education v. Loudermill*, 470 U.S. 532, 541 (1985).
11. *Supra* note 7.
12. *See Gilbert v. Homar*, 520 U.S. 924, 935–36 (1997) (state employee suspension); *supra note 10* (state employee removal); *Stone v. Federal Deposit Insurance Corporation*, 179 F.3d 1368 (Fed. Cir. 1999) (federal employee removal); *Do v. Department of Housing and Urban Development*, 913 F.3d 1089 (Fed. Cir. 2019) (federal employee demotion and suspension).
13. *Stone v. Federal Deposit Insurance Corporation*, 179 F.3d 1368 (Fed Cir. 1999).
14. *See* Civil Service Reform Act of 1978, 5 USC §7511.
15. Excepted Service employees, who have passed their probationary period, like competitive service employees, are currently covered by the Act and have due process rights. However, prior to the enactment of the Civil Service Due Process Amendments of 1990, Pub. L. No. 101–376, 104 Stat. 461 (1990), a nonpreference eligible employee in the excepted service, such as an attorney, was not included within the definition of "employee" in 5 USC §7511 (a) and, therefore, did not have the statutory and regulatory protections provided to an "employee" subjected to a removal action; *see Huber v. Merit Systems Protection Board* 793 F.2d 284 (Fed. Cir. 1986) (Petitioners, as excepted service employees without preference eligibility, could have been removed at any time, with or without cause. *Chu v. United States*, 773 F.2d 1226, 1228 (Fed. Cir. 1985)).

The Act does not confer a property interest in the jobs of probationary employees;[16] at will employees, such as Schedule C appointees; and employees with term appointments that have expired. Such employees can be removed without cause, do not have an expectation of continued employment, and are not entitled to due process protections prior to removal. Accordingly, the federal manager is well advised to address performance or conduct problems prior to the completion of the probationary period. However, this does not mean a probationary employee does not have legal protections. A probationary employee can still file an EEO complaint alleging discrimination,[17] a whistleblower retaliation complaint,[18] or a complaint based on partisan political reasons or discrimination due to marital status with the U.S. Merit Systems Protection Board.[19]

In addition to 5 U.S.C. § 7503, 5 U.S.C. § 7511, and 5 USC § 4303, other statutory provisions have been passed by Congress that are applicable to different segments of the federal workforce, such as the

16. Under the Act, veterans must serve a one-year probationary period and non-veteran employees must serve a two-year probationary period. *See* Civil Service Reform Act of 1978, 5 USC §§ 7501, 7511, and 4301.
17. See Federal Sector Equal Employment Opportunity, 29 CFR § 1614, which provides the rights of federal employees, including probationary employees, to file a complaint alleging discrimination under civil rights laws enforced by the Equal Employment Opportunity Commission (EEOC) under Title VII of the 1964 Civil Rights Act as amended (prohibiting employment discrimination based on race, color, national origin, gender, and religion); the Pregnancy Discrimination Act, Pub. L. 95–555, which makes it illegal to discriminate against a woman because of pregnancy, childbirth, or a medical condition related to pregnancy or childbirth; the Age Discrimination and Employment Act, 29 U.S.C. §§ 621–634, prohibiting employment discrimination for employees over 40; the Equal Pay Act, Pub. L. 88–38, which makes it illegal to pay different wages to men and women if they perform equal work in the same workplace; Sections 501 and 505 of the Rehabilitation Act of 1973, Pub. L. 93–112 §§ 501, 505, as amended, which prohibits discrimination based on disability and requires reasonable accommodation that will permit an employee to perform the essential functions of the job without causing undue hardship, and reasonable accommodation in the application process and reasonable accommodation, which will permit the individual to enjoy the benefits and privileges of the workplace; the Genetic Information Nondiscrimination Act of 2008, 81 FR 31143, which makes it illegal to discriminate against employees or applicants because of genetic information. See also U.S. Equal Employment Opportunity Commission, Laws Enforced by EEOC, http://www.eeoc.gov/laws/statutes/index.cfm for more detail about these laws.
18. In accordance with 5 USC 2302(b)(8) and as will be discussed in more detail in the whistleblower chapter herein, a probationary employee may file an individual right of action (IRA) with the Office of Special Counsel (OSC), alleging whistleblower retaliation, and if the OSC dismisses the complaint, the employee can file the IRA complaint and receive a hearing before the MSPB.
19. *See* Termination of Probationers for Conditions Arising Before Appointment, 5 C.F.R. §§315.805 and 315.806(b).

career Senior Executive Service[20] and employees of the Veterans Administration.[21] These services provide covered employees, due process protection.

What Process Is Due?

Once the employee has established a property interest in their job, the next step is determining what process they are due.[22] In the federal employment context, due process requires written notice of the charges against the employee, an explanation of the federal agency's evidence to support the charges,

20. Career members of the Senior Executive Service (SES) have a property interest in their job, and can be suspended for more than fourteen days up to removal if the SES member engaged in "misconduct, neglect of duty, malfeasance, or failure to accept a directed reassignment or to accompany a position in a transfer of function," in accordance with Senior Executive Service, 5 U.S.C. §§ 7541–7543. This action may be formally appealed to the MSPB. There is no statutory authority to suspend a career SES for misconduct for fourteen days or less. In addition, a career appointee who is removed from the SES for less than fully successful performance is only entitled to an informal hearing, which does not delay their removal from the SES, and they do not have a formal right to appeal their removal from the SES to the MSPB. *See* Removal from the Senior Executive Service, 5 U.S.C. § 3592(a)(2). Instead, in accordance with Guaranteed Placement in Other Personnel Systems, 5 U.S.C. § 3594(b), the career SES appointee removed from the SES for less-than-satisfactory performance is entitled to a guaranteed placement to a non-SES GS-15 position and is not removed from the civil service. Additional information about this process is set forth at U.S. Office of Personnel Management, Suspension & Removal, https://www.opm.gov/policy-data-oversight/senior-executive-service/adverse-actions/.
21. In 2017, Congress passed the Department of Veterans Affairs Accountability and Whistleblower Act of 2017, Public L. No. 115–41, 131 Stat 862 and codified, in part, at 38 USC § 714, which provides less rigorous standards and expedited procedures under which the Secretary of the VA ("the Secretary") "may remove, demote, or suspend" VA employees "if the Secretary determines the performance or misconduct of the covered individual warrants such removal, demotion, or suspension." Employees: Removal, Demotion, or Suspension Based on Performance or Misconduct, 38 U.S.C. § 714(a)(1). "The aggregate period for notice, response, and final decision ... may not exceed 15 business days" and the employee must appeal the adverse action to the Board within ten business days. *Id.* at § 714(c)(1)(A), (4)(B). The appeal is subject to expedited review, and "the administrative judge shall uphold the decision of the Secretary ... if the decision is supported by substantial evidence." *Id.* at §714(d)(1)–(2)(A). "[I]f the decision of the Secretary is supported by substantial evidence, the administrative judge shall not mitigate the penalty prescribed by the Secretary." *Id.* at § 714(d)(2)(B). *See Brenner v. Department of Veterans Affairs*, 990 F.3d 1313 (Fed Cir. 2021) (quoting *Sayers v. Department of Veterans Affairs*, 954 F.3d 1370 (Fed. Cir 2020)).
22. There may be some unusual exceptions to constitutional due process requirements when it comes to disciplinary actions short of removal. In *Do v. Department of Housing and Urban Development*, 913 F.3d 1089 (2019), the Federal Circuit Court of Appeals stated, "To be sure, not every disciplinary action requires pre-deprivation notice and opportunity to be heard. For example, in *Gilbert v. Homar*, 520 U.S. 924, 933, 117 S.Ct. 1807, 138 L.Ed.2d 120 (1997), the Supreme Court held that a pre-disciplinary hearing was not required where the disciplinary action—suspension—was only temporary, and 'the State ha[d] a significant interest in immediately suspending' an employee who had been arrested and charged with a felony." Accordingly, under what has been commonly referred to as the "crime provision," an agency is permitted to shorten that notice period when "there is reasonable cause to believe the employee has committed a crime for which a sentence of imprisonment may be imposed." Adverse Actions. 5 C.F.R. § 752.404(d)(1). *See Lockwood v. Department of Veterans Affairs*, 725 F. Appendix 938, 941 (Fed. Cir. 2018) (VA invoked the crime provision and reduced the length of the written notice period from the normal thirty-day period and provided him with the statutory minimum of seven days to respond to the charges.); *see* Cause and Procedure, 5 U.S.C. § 7513(b)(2). Indefinite suspension will be discussed in more detail in the security clearance section of this chapter.

and an opportunity for the employee to present their side of the story in some kind of hearing before termination.[23]

The federal employee is not entitled to a pretermination trial, like welfare recipients are, as required by *Goldberg v. Kelly.*[24] Rather, the employee is only entitled to a written proposal from the proposing official (usually the employee's first-level supervisor) that clearly places the employee on notice of the charges and specifications against the employee, so they can make a meaningful reply, they have an opportunity to make an oral or written reply to the Deciding Official (usually the employee's second-level supervisor), and they can receive a final written decision from the Deciding Official.[25]

Congress has set forth statutory procedures that protect federal employees accused of misconduct or unacceptable performance. Specifically, before an agency suspends an employee for fourteen days or less for misconduct, which is referred to as a "disciplinary action," the agency must comply with the procedural requirements set forth at 5 U.S.C. § 7503.[26] Before an agency takes an "adverse action," defined as suspending an employee for more than fourteen days, reducing the employee in grade or pay, or removing the employee, the agency must comply with the procedural protections set forth at 5 U.S.C. § 7511.[27] Before an agency removes, reassigns, or downgrades an employee for "unacceptable performance," the agency must comply with the procedural requirements set forth in 5 U.S.C. § 4303.[28]

An agency may take a disciplinary action under § 7503 or an adverse action under § 7511 if the agency

23. *See Do v. Department of Housing and Urban Development*, 913 F.3d 1089, 1093 (Fed. Cir. 2019) (citing *Cleveland Board of Education v. Loudermill*, 470 U.S. 532, 542–546 (1985); *Supra note 13* at 1376; *Young v. Department of Housing and Urban Development*, 706 F.3d 1372, 1377 (Fed. Cir. 2013).
24. *Supra* note 5.
25. *See supra note 13.* However, at the pretermination stage, it is not a violation of due process when the proposing and deciding roles are performed by the same person. *See also Robinson v. Department of Veteran's Affairs*, 923 F.3d 1004, 1022 (Fed. Cir. 2019).
26. In accordance with Cause and Procedure, 5 U.S.C. §7503, a federal employee suspended for fourteen days or less is entitled to the following procedures: (1) an advance written notice stating the specific reasons for the proposed action; (2) a reasonable time to answer orally and in writing and to furnish affidavits and other documentary evidence in support of the answer;
(3) be represented by an attorney or other representative; and (4) a written decision and the specific reasons therefor at the earliest practicable date. Further, the Office of Personnel Management set forth regulations at Procedures, 5 C.F.R. § 752.203(c) that provide that the employee's period to reply to a proposed suspension of fourteen days or less cannot be less than twenty-four hours.
27. In accordance with Definitions; Application, 5 U.S.C. §7511, if an agency imposes a suspension for more than fourteen days, a change to lower grade, reduction in pay, or removal action, an employee is entitled to: (1) at least thirty days' advance written notice, unless there is reasonable cause to believe the employee has committed a crime for which a sentence of imprisonment may be imposed, stating the specific reasons for the proposed action; (2) a reasonable time, but not less than seven days, to answer orally and in writing and to furnish affidavits and other documentary evidence in support of the answer; (3) be represented by an attorney or other representative; and (4) a written decision and the specific reasons therefor at the earliest practicable date.
28. See Actions Based on Unacceptable Performance, 5 U.S.C. § 4303, in which an employee charged with "unacceptable performance" is entitled to: (1) thirty days' advance written notice of the proposed action which identifies the specific instances of unacceptable performance by the employee on which the proposed action is based and the critical elements of the employee's position involved in each instance of unacceptable performance; (2) be represented by an attorney or other representative; (3) a reasonable time to answer orally and in writing; and (4) a written decision" that specifies the instances of unacceptable performance and that has been "concurred in" by an official at a higher level than that of the proposing official.

can prove, by a preponderance of the evidence,[29] that misconduct occurred, there is a nexus between the misconduct and the efficiency of the service, and the penalty for the misconduct is reasonable.[30]

An agency taking an unacceptable performance action under § 4303 must meet the lesser substantial evidence standard[31] and show the existence of an OPM-approved performance appraisal system; that the performance standards were fair, reasonable, and objective; that the standards were communicated to the employee; that the employee was given a reasonable opportunity to improve, otherwise known as a performance improvement plan (PIP); and that the employee failed one or more critical elements under the PIP. Once the foregoing elements have been satisfied, the employee can be removed, reassigned, or demoted from their position, and this penalty cannot be mitigated by the MSPB, an arbitrator, or the courts. An important recent development in unacceptable performance cases is the added agency burden of showing by substantial evidence that the employee engaged in unacceptable performance prior to being placed on the PIP.[32]

Due Process in Disciplinary or Performance-Based Actions

Whether taking an adverse or disciplinary action or an unacceptable performance action, due process issues may arise if the proposal is insufficiently clear to put the employee on notice of the charged wrongdoing. The proposal must be "in sufficient detail to allow the employee to make an informed reply."[33]

Due process requires "notice and an opportunity to be heard."[34] The right to due process may have been violated if, related to any reason for the ultimate removal decision, the notice of proposed removal did not "fully inform the employee of the grounds"[35] to provide "an opportunity to make an informed response before the agency"[36] on that basis. In the civil service system, "[o]nly the charge and specifications set out in the Notice may be used to justify punishment."[37]

The agency also violates due process when an employee is disciplined for reasons not expressly

29. Preponderance of the evidence means "the degree of relevant evidence that a reasonable person, considering the record as a whole, would accept as sufficient to find that a contested fact is more likely to be true than not true." General Definitions, 5 C.F.R. § 1201.4(q).
30. *Pope v. United States Postal Service*, 114 F.3d 1144 (Fed. Cir. 1997).
31. Substantial evidence is defined as the "degree of relevant evidence that a reasonable person, considering the record as a whole, might accept as adequate to support a conclusion, even though other reasonable persons might disagree." General Definitions, 5 C.F.R. § 1201.4(p).
32. *Santos v. NASA*, 990 F.3d 1355 (Fed Cir. 2021).
33. *Braun v. Department of Health and Human Services*, 983 F.3d 1295, 1304 (Fed Cir. 2020).
34. *Id.*
35. *Id.*
36. *Id.*
37. *Id.* (citations omitted).

included in the proposal.[38] The omission of some of the pertinent dates, times, and places in the charges is not improper, per se, if the employee was otherwise capable of defending themself at the oral reply.[39]

Due process issues may arise in the context of an allegedly biased Deciding Official,[40] or an issue may arise from the agency changing the Proposing or Deciding Official after reaching a decision.[41] If the employee can establish a defense of laches (i.e., an extensive delay before the employee is disciplined) by proving both (1) an unreasonable delay in bringing an action and (2) material prejudice from the delay,[42] there is potential for a due process issue. Similarly, issues may arise in circumstances in which the employee has been placed on enforced leave (against their will) for more than fourteen days—which is considered a suspension by the MSPB—without providing the employee due process procedures.[43]

38. *Do v. Department of Housing and Urban Development*, 913 F.3d 1089, 1093 (Fed. Cir. 2019) (An employee's due process rights were violated when he was charged in the proposal for violating a rule that prohibited hiring an Auditor who did not have a degree in accounting, but when it subsequently turned out that there was no such rule, because an applicant could possibly qualify by showing a combination of education and experience, the Deciding Official demoted and suspended him for negligence, and the employee was not on notice that she needed to defend against a charge of negligence for allegedly failing to investigate whether the applicant was qualified based on a combination of education and experience.).
39. *Pope v. United States Postal Service*, 114 F.3d 1144, 1148–49 (Fed. Cir. 1997).
40. An appellant's right to due process is violated when his "basic rights are determined either by a biased decision maker or by a decision maker in a situation structured in a manner such that the 'risk of unfairness is intolerably high.'" *Martinez v. Department of Veterans Affairs*, 119 MSPR 37, 40 (2012) (quoting Svejda *v. Department of the Interior*, 7 MSPR 108, 111 (1981)). The burden is on the appellant to establish actual bias or an intolerable risk of unfairness. *See Holton v. Department of the Navy*, 123 MSPR 688, 700 (2016)("To establish a due process violation based on the identity of a Deciding Official, an appellant must assert specific allegations indicating that the agency's choice of Deciding Official made the risk of unfairness to the appellant intolerably high."), aff'd, 884 F.3d 1142 (Fed. Cir. 2018). The MSPB explained in *Martinez* that a Deciding Official's awareness of background information regarding the appellant, his concurrence in the desirability to take an adverse action, or his predisposition to impose a severe penalty does not disqualify him from serving as a Deciding Official on due process grounds. *Martinez v. VA*, 119 MSPR 37, 40. *See also Norris v. Securities and Exchange Commission*, 675 F.3d 1349, 1354 (Fed. Cir. 2012) (Nothing in the regulation requires that the Deciding Official be unfamiliar with the individual, the facts of the case, or the employee's prior conduct.).
41. *See Goeke v. Department of Justice*, 122 MSPR 69, 76 (2015) (citing *Bross v. Department of Commerce*, 389 F.3d 1212, 1216 (Fed. Cir. 2004) and *Boddie v. Department of the Navy*, 827, F.2d 1578, 1580 (Fed. Cir. 1987)) (Due process barred a change in the Proposing or Deciding Officials after the lower-level official actually reached a decision and a detailed e-mail from the proposing official indicating he did not believe removal was an appropriate penalty for the specific professional misconduct issue and barred the agency from changing the proposing official at that time.).
42. Lengthy delays should be avoided, where possible, to avoid due process allegations from raising. However, a lengthy delay in and of itself does itself create reversable error. *See Salter v. Department of the Treasury, 432 F.2d 697* (citing *Social Security Administration v. Carr* (citing *Carr v. Social Security Administration*, 78 MSPR 313, 330–31(1998) *aff'd* 185 F.3d 1318 (Fed. Cir. 1999)) (three-year delay in bringing an action after the misconduct occurred did not in and of itself create reversable error). The appellant must show that the delay caused a material prejudice that harmed their ability to make a meaningful reply. Where the appellant is unable to articulate any specific prejudice or harm to their ability to defend against the charge, the laches defense will be defeated. *Salter v. Department of the Treasury*, 432 F.2d 697.
43. *Menoken v. Equal Employment Opportunity Commission,* No. DC-0752-19-0297-I-1, 2022 WL 3137714, at *3 (M.S.P.B. Aug. 5, 2022) ("Because a tenured federal employee has a property interest in continued employment, an agency is prohibited from placing an appellant on enforced leave for more than fourteen days without providing the due process required under the Fifth Amendment. *Cleveland Board of Education v. Loudermill*, 470 U.S. 532, 546 (1985); *see Martin v. U.S. Postal Service*, 123 MSPR 189, (2016)").

Due Process and Ex Parte Communications in Disciplinary Actions

Ex parte communications with the Deciding Official may also violate due process. In *Stone v. Federal Deposit Insurance Corp., supra*, the Court of Appeals explored whether communications with the Deciding Official, in the form of written memoranda unknown to the employee at the time of his oral reply to the proposed removal, violated due process. The Court held: "Procedural due process guarantees are not met if the employee has notice only of certain charges or portions of the evidence and the Deciding Official considers new and material information."[44] In short, the employee is not given a meaningful opportunity to reply to proposed charges if the Deciding Official is considering substantive evidence without giving the employee the opportunity to respond to that evidence first. However, not every *ex parte* communication violates due process:

> Among the factors that will be useful for the Board to weigh are whether the ex parte communication merely introduces "cumulative" information or new information; whether the employee knew of the error and had a chance to respond to it; and whether the ex parte communications were of the type likely to result in undue pressure upon the deciding official to rule in a particular manner. Ultimately, the inquiry of the Board is whether the *ex parte* communication is so substantial and so likely to cause prejudice that no employee can fairly be required to be subjected to a deprivation of property under such circumstances.[45]

Accordingly, a Deciding Official should avoid any communications with anyone about the proposed disciplinary action, other than their legal counsel or their assigned Employee Relations Specialist, while they are considering the merits of the action. If the Deciding Official receives new *ex parte* evidence, they should consult with the foregoing advisors to determine whether the employee subject to the proposed disciplinary action should be provided notice and an opportunity to respond to the new evidence prior to the Deciding Official considering it and rendering a final decision.

In *Ward v. U.S. Postal Service*,[46] the Court of Appeals held that the prohibition of the Deciding Official considering new and material *ex parte* evidence extended not only to evidence concerning the charges and specifications but to consideration of the appropriate penalty as well. An appropriate penalty in a disciplinary or adverse action is determined by the application of mitigating and aggravating factors set forth in the landmark MSPB case *Douglas v. Veterans Administration*.[47]

- the nature and seriousness of the offense, and its relation to the employee's duties, position, and responsibilities, including whether the offense was intentional or technical or inadvertent, or was

44. *Supra note 13.*

45. *Id.* at 1377.

46. *Ward v. U.S. Postal Service*, 634 F.3d 1274 (Fed. Cir. 2011).

47. *Douglas v. Veterans Administration*, 5 MSPR 280 (1981). The "*Douglas* factors" include the following non-exhaustive list of mitigating and aggravating factors:

committed maliciously or for gain, or was frequently repeated;

- the employee's job level and type of employment, including supervisory or fiduciary role, contacts with the public, and prominence of the position;
- the employee's past disciplinary record;
- the employee's past work record, including length of service, performance on the job, ability to get along with fellow workers, and dependability;
- the effect of the offense upon the employee's ability to perform at a satisfactory level and its effect upon supervisors' confidence in the employee's work ability to perform assigned duties;
- consistency of the penalty with those imposed upon other employees for the same or similar offenses;
- consistency of the penalty with any applicable agency table of penalties;
- the notoriety of the offense or its impact upon the reputation of the agency;
- the clarity with which the employee was on notice of any rules that were violated in committing the offense, or had been warned about the conduct in question;
- the potential for the employee's rehabilitation;
- mitigating circumstances surrounding the offense such as unusual job tensions, personality problems, mental impairment, harassment, or bad faith, malice, or provocation on the part of others involved in the matter; and
- the adequacy and effectiveness of alternative sanctions to deter such conduct in the future by the employee or others. The agency removed the employee based on a single incident of shouting, threatening, and disobeying a supervisor. The Deciding Official considered *ex parte* communications of other supervisors who alleged the employee engaged in similar past misconduct. These communications were referenced in the penalty analysis of the final decision that sustained the removal of the employee but not in the proposal. The Court remanded the case to the MSPB to determine whether the *ex parte* communications were merely cumulative or new and material, as described in *Stone.* It clarified that if the information was new and material, the decision must be reversed as a violation of due process. If the information was merely cumulative, the agency would still have violated a government-wide regulation that provides it is a violation for "an agency to rely on matters affecting the penalty it imposes without including those matters in the proposal notice."[48] Under these circumstances, the Court directed the MSPB to conduct a harmful error analysis.[49] Either way, it is advisable for the proposal to lay out in detail all the reasons and rationales for taking the proposed action. If the Deciding Official wishes to rely on any other information, they are well advised to carefully consult with legal counsel to potentially avoid reversable error.

Furthermore, when determining whether a due process violation has occurred, there is no basis for distinguishing between ex parte information provided to the Deciding Official and information personally

48. *See* Procedures, 5 C.F.R. §752.404(f).

49. *See* Burden and Degree of Proof, 5 C.F.R. §1201.56(c)(3), which defines a harmful error as "an error by the agency in the application of its procedures that is likely to have caused the agency to reach a conclusion different from the one it would have reached in the absence or cure of the error."

known by the Deciding Official, if the information was considered in reaching the decision and not previously disclosed to the appellant in the proposal.[50] In *Lopes v. Department of the Navy, supra*, the agency proposed to remove the appellant based on the charges of misuse of her government telephone, misuse of her government laptop computer, and misuse of her government desktop computer. No reference was made in the proposal to the employee's prior three-day suspension for misuse of a credit card. The Deciding Official was personally aware of the three-day suspension and referenced it during a hearing with the MSPB Administrative Judge (AJ) as support for why he sustained the removal. The AJ sustained the removal, but on appeal, the full MSPB reversed. The MSPB found the Deciding Official violated the employee's due process rights. The MSPB explained that even though the employee was clearly aware of her prior three-day suspension, it was not cumulative evidence because the suspension was not previously referenced in the proposal. The employee's due process rights were violated because by failing to include the three-day suspension in the proposal, the employee did not have an opportunity to respond to it at the oral reply before the Deciding Official rendered his final decision. Accordingly, it is advisable that when an agency intends to rely on aggravating factors as the basis for imposing a penalty for misconduct, such as a prior disciplinary record or poor work history, such factors must be included in the proposed notice of adverse action so that the employee will have a fair opportunity to respond before the Deciding Official considers their case.

Due Process and Security Clearances

When an Agency Personnel Security Office determines an employee's security clearance should be revoked, it follows Executive Order 12968: Access to Classified Information and agency rules. The Office then provides certain notice and appeal rights to the employee. Specifically, the agency suspends the clearance, gives the employee notice of the reasons why the clearance is suspended and provides the employee with an opportunity for a hearing before an impartial Hearing Officer to respond and adjudicate the merits of the clearance suspension. This process is separate and apart from the disciplinary action process set forth previously. If the Hearing Officer sustains the agency, the employee's clearance will be revoked.[51]

The MSPB does not have subject matter jurisdiction over an agency's security clearance substantive

50. *See Lopes v. Department of the Navy*, 116 MSPR 470 (2011).

51. The Agency Personnel Security Office and the independent and impartial Hearing Officer will apply the Adjudication Guidelines for Determining Eligibility for Access to Classified Information and the "whole person test" to the facts and evidence gathered. Any doubt whether access to classified information is clearly consistent with national security will be resolved in favor of national security. These guidelines include (1) allegiance to the United States; (2) foreign influence; (3) foreign preference; (4) sexual behavior; (5) personal conduct; (6) financial considerations; (7) alcohol consumption; (8) drug involvement; (9) psychological conditions; (10); criminal conduct; (11) handling protected information; (12) outside activities; and (13) use of information technology systems. Code of Federal Regulations, Title 32 – National Defense, https://www.govinfo.gov/content/pkg/CFR-2012-title32-vol1/xml/CFR-2012-title32-vol1-part147.xml.

determinations.[52] In *Department of Navy v. Egan,*[53] the Supreme Court held that the MSPB lacks jurisdiction to examine the substantive reasons for the revocation of a security clearance. The Supreme Court emphasized that "no one has a 'right' to a security clearance," particularly since the substantive decision of an agency to grant or deny a security clearance is a decision "clearly consistent with the interests of the national security."[54] The MSPB may only determine whether the position requires a clearance, whether the clearance was denied or revoked, and whether the employee was provided minimal procedural protections, such as notice of the charges, an opportunity to respond to the charges, and representation by legal counsel or otherwise.[55] The MSPB has jurisdiction to ensure the agency followed its own security clearance process procedures.[56]

While this security clearance process is proceeding, the agency can simultaneously decide to indefinitely suspend the employee.[57] An indefinite suspension means placing an employee in a temporary status without duties and pay for an indeterminate period while the foregoing clearance revocation procedures are proceeding. The indefinite suspension must come to an end once the matter has been fully adjudicated and a decision on the clearance suspension has been rendered. The indefinite suspension may be appealed to the MSPB, and the employee is entitled to due process. An agency provides minimal due process protections when it informs the employee, in the proposal, of the basis for the indefinite suspension action—that is, that the employee's position requires access to classified information and that their access has been suspended. The agency further complies with minimum due process requirements by informing the employee of the reasons for the suspension of access to classified information.[58]

If the agency's internal security clearance and adjudication process leads to a revocation of the

52. *See Skees v. Department of the Navy*, 864 F.2d 1576, 1578 (Fed. Cir. 1989). (The Board does not have the authority to review a security clearance determination or whether a position should be subject to a certain clearance level—or to a security clearance at all.).
53. *Department of the Navy v. Egan*, 484 U.S. 518, 530–31 (1988).
54. *Id.* at 528.
55. *Id.* at 530. Further, *Egan* has been broadly interpreted to restrict MSPB jurisdiction, not only for agency determinations regarding employee eligibility for a position requiring a security clearance but also to employee eligibility for sensitive positions. *See Kaplan* v. *Conyers,* 733 F.3d 1148 (Fed. Cir. 2013) (*en banc*), *cert. denied sub nom. Northover v. Archuleta*, 572 U.S. 1033 (2014).
56. *Romero v. Department of Defense*, 527 F.3d 1324 (2008).
57. Agencies are authorized to indefinitely suspend an employee, not only while seeking to revoke a clearance but also when there is reasonable cause to believe that the employee has committed a crime for which a sentence of imprisonment could be imposed, usually after an indictment, pending the outcome of criminal proceedings. Another recognized basis to support an indefinite suspension is where there are legitimate concerns that an employee's medical condition makes their continued presence in the workplace dangerous or inappropriate, pending determination that the employee is fit for duty. *See Gonzalez v. Department of Homeland Security*, 144 MSPR 118, 126 (2010). In these cases, the agency must be prepared to show there is a nexus between the charged conduct and the efficiency of the Service and that the penalty is reasonable. *See Hernandez v. Department of Homeland Security*, 120 MSPR 14, 16 (2013).
58. *See Palafox v. Department of Navy*, 124 MSPR 54, 60 (2016) (citing *King v. Alston*) (finding that the agency provided the employee with sufficient information to make an informed reply when it notified him that his security clearance was being suspended because of potential medical condition and then informed him that he was being indefinitely suspended from duty based on the suspension of his security clearance); *cf. Cheney v. Department of Justice*, 720 F.2d 1280 (finding that the employee was not provided with the opportunity to make a meaningful response to the notice of proposed suspension when he had to guess at the reasons for his security clearance suspension).

clearance and the agency removes the employee, the agency first needs to initiate adverse action procedures. Specifically, the agency proposes that the employee be removed, based upon the revocation of the clearance; offers the employee an oral reply; and issues a final decision. Again, the MSPB may only determine whether the position requires a clearance, whether the clearance was revoked, and whether the employee was provided minimal procedural protections, such as notice of the charges, an opportunity to respond to the charges, and representation by legal counsel or otherwise.[59] The MSPB lacks authority to review the feasibility of reassignment or the adequacy of the agency's reassignment efforts in a security clearance case, in the absence of an agency regulation that would require such efforts.[60]

Leadership in the Context of a Constitutional Government and Due Process

The federal manager should embrace due process, not only because it is required by the Constitution and statute, but because providing due process is consistent with the traits of an effective leader. The effective leader is fair, transparent, accountable, a clear communicator, and a careful listener. The procedural requirements of the Due Process Clause help the federal manager achieve these goals. The process of providing a detailed written proposal explaining all the reasons and evidence to justify a disciplinary action requires the manager to communicate clearly and be transparent; the oral and written reply period provides a unique opportunity for a manager to listen carefully before deciding; and the final written decision provides a measure of accountability, as the decision must explain why the discipline is fair and justified, given the reply of the employee. It is understandable why a manager would complain about the delay and difficulty satisfying due process requirements. The effective leader does not take shortcuts at the risk of compromising their commitment to fairness, transparency, and accountability.

A proposing official embraces due process by consulting with human resources and legal counsel when there are poor-performance or misconduct issues. In a misconduct case the Proposing Official thoughtfully decides what the charges and specifications should be after a thorough collection and examination of the evidence The Official also determines whether the proposed action is supported by a preponderance of the evidence; carefully assesses how the misconduct adversely affects the efficiency of the federal government; carefully considers the appropriateness of the proposed penalty after examining all of the *Douglas* factors in a disciplinary action; and, with the help of the Human Resources department, drafts a proposed disciplinary action letter.

The Deciding Official embraces due process by avoiding *ex parte* communication and does not consider reasons or evidence unknown to the employee; welcomes the reply period of an employee as an opportunity to test whether the proposed disciplinary action is fair and objectively assesses its strengths and weaknesses; carefully considers all the evidence in the record, the reply of the employee, and all the *Douglas* factors; ensures the final decision clearly explains the reasons and rationale for sustaining or overturning the charge, the reasons and rationale for sustaining or mitigating the proposed penalty, and whether the misconduct adversely affects the efficiency of the federal government; and issues a final

59. *Supra* note 50 at 530.

60. *See Ryan v. Department of Homeland Security*, 793 F.3d 1368, 1372–73 (Fed. Cir. 2015).

decision after taking into account the wisdom and experience of the Human Resources department and legal counsel.

The legal requirements in an unacceptable performance action under Chapter 43 of the Civil Service Reform Act are different than in a misconduct action under Chapter 75, as previously discussed, but the same principals of fairness, transparency, accountability, communicating clearly, and listening carefully are all on display in an unacceptable performance action. The proposing official embraces due process by carefully gathering all evidence to justify placing the employee on a PIP, the reasonable efforts made to help the employee improve, and why the employee's performance remained unacceptable; providing the employee with all the evidence relied upon and a written proposal explaining why the proposed removal is justified; and then providing the employee the right to present their side of the story at the oral reply. The Deciding Official embraces due process by listening carefully to the oral and/or written reply, avoiding any *ex parte* communication that produces new and material evidence and renders a clearly written decision after consideration of advice from the Human Resources department and legal counsel, which includes consideration of the employee's arguments.

Whether they are the Proposing Official or Deciding Official in a performance or conduct action, the effective leader embraces due process and provides the employee their constitutional pretermination right to defend themselves prior to losing the property right that is their job.

Cases and Review Questions

Directions: Use the provided links to access each case of note. Then, provide complete and detailed responses to the questions and prompts about each case.

Cleveland Board of Education v. Loudermill, 470 U.S. 532 (1985)

https://tile.loc.gov/storage-services/service/ll/usrep/usrep470/usrep470532/usrep470532.pdf

1. In *Loudermill*, how did the Court arrive at the conclusion that a public employee's job is property?
2. What kind of public employee jobs are not property?
3. Do you agree with the Court's reasoning that a full trial is not required before termination?
4. How impartial does the pretermination decision-maker have to be in *Loudermill*, and should the decision-maker be impartial?
5. Discuss how this case renders the government more or less efficient. Would you change any policies or practices in your workplace because of *Loudermill*?
6. Do you believe *Loudermill* hurts or helps the government?
7. Does this case make the job of a manager harder or easier? Explain.

LaChance v. Erickson, 522 U.S. 262 (1998)

https://tile.loc.gov/storage-services/service/ll/usrep/usrep522/usrep522262/usrep522262.pdf

1. In *La Chance v. Erickson*, how does the Fifth Amendment due process protection and the due

process protection against self-incrimination intersect?
2. Does due process include the right to make false statements during an investigation or during an oral reply to a proposed disciplinary action?
3. If the same charges of alleged misconduct at issue in an MSPB appeal were the issue of criminal charges, what should happen to the appeal?

Stone v. Federal Deposit Insurance Corporation, 179 F.3d 1368 (Fed Cir. 1999)

https://caselaw.findlaw.com/us-federal-circuit/1414122.html

1. In *Stone*, what is an ex parte communication, and what does the prohibition against such a communication have to do with due process?
2. How did Mr. Stone learn about the ex parte communications at the Merit Systems Protection Board hearing in the first place?
3. How will *Stone* affect a decision-maker's reliance on the advice of the proposing official, colleagues, higher-level supervisors, agency legal counsel, and the Human Resources department prior to rendering a final decision on a proposed disciplinary action?
4. In what ways, if any, would you change the test imposed by *Stone* to determine whether an ex parte communication violates due process?
5. How does *Stone* affect government efficiency?
6. How would *Stone* affect you as a manager prior to disciplining an employee?
7. What is discovery, and what are the different kinds of discovery before the Merit Systems Protection Board and the Courts?
8. How does discovery affect the importance of the *Stone* decision?

Ward v. U.S. Postal Service, 672 F.3d 1294 (Fed Cir. 2012)

https://caselaw.findlaw.com/us-federal-circuit/1555841.html

1. How is *Ward* different from *Stone?*
2. Do you agree that the ex parte communications prohibition should apply to determining the appropriateness of a penalty?
3. What are the *Douglas v. Veterans Administration* factors for assessing the appropriateness of the penalty, and after reading *Ward*, how will the case affect the proposal stage of the disciplinary process?
4. How does the Court differentiate between due process violations and harmful error violations?
5. What can the Deciding Official do to avoid ex parte communications?
6. How will *Ward* affect a manager's reliance on agency counsel and the Human Resources department prior to proposing discipline or rendering a final decision?

Boss v. Department of Homeland Security, No. 17-2231 (Fed. Cir. 2018)

https://caselaw.findlaw.com/us-federal-circuit/1963045.html

1. In *Boss v. Department of Homeland Security*, what is the significance of the Court's holding that due process violations will be examined charge by charge in a disciplinary action, rather than automatically negating the entire disciplinary action?
2. What insight does this case provide regarding the sharing of ex parte documents on agency policies without additional communication about these policies?
3. What lessons can be learned about failure to disclose to the employee and their union representative all documents relied upon by the Deciding Official in sustaining the charges?
4. In the future, what can a manager do to ensure all documents relied upon are disclosed to the employee being disciplined?

Villareal v. Bureau of Prisons, 901 F.3d 1361 (Fed. Cir. 2018)

https://caselaw.findlaw.com/us-federal-circuit/1949776.html

1. In *Villareal v. Bureau of Prisons*, what did the court rule about the impact of substantial delay in disciplining an employee for misconduct.
2. Under what circumstances, if any, does delay create reversable error?
3. What can an agency manager or a Human Resources department do to minimize delay in the disciplinary action process?

Santos v. National Aeronautics and Space Administration, 990 F.3d 1355 (2021)

https://law.justia.com/cases/federal/appellate-courts/cafc/19-2345/19-2345-2021-03-11.html

1. How has the Santos case changed the proof required in a 4303 unacceptable performance action?
2. What impact do you believe the Santos case will have on supervisors seeking to place an employee on a performance improvement plan?
3. What impact do you believe the Santos case will have on whether s supervisor will consider whether to take an unacceptable performance action at all?

Chapter 4

Free Speech and the First Amendment

Introduction

This chapter addresses the general principles of the right of freedom of speech provided by the First Amendment, including its applicability to speech by members of the public as well as separate sections on speech by government employees and speech by federal employees. The chapter concludes with a section on leadership in the context of a limited government and a list of cases with questions for class discussion.

General Principals Applicable to the First Amendment Right of Free Speech by Members of the Public

The First Amendment provides the following:

> Congress shall make no law respecting an establishment of religion or prohibiting the free exercise thereof; or abridging the freedom of speech,

or of the press; or the right of the people peaceably to assemble, and to petition the Government for a redress of grievances.[1]

The First Amendment protects five freedoms: freedom of religion (and prohibits the government from establishing a religion), freedom of speech, freedom of the press, freedom to peaceably assemble and the freedom to petition the government. This chapter focuses specifically on the freedom of speech affecting the public and the freedom of speech of government employees, with a particular emphasis on the rights and responsibilities of federal employees.

Speech is interpreted broadly as covering various forms of communication, including, but not limited to, speaking, writing, and various forms of symbolic expression.[2] Examples of symbolic speech include but are not limited to burning flags,[3] wearing armbands[4], or burning crosses[5]. The Supreme Court has adopted an "expressive conduct test" to determine coverage under the First Amendment, which considers "whether 'an intent to convey a particularized message was present, and whether the likelihood was great that the message would be understood by those who viewed it.'"[6]

The First Amendment limits all forms of government, including federal, state, and local governments, from interfering with free speech and other rights protected by the Amendment. Laws, regulations, or government policies that are overbroad[7] or unduly vague[8] may also violate the First Amendment. Similarly,

1. U.S. Const amend. 1. The Constitution annotated describes the history of the First Amendment as follows: "Madison's version of the speech and press clauses, introduced in the House of Representatives on June 8, 1789, provided: 'The people shall not be deprived or abridged of their right to speak, to write, or to publish their sentiments; and the freedom of the press, as one of the great bulwarks of liberty, shall be inviolable.' The special committee rewrote the language to some extent, adding other provisions from Madison's draft, to make it read: 'The freedom of speech and of the press, and the right of the people peaceably to assemble and consult for their common good, and to apply to the government for redress of grievances, shall not be infringed.' In this form, it went to the Senate, which rewrote it to read: 'That Congress shall make no law abridging the freedom of speech, or of the press, or the right of the people peaceably to assemble and consult for their common good, and to petition the government for a redress of grievances.' Subsequently, the religion clauses and these clauses were combined by the Senate. The final language was agreed upon in conference." Constitution Annotated, First Amendment, https://constitution.congress.gov/constitution/amendment-1/.
2. Geoffrey R. Stone and Eugene Volokh, Freedom of Speech and the Press, the National Constitution Center.
3. *Texas v. Johnson*, 491 U.S. 397, 408 (1989) (The state's interest in preventing breaches of peace did not justify the defendant's conviction for violation of the Texas flag desecration statute when he burned an American flag as part of a protest; no actual breach of peace occurred at the time of the flag burning or in response to the flag burning, and mere potential for breach of peace could not serve to justify prosecution.).
4. *Tinker v. Des Moines Independent Community School District*, 393 U.S. 503 (1969)
5. *Virginia v. Black*, 538 U.S. 343 ((2003)
6. *Texas v. Johnson, supra.*
7. *Virginia v. Hicks*, 513 U.S. 109, 118-119 (2003)
8. *Baggett v. Bullitt*, 377 U.S. 360 , 373(1964)

laws that limit the content of speech[9] or create a "prior restraint"[10] on speech will need to satisfy a heavy burden to be deemed constitutional.[11] Additionally, laws or government actions that constitute "viewpoint discrimination" are also prohibited.[12]

The First Amendment does not apply to actions taken by private employers or other private persons or entities. For example, if a private employer chose to discipline an employee for speech made to the press or posted on Facebook, that speech would not be protected by the First Amendment. However, if the government prohibited such speech, regulated the speech, or took action that adversely affected the speaker because of the speech, there may be a First Amendment issue. Accordingly, in determining whether there is a potential constitutional violation, it is critical to initially identify what role, if any, the government played in limiting the free speech rights of the communicator. If there is no nexus between the government and the speech at issue, there cannot be a First Amendment violation.

If the government is involved, it is important to assess who the speaker is before assessing whether the First Amendment has been violated. Members of the public and government employees both have free speech protections, but members of the public who are not employed by the government enjoy the greatest free speech protections; their speech has broad constitutional protection.

In *Brandenburg v. Ohio*[13], the Supreme Court held that the government may only limit speech by the public if it is "directed to inciting or producing imminent lawless action" and the speech is "likely to incite or produce imminent lawless action."[14]As discussed in depth shortly, the government as an employer has

9. *Twitter, Inc. v. Sessions*, 263 F. Supp. 3d 803, 810 (N.D. Cal. 2017), citing *Reed v. Town of Gilbert, Ariz.*, --- U.S. ----, 135 S.Ct. 2218, (2015)("content-based laws—those that target speech based on its communicative content—are presumptively unconstitutional and may be justified only if the government proves that they are narrowly tailored to serve compelling state interests.")

10. *Twitter, Inc. v. Sessions*, 263 F. Supp. 3d 803, 810 (N.D. Cal. 2017), citing *Alexander v. United States*, 509 U.S. 544, 550 (1993) ("The term prior restraint is used to describe administrative and judicial orders forbidding certain communications when issued in advance of the time that such communications are to occur.")

11. *Twitter, Inc. v. Sessions*, 263 F. Supp. 3d 803, 810 (N.D. Cal. 2017), citing *Nebraska Press Ass'n,* 427 U.S. 539, 571 (1976) ("In order to justify a prior restraint, the government must demonstrate that the restraint is justified without reference to the content of the speech, and is narrowly tailored to serve a compelling governmental interest.")

12. *Rosenberger v. Rector & Visitors of Univ. of Virginia*, 515 U.S. 819, 829(1995) "When the government targets not subject matter, but particular views taken by speakers on a subject, the violation of the First Amendment is all the more blatant. Viewpoint discrimination is thus an egregious form of content discrimination. The government must abstain from regulating speech when the specific motivating ideology or the opinion or perspective of the speaker is the rationale for the restriction." Internal citations omitted.

13. *Brandenburg v. Ohio*, 395 U.S. 444, 447 (1969) (reversed the conviction of a Ku Klux Klan leader for threatening "revengeance" if the "suppression" of the white race continued, holding that advocacy of the use of force or of law is permitted "except where such advocacy is directed to inciting or producing imminent lawless action and is likely to incite or produce such action."). *Brandenburg* has been raised in connection with Former President Trump's January 6, 2021, speech and discussed at length during the impeachment proceedings. An excellent article, Debra Cassens Weiss, *Could Trump Face Charges for Speech Before Capitol Riot? Experts Differ on Brandenburg Impact*, American Bar Association, Jan. 21, 2021, https://www.abajournal.com/news/article/could-trump-face-charges-for-speech-before-capitol-riot-experts-differ-on-brandenburg-impact, summarizes the differing views of constitutional law experts on his January 6 speech.

14. *Brandenburg v. Ohio*, 395 U.S. 444, 447 (1969).

much broader discretion to regulate the speech of its employees compared to members of the public. Thus, it is important to determine the speaker's constitutional rights by identifying who the speaker is.

There are, however, certain types of speech that are not protected by the Constitution regardless of who is speaking. The First Amendment will not protect "fighting words,"[15] "obscenity"[16] "true threats,"[17] or "defamatory statements."[18] Further, the government is permitted to engage in content-neutral regulation involving the time, place, and manner of speech.[19]

However, in *Mahanoy Area School District v. B. L.*,[20] the Supreme Court recently reminded us, yet again, of the heavy burden the government has to regulate the content of speech, even if it is a student complaining on Snapchat that she did not make the varsity cheerleading team:

> Our representative democracy only works if we protect the 'marketplace of ideas' ... . That protection must include the protection of unpopular ideas, for popular ideas have less need for protection. ..." Consider B. L.'s speech. Putting aside the vulgar language, the listener would hear criticism, of the team, the team's coaches, and the school—in a word or two, criticism of the rules of a community of which B. L. forms a part. This criticism did not involve features that would place it outside the First Amendment's ordinary protection. B. L.'s posts, while crude, did not amount to fighting words. ... And while B. L. used vulgarity, her speech was not obscene as this Court has understood that term. ... To the contrary, B. L. uttered the kind of pure speech to which, were she an adult, the

15. *See* Constitution Annotated, First Amendment, *Fighting Words, Hostile Audiences and True Threats*, https://constitution.congress.gov/browse/essay/amdt1-2-3-2-1/ALDE_00000742; *Chaplinsky v. New Hampshire*, 315 U.S. 568 (1942) ("... still remains viable for the principle that the States are free to ban the simple use, without a demonstration of additional justifying circumstances, of so-called 'fighting words,' those personally abusive epithets which, when addressed to the ordinary citizen, are, as a matter of common knowledge, inherently likely to provoke violent reaction. But, in actuality, the Court has closely scrutinized statutes on vagueness and overbreadth grounds and set aside convictions as not being within the doctrine. *Chaplinsky* thus remains formally alive but of little vitality.")
16. *See* Constitution Annotated, First Amendment, *Obscenity: Overview*, https://constitution.congress.gov/browse/essay/amdt1-2-3-4-1/ALDE_00000747/ (discussing *Roth v. United States,* 354 U.S. 476 (1957) ("The standard that the Court thereupon adopted for the designation of material as unprotected obscenity was whether to the average person, applying contemporary community standards, the dominant theme of the material taken as a whole appeals to prurient interest. The Court defined material appealing to prurient interest as material having a tendency to excite lustful thoughts, and defined prurient interest as a shameful or morbid interest in nudity, sex, or excretion."); *see also Miller v. California, 413 U.S. 15 (1973)* ("Laws that regulate pornography must be carefully limited; their scope is to be confined to materials that depict or describe patently offensive 'hard core' sexual conduct specifically defined by the regulating state law, as written or construed. The law must also be limited to works which, taken as a whole, appeal to the prurient interest in sex, which portray sexual conduct in a patently offensive way, and which, taken as a whole, do not have serious literary, artistic, political, or scientific value.").
17. *Elonis v. United States,* 575 U.S. 573 (2015) (Facebook posts did not create a true threat.); *see Virginia v. Black,* 538 U.S. 343, 359 (2003) (A "true threat" occurs when the speaker communicates "a serious expression of intent to commit an act of unlawful violence" toward an individual or group.).
18. *See New York Times v. Sullivan,* 376 U.S. 264 (1964) (especially when the speaker knew the statements to be untrue).
19. *Thomas v. Chicago Park District,* 534 U.S. 316 (2002) (upheld a Chicago ordinance requiring individuals holding events in a public park to obtain a permit under circumstances); *Ward v. Rock Against Racism*, 491 U.S. 781 (1989) (Speech neutrality applies if ordinance provisions apply to speech generally or only to the specific message it conveys.).
20. *Mahanoy Area Sch. Dist. v. B. L.*, 141 S. Ct. 2038 (2021).

> First Amendment would provide strong protection. ... It might be tempting to dismiss B. L.'s words as unworthy of the robust First Amendment protections discussed herein. But sometimes it is necessary to protect the superfluous in order to preserve the necessary.[21]

While *Mahanoy* is a case involving off campus student speech, it is reasonably foreseeable that it will be cited as precedent to protect off-duty government employee speech, in a case where the employee argues the speech does not adversely affect the government. However, any discussion of free speech rights herein must begin with well-established Supreme Court precedent set forth below in the sections examining the rights of all government employee and federal employees in particular.

On January 17, 2025 the Supreme Court issued its decision, *TikTok v. Merrick Garland,*[22] which unanimously upheld a federal law that will ban TikTok in the United States unless its Chinese parent company sells it to a business that did not present national security concerns. The Supreme Court found that the government's concerns regarding TikTok's data collection practices of 170 million Americans and the United States' adversarial relationship with China satisfied the "intermediate scrutiny" test. Specifically, the Court found that the law satisfied an "important government interest" related to national security, since China could leverage its control over a platform that collected personal data of millions of Americans. The Court also found that that the law was "sufficiently tailored" to address these concerns. The Court acknowledged that while "strict scrutiny" is warranted when laws are intended to restrict specific speakers, the unique circumstance of this case, dealing with the ownership of a platform by a foreign adversary warranted the less intrusive intermediate scrutiny test.

Free Speech and Government Employees

The Supreme Court has recognized that government employees, including federal employees, do not relinquish their constitutionally protected First Amendment right of freedom of speech simply because they work for the government.[23] However, the government as an employer has greater discretion to regulate the speech of its employees than it does for members of the public but only where the speech adversely affects government operations:

> [Although a] government entity has broader discretion to restrict speech when it acts in its role as employer ... the restriction it imposes must be directed at speech that has some potential to affect the entity's operations. ... So long as employees are speaking as citizens about an issue of public concern, they must face only those speech restrictions that are necessary for their employers to operate efficiently and effectively. ... [S]uch

21. 141 S. Ct. 2038, 2046–2048 (2021) (student was improperly suspended from the Junior Varsity Cheerleading squad when, upon learning she did not make varsity cheerleading, posted off campus on Snapchat: "Fuck school fuck softball fuck cheer fuck everything." The Court emphasized that the speech was off campus, was not directed at any individual in particular and did not constitute bullying or harassment, which might justify intervention by the school in the future.).
22. *TikTok v. Merrick Garland, Case No. 24-656 (January 17, 2025).*
23. *United States v. National Treasury Employees Union*, 513 US 454, 465 (1995) (citing *Pickering v. Board of Education*, 391 U.S. 563 (1968)).

cause as will promote the efficiency of the service' excludes constitutionally protected speech, and that the statute is not overbroad.[24]

The Courts have routinely applied the Pickering-Connick balancing test to determine whether the speech of a government employee is constitutionally protected. This test is based on two Supreme Court decisions: *Pickering v. Board of Education*[25] and *Connick v. Meyers.*[26]

The test initially measures the degree to which the government employee is speaking as a "citizen" on a "matter of public concern" or as an "employee" concerned with their personal grievance or complaint.[27] Speech deals with matters of public concern when it can "be fairly considered as relating to any matter of political, social, or other concern to the community ... or when it 'is a subject of legitimate news interest; that is, a subject of general interest and of value and concern to the public' ... . The arguably 'inappropriate or controversial character of a statement is irrelevant to the question whether it deals with a matter of public concern.'"[28]

The next part of the test is to balance the employee's right to speak on a manner of public concern with the degree the speech interferes with the effective functioning of the public employer. This balancing test includes "whether the statement impairs discipline by superiors or harmony among co-workers, has a detrimental impact on close working relationships for which personal loyalty and confidence are necessary, or impedes the performance of the speaker's duties or interferes with the regular operation of the enterprise."[29] Further, "The more central a matter of public concern is to the speech at issue, the stronger the employer's showing of counter-balancing governmental interests must be."[30]

Applying the two-part test outlined above to both the *Pickering* and *Connick* cases helps to explain the reasoning of the Supreme Court. Mr. Pickering's letter, which criticized the School Board's allocation of its budget for in-class activities versus after-school sports, was deemed to focus on a clear matter of public concern. The Court emphasized that the community would be particularly interested in the views of a teacher in the classroom on this important subject. In contrast, Ms. Meyers' questionnaire in *Connick* had only one question involving a matter of public concern—whether staff felt pressured to support a particular political candidate—but most of the questionnaire related to her personal complaint about her reassignment as an employee.

The Supreme Court found little evidence of disruption caused by the speech in *Pickering*, and thus,

24. *Garcetti v. Ceballos*, 547 U.S. 410, 418 (2006). *See Arnette v. Kennedy* (false statements made by a federal employee alleging his supervisor took a bribe was not protected speech and the standard for suspending or removing an employee in the federal government.).

25. *Pickering v. Board of Education*, 391 U.S. 563 (1968) (where a high school teacher was wrongfully terminated because of protected speech in the form of a letter to a newspaper that was openly critical of the way the Board of Education handled past proposals to raise new revenue for the schools).

26. *Connick v. Meyers*, 461 U.S. 137 (1983) (where an Assistant District Attorney did not engage in protected speech in the form of a questionnaire she drafted and distributed office wide, prompted by the decision of management to reassign her to a different section of the criminal court).

27. *Id.*

28. *Snyder v. Phelps,* 562 U.S. 443, 453 (2011) (citations omitted).

29. *Rankin v. McPherson,* 483 U.S. 378, 388, (1987).

30. *Coughlin v. Lee,* 946 F.2d 1152, 1157 (5th Cir. 1991).

Mr. Pickering's speech was protected. In *Connick*, however, Ms. Meyer's speech was intended to cause "a mini-insurrection" in the office and was unprotected because the adverse impact of the speech on government efficiency and effectiveness outweighed the employee's right to speak as a citizen on matters of public concern.

We provide a word of caution: matters related to the First Amendment require careful consideration of the totality of facts and circumstances surrounding the speech before conducting the balancing test. As such, "In performing the balancing, the statement will not be considered in a vacuum; the manner, time, and place of the employee's expression are relevant, as is the context in which the dispute arose."[31]

The First Amendment also does not protect speech made by an employee "pursuant to their official duties."[32] Specifically, the Supreme Court ruled the following: "We hold that when public employees make statements pursuant to their official duties, the employees are not speaking as citizens for First Amendment purposes, and the Constitution does not insulate their communications from employer discipline."[33]

Garcetti substantially limited free speech rights of government employees because most employee speech in the workplace is made pursuant to their official duties. The Supreme Court acknowledged in *Garcetti* that while "[e]xposing government inefficiency and misconduct is a matter of considerable significance" and that public employers should be "receptive to constructive criticism," such speech is best protected by the passage of "whistleblower protection laws and labor codes—available to those who seek to expose wrongdoing."[34] The Supreme Court emphasized, however, that the First Amendment does not "shield from discipline the expressions made pursuant to their professional duties," and there is not "a constitutional cause of action behind every statement a public employee makes in the course of doing [their] job."[35]

In *Lane v. Franks* the Supreme Court carefully examined *Garcetti* in the context of an employee testifying in court under oath in a criminal proceeding regarding information they learned while doing their job.[36] The Supreme Court held that his speech was protected speech because:

> [T]he mere fact that a citizen's speech concerns information acquired by virtue of his public employment does not transform that speech into employee-rather than citizen

31. *Rankin v. McPherson*, 483 U.S. 378, 388, (1987) (where a Deputy Constable, upon hearing of the assassination attempt of President Reagan, was fired, in violation of the First Amendment, for stating, "I hope next time they get him," since she was a clerical employee and had communicated her view to a single coworker in their office.).
32. *See Garcetti v. Ceballos*, 547 U.S. 410 (2006) (Deputy Assistant United States Attorney's (AUSA) complaints to supervisors that the case he was assigned should not be prosecuted because of his belief that the warrant issued by the police contained serious misrepresentation of facts was not protected speech, where the concerns he raised were made pursuant to his official duties as an AUSA).
33. *Id.* at 421.
34. *Id.* at 425–426. The impact of *Garcetti* was to place additional importance on the need for effective whistleblower laws, which are discussed in chapter 5.
35. *Id.* at 426.
36. *Lane v. Franks*, 573 U.S. 228 (2014).

speech. The critical question is whether the speech is *ordinarily* within the scope of an employee's duties, not whether it merely concerns those duties.[37]

Recently some Courts have combined *Pickering*, *Connick,* and *Garcetti* into a five-part test for analyzing a First Amendment retaliation case. The five criteria are as follows: (1) whether the speech was made pursuant to an employee's official duties; (2) whether the speech was on a matter of public concern; (3) whether the government's interests, as employer, in promoting the efficiency of the public service are sufficient to outweigh the plaintiff's free speech interests; (4) whether the protected speech was a motivating factor in the adverse employment action; and (5) whether the defendant would have reached the same employment decision in the absence of the protected conduct.[38] Finally, the same First Amendment protections that apply to government employees also apply to government contractors.[39]

Free Speech and Federal Employees

Federal employees who allege reprisal for exercising their constitutional free speech rights typically must satisfy the same *Pickering-Connick* balancing test before the Merit Systems Protection Board (MSPB)[40] and federal courts.[41] Further, the same *Garcetti* rule, which finds speech unprotected if it is made "pursuant to official job duties" of the employee is also equally applicable to the federal government.[42]

There are, however, First Amendment free speech issues unique to the federal government. Federal employees may be disciplined under the Lloyd-La Follette Act, as incorporated into the Civil Service

37. *Id.* at 240 (emphasis added). Some courts have limited the application of *Lane* to cases involving compelled speech on a witness stand and have downplayed the significance of the word "ordinary" referenced in the decision. *See* Anderson v. Valdez, 845 F.3d 580 (5th Cir. 2016) (Although Lane added "ordinarily" to the formulation used in Garcetti ....we have since noted that, "whatever change in the jurisprudence 'ordinary' may augur, we are unable to discern any change in *Garcetti*'s rule from Lane ..., for any change resulting from Lane cannot be said to have been 'clearly established.'" *Citing Gibson v. Kilpatrick*, 773 F.3d 661, 669 (5th Cir. 2014).
38. *Duda v. Elder*, 7 F.4th 899 (10th Cir. 2021).
39. *Board of County Commissioners v. Wabaunsee County*, 518 U.S. 668 (1996); *Kansas v. Umbehr*, 518 U.S. 668 (1996).
40. *See Smith v. Department of Transportation*, 106 MSPR 59 (2007); *Ledeaux v. Veteran's Administration, 29 MSPR 440 (1985)* (In addressing the issue of whether employee speech is protected by the First Amendment, the Board must determine: (1) whether the speech addressed a matter of public concern and, if so, (2) whether the agency's interest in promoting the efficiency of the service outweighs the employee's interest as a citizen).
41. *See Mings v. Department of Justice*, 813 F.2d 384, 387 (1987) (quoting Connick, "Federal employees' free speech rights must be balanced, however, against the need of Federal government agencies to exercise 'wide latitude in managing their offices, without intrusive oversight by the judiciary in the name of the First Amendment'") (the potentially disruptive effect a letter by an employee to the Director of Immigration and Naturalization Service could have on agency operations substantially outweighed whatever public interest the letter addressed, being critical of I-293 Immigration Form, and the letter was properly relied on in part as basis for removal of employee, without showing employee's continued employment actually diminished the efficiency of the service; the letter reflecting virulent anti-Hispanic and anti-Catholic bias and accusing the employee's superiors and fellow employees of incompetence); *see also Harnishfeger v. United States*, 943 F. 3d 1105 (7th Cir. 2019).
42. *Id.*

Reform Act[43] for "for such cause as will promote the efficiency of the Service,"[44] which may apply to their speech and conduct. This law, while general and flexible, is not "vague" or "overbroad" and does not violate the Constitution, since it is understood that the law must be applied consistently with constitutional requirements and is designed to address a wide array of misconduct that adversely affects the government.[45]

Further, a federal employee who wishes to raise a constitutional violation must comply with the statutory scheme set forth in the Civil Service Reform Act (CSRA) before going into federal court.[46] Thus, the federal employee must first exhaust administrative remedies by filing an appeal before the Merit Systems Protection Board (MSPB), if there is a suspension of fifteen days or more, up to removal. For allegations of a prohibited personnel practice under 5 U.S.C. 2302(b) involving suspensions of less than fifteen days or other personnel actions, such as denial of promotion or involuntary reassignment, the federal employee must first raise a claim before the Office of Special Counsel (OSC).[47] Matters may also be raised under an applicable broad scope collective bargaining agreement before going into federal court. In the unusual case that the allegation does not fall under any forum set forth under the CSRA, the employee can raise the issue directly to federal court.[48]

Issues involving free speech and partisan political speech of federal employees also arise under the Hatch Act: "The purpose of the Act is to maintain a federal workforce that is free from partisan political influence or coercion."[49] The Hatch Act was upheld in *U.S. Civil Service Commission v. National Association of Letter Carriers, AFL-CIO*[50] *and Public Works v. Mitchell.*[51] In *American Federation of Government Employees v. Office of Special Counsel,* the Fourth Circuit Court of Appeals provided an outstanding historical summary of efforts made to establish a neutral federal civil service that does not trod on the First Amendment rights of federal employees, from President Thomas Jefferson in 1791 through the

43. *See* Civil Service Reform Act, 5 U.S.C. 7503(a) (applicable to suspensions of fourteen days or less and 7513(a) applicable to demotions, suspensions of fifteen days or more, up to removal from the federal government).

44. *Id.*

45. *See Arnette v. Kennedy*, 416 U.S. 134, 162, (1974) ("Since Congress when it enacted the Lloyd-La Follette Act did so with the intention of conferring job protection rights on federal employees which they had not previously had, it obviously did not intend to authorize discharge under the Act's removal standard for speech which is constitutionally protected. The Act proscribes only that public speech which improperly damages and impairs the reputation and efficiency of the employing agency, and it thus imposes no greater controls on the behavior of federal employees than are necessary for the protection of the Government as an employer. Indeed the Act is not directed at speech as such, but at employee behavior, including speech, which is detrimental to the efficiency of the employing agency. We hold that the language 'such cause as will promote the efficiency of the service' in the Act excludes constitutionally protected speech, and that the statute is therefore not overbroad.").

46. *Elgin v. Department of Treasury*, 567 U.S. 1 (2012).

47. *Harnishfeger v. United States*, 943 F. 3d 1105, 1113 (7th Cir.).

48. *See Turner v. U.S. Agency for Global Media*. 502 F. Supp. 3d 333 (D.C. 2020) (citing *Steadman v. Governor, U.S. Soldier' and Airmen's Home*, 918 F.2d 963).

49. The Hatch Act, 5 U.S.C. § 7323 *et seq; see, e.g.*, Office of Special Counsel, A Guide to the Hatch Act for Federal Employees, https://osc.gov/Documents/Outreach%20and%20Training/Handouts/A%20Guide%20to%20the%20Hatch%20Act%20for%20Federal%20Employees.pdf.

50. *U.S. Civil Service Commission v. National Association of Letter Carriers*, AFL-CIO, 413 U.S. 548 (1973).

51. *Public Works v. Mitchell*, 330 U.S. 75 (1947).

Pendleton Act of 1883 and its elimination of the "spoils system" to the date of the decision in June, 2021, upholding the Hatch Act and its amendments:

> It is not for the judicial branch to second-guess the sober judgment of Congress that some separation of the civil service from partisan electioneering remains necessary. ... For Congress could well believe that the project of realizing a politically neutral civil service, a project now over two centuries old, was more essential than ever in this most partisan and intolerant of times. An efficient and meritocratic civil service of federal employees devoted above all "to serve this great end of Government—the impartial execution of the laws," Letter Carriers, 413 U.S. at 565, 93 S.Ct. 2880, may yet help to restore a fraying popular faith in our basic public bodies. Or so the legislative branch is entitled to conclude. That "great end of Government" is the great end of the Hatch Act too, and we hesitate to gainsay Congress' judgment to this effect.[52]

Another unique issue applicable to the federal government arose in *United States v. National Treasury Employees Union*, wherein the Supreme Court struck down section 501(b) of the Ethics in Government Act that prohibited federal employees from receiving honoraria for writing and speaking on matters unrelated to political activities covered by the Hatch Act or their official duties (e.g., a mail handler paid for lecturing on Quaker history, an aerospace engineer paid for lecturing on African American history, and a biologist paid for writing and speaking about dance performances).[53] The Supreme Court took judicial notice that authors Nathaniel Hawthorne, Herman Melville and Walt Whitman had all published and been paid for their famous literary works while employed by various federal agencies. The Court held that when the speech is unrelated to the employee's job or agency, occurs outside the workplace, and is addressed to a public audience, the employer must show that the speech was linked somehow to the agency's mission, purpose, or image. If the agency cannot do so, and the employee is speaking on a matter of public concern, consistent with *Pickering,* the employee will prevail in their First Amendment claim.[54] The Supreme Court emphasized that it was unnecessary to examine the applicability of *Garcetti*

52. *American Federation of Government Employees v. Office of Special Counsel, 1 F.4th 180, 185 (4th Cir. 2021)* ("In 1993, Congress observed that political patronage was no longer the problem it had once been. Instead, excessively partisan speech and conduct within the federal workplace was the danger most in need of being curbed. So, in the Hatch Act Reform Amendments of 1993, Congress loosened restrictions on federal employees' ability to participate in political campaigns outside of work and tightened restrictions on political activity undertaken in the course of civil service business. See *Burrus v. Vegliante*, 336 F.3d 82, 86 (2d Cir. 2003). On-duty federal civil servants were thereby prohibited from engaging in 'political activity,' 5 U.S.C. § 7324, where 'political activity' came to mean 'an activity directed toward the success or failure of a political party, candidate for partisan political office, or partisan political group,' 5 C.F.R. § 734.101. And that remains the law today.")
53. *United States v. National Treasury Employees Union*, 513 U.S. 454, 467 (1995).
54. *See Harnishfeger v. United States*, 943 F.3d 1105, 1113–1114 (7th Cir. 2019) (summarizing *United States v. NTEU, 513 U.S. 454 (1995).*

or *Connick,* where the applicable law issues broad sweeping changes unrelated to whether an individual is speaking pursuant to their official duties or speaking as an employee.[55]

Leadership in the Context of a Constitutional Government and First Amendment Free Speech Rights

The effective government leader should always keep the bedrock principle of the First Amendment in mind: protect the free flow of information, ideas, and debate on matters of public concern.[56] The Constitution demands the greatest tolerance of speech by the public, but government employees have First Amendment protections as well. As Justice Sandra Day O'Connor stated, "Government employees are often in the best position to know what ails the agencies for which they work; public debate may gain much from their informed opinions."[57] The model manager strives to create an environment that encourages differing views. Accordingly, a certain degree of tolerance, even for ideas the manager may disagree with, should be respected. It is out of such an environment that productive ideas, as well as mutual respect for the manager and employer, may emerge.

Another leadership lesson learned comes from the *Pickering* court, where the school board was particularly thin-skinned when considering criticism from a teacher of its decision to fund school sports over increasing the budget for classroom activities. The government manager must be prepared to be receptive to such criticism and avoid retaliating against the critical employee. This is not to say there are not times when the disruption caused by the employee is so significant as to outweigh the public concern caused by the speech; however, the effective leader makes a reasonable effort to err on the side of tolerance.

Further, the model leader avoids a reflexive reaction to an employee's speech and does not consider the speech in a vacuum. Rather, they remember the lesson taught by the *Rankin* court and carefully consider the totality of circumstances before applying the balancing test.

Finally, it is advisable to seek legal counsel whenever a First Amendment issue emerges, as these cases are often complex and confusing to the layperson.

Cases and Review Questions

Directions: Use the provided links to access each noteworthy case. Then, provide complete and detailed responses to the questions and prompts about each case.

55. *See id.* (Volunteers in Service to America (VISTA) and the National Guard violated the First Amendment when they removed a clerical employee upon discovering she had written a book providing a candid account of her experiences as a phone-sex operator, describing some of the callers as "vile" and "monsters," which was found by the Court to be a matter of public concern, where the book was published before she was hired, involved content unrelated to her job or the agency, was written for a general audience, and the National Guard could not show the book was linked to her employment or the agency's mission or image or reflected badly on the National Guard.).
56. U.S. Const amend. 1.
57. *Waters v. Churchill,* 511 U.S. 661, 674 (1994).

Brandenburg v. Ohio, 395 U.S. 444 (1969)

https://supreme.justia.com/cases/federal/us/395/444/

1. Why did the Supreme Court reverse the Ohio Criminal Syndicalism statute referenced in this case?
2. Under what circumstances can the government intervene to stop public advocacy?
3. Must all hate speech be tolerated?
4. Do you agree with the court's tolerance of the KKK's hurtful public advocacy?
5. Do the broad free speech protections described in *Brandenburg* help or hinder society?

Pickering v. Board of Education, 391 U.S. 563 (1968)

https://supreme.justia.com/cases/federal/us/391/563/

1. Why was Mr. Pickering's letter protected by the First Amendment?
2. How can you determine whether speech is a matter of public concern?
3. Is advocacy protected when factual assertions are incorrect?
4. Does a government employee share the same free speech protections as a member of the public?
5. How do you think the school board should have reacted upon seeing the Pickering article. What lessons can be learned about leadership from the reaction of the school board to the criticism of the budget decisions of the school board described in the Pickering letter?

Connick v. Myers, 461 U.S. 138 (1983)

https://supreme.justia.com/cases/federal/us/461/138/

1. Was any part of the Meyers questionnaire a matter of public concern?
2. How can you determine whether an employee is speaking as a citizen or an employee?
3. What is the balancing test in *Connick?*
4. How do you apply the balancing test?
5. Do you feel Ms. Meyers was treated fairly in this case?
6. How does *Connick* impact the right of free speech of government workers?

Garcetti v. Ceballos, 547 U.S. 410 (2006)

https://supreme.justia.com/cases/federal/us/547/410/

1. How can you determine whether an employee is speaking out as a citizen or an employee?
2. Why is it that speech "pursuant to your official job duties" is considered employee speech? Is anything you learn and speak out about considered pursuant to your job duties?
3. How is whistleblowing treated under *Garcetti*?
4. What is the impact of *Garcetti* on First Amendment speech of government employees? Do you

agree with the reasoning of the court?

Lane v. Franks, President of Central Alabama Community College, 570 U.S. 228 (2014)

https://supreme.justia.com/cases/federal/us/573/228/

1. The employees in Garcetti and Lane both engaged in speech related to information they learned while performing their jobs. Garcetti's speech was unprotected by the First Amendment whereas Mr. Lane's speech was protected. How did the Supreme Court distinguish between *Lane* from *Garcetti*?
2. How significant was it that Lane was subpoenaed and testified under oath on the witness stand? Why was the individual who fired Mr. Lane not personally liable?
3. Under what circumstances would he have been personally liable?
4. What are the lessons learned from Lane regarding the importance of government managers complying with the Constitution?

Rankin v. McPherson, 483 U.S. 378 (1987)

https://supreme.justia.com/cases/federal/us/483/378/

1. Upon learning of the attempted assassination of President Reagan, Deputy Constable McPherson stated, in part, "[I]f they go for him again, I hope they get him."
2. Why did the state government employer find that such speech warranted her removal?
3. How did the Court conclude that this speech was protected by the First Amendment?
4. How did the Court weigh McPherson's speech after learning President Reagan was shot, considering she held the position of deputy constable?
5. What are the lessons learned can be taught from this case regarding carefully considering the totality of facts in the case?
6. Under what circumstances could the foregoing speech justify a government employee's removal?

United States v. National Treasury Employees Union, 513 U.S. 454 (1995)

https://www.law.cornell.edu/supct/html/93-1170.ZO.html

1. How did the Supreme Court's First Amendment analysis differ in this case as compared to the typical free speech retaliation case?
2. What must the government prove to justify a broad restraint on speech?
3. Why are the Hatch Act's restrictions constitutional but the honoraria ban unconstitutional?

Mahanoy Area School District, Petitioner, v. B.L., 141 S. Ct. 2038 (2021)

https://www.supremecourt.gov/opinions/20pdf/20-255_g3bi.pdf

1. Why were B. L.'s posts on social media protected speech?
2. What kind of speech on social media is not protected?
3. How does this case affect students' varying types of off-duty speech?
4. How might this case be relevant to off-duty conduct in other contexts, such as employment?

TikTok Inc. v. Merrick Garland, Attorney General, Case No. 24-656 (2025)

https://www.supremecourt.gov/opinions/24pdf/24-656_ca7d.pdf

1. Why did the government ban TikTok?
2. What level of scrutiny did the Supreme Court apply to the ban of TikTok and why?
3. What was the rationale the Supreme Court reached in its decision to uphold the government ban of TikTok?
4. How would the Supreme Court decision have changed if the government was directing the ban of specific individualized speech?

Chapter 5

Whistleblowing

Introduction

There are numerous whistleblower statutes.[1] The Occupational Safety and Health Administration alone enforces 20 of such statutes.[2] This chapter focuses on the rights and protections afforded most federal employee whistleblowers under the Whistleblower Protection Enhancement Act of 2012 (WPEA).[3] There are some federal employees not covered under the WPEA.[4] The intelligence community whistleblowers are covered under different whistleblower laws and currently do not receive the same level of protection against whistleblower retaliation as those covered under the WPEA.[5]

1. *See* National Whistleblower Center, https://www.whistleblowers.org/law-library/, for a listing of such federal and state whistleblowing laws.
2. Occupational Safety and Health Administration, Directorate of Whistleblower Protection Programs (DWPP) Whistleblower Statutes Summary Chart (2021), https://www.whistleblowers.gov/sites/wb/files/2021-06/Whistleblower_Statutes_Summary_Chart_FINAL_6-7-21.pdf.
3. Whistleblower Protection Enhancement Act of 2012, 5 U.S.C. 2302 (b)(8); *see Hicks v. Merit Systems Protection Board*, 819 F.3d 1318, 1319 (Fed. Cir. 2016) (citing the Whistleblower Protection Enhancement Act of 2012 as Pub. L. No. 112–199, 126 Stat. 1465).
4. The WPEA does not apply to employees of the Federal Bureau of Investigation, Government Accountability Office, U.S. Postal Service, National Security Agency, Central Intelligence Agency, and other various intelligence and counterintelligence agencies. It also does not apply to Schedule C policymaking positions. *See supra* note 3 at (a)(2)(B) and (C).
5. For an update on intelligence community whistleblowing, see Congressional Research Service, Intelligence Community Whistleblower Provisions (2022), https://sgp.fas.org/crs/intel/R45345.pdf.

A Brief History of Whistleblowing Law Impacting Federal Employees

The Civil Service Reform Act of 1978 (CSRA), effective in January 1979, established eleven prohibited personnel practices.[6] There are now fourteen prohibited personnel practices.[7]

Section 2302 (b)(8) makes it a prohibited personnel practice to retaliate against a whistleblower. The CSRA also created the Office of the Special Counsel (OSC) to receive and investigate allegations of prohibited personnel violations, including allegations of whistleblower retaliation. OSC also had the authority to file a petition for corrective or disciplinary action with the Merit Systems Protection Board (MSPB), which replaced the previous Civil Service Commission. At its inception, OSC served as an "autonomous arm" of the MSPB.[8]

Subsequently, Congress enacted the Whistleblower Protection Act of 1989 (WPA).[9] Under the WPA, OSC became an independent agency, separate and apart from the MSPB, with authority, among other things, to receive, investigate, and prosecute prohibited personnel practices.[10]

Subsequently, "The Whistleblower Protection Enhancement Act of 2012 (WPEA) was signed into law in November 2012 and strengthened the WPA. This law overturned legal precedents that narrowed protections for government whistleblowers; provided whistleblower protections to employees who were not previously covered, including Transportation Security Administration (TSA) officers; restored OSC's ability to seek disciplinary actions against supervisors who retaliate; and held agencies accountable for retaliatory investigations."[11]

Prior to the WPEA, the federal courts and the MSPB determined that an employee was not a covered whistleblower, regardless of how serious and substantial the disclosure of wrongdoing was, if the disclosure was about matters involving the regular course of the employee's job, was disclosed to a supervisor or coworker, or was previously reported on by another employee. This judicial precedent discouraged whistleblowing.[12] Congress passed the WPEA to make it easier to qualify as a whistleblower and encourage whistleblowing by ensuring the foregoing judicial precedent was no longer applicable. Thus, a current employee under the WPEA can qualify as covered whistleblower and is protected against

6. *Supra* note 3 at 2302 (b).
7. *See supra* note 3 at 2302 (b), for a listing of the fourteen prohibited personnel practices.
8. OSC also had the authority to receive, investigate and litigate allegations of Hatch Act violations. *See* https://osc.gov/Services/Pages/HatchAct-Federal.aspx.
9. *Supra* note 3 at 2302 (b).
10. *Id.* It was also given the authority to receive and investigate and seek corrective action for violations of Uniformed Services Employment and Reemployment Rights Act of 1994 (USERRA). Subsequently, OSC's 1994 Reorganization Act expanded protections for federal employees. For a full description of this Act, *see supra* note 8 at 7.
11. *Id.* at 8.
12. *See* Merit Systems Protection Board, Blowing the Whistle: Barriers to Federal Employees Making Disclosures (2010), https://www.mspb.gov/studies/studies/Blowing_The_Whistle_Barriers_to_Federal_Employees_Making_Disclosures_662503.pdf

retaliation, even if the disclosure involved their regular job duties, was disclosed to a supervisor or coworker, or was previously reported on by a coworker.[13]

The Whistleblower Protection Enhancement Act of 2012

The WPEA provides the following:

> Any employee who has the authority to take, direct others to take, recommend, or approve any personnel action, shall not, with respect to such authority ...
>
> (8) take or fail to take, or threaten to take or fail to take, a personnel action with respect to any employee ... because of—
>
> (A) any disclosure of information by an employee ... which the employee ... reasonably believes evidences—
>
> (i) any violation of any law, rule, or regulation, or
>
> (ii) gross mismanagement, a gross waste of funds, an abuse of authority, or a substantial and specific danger to public health or safety ... .[14]

"Whistleblowing" is defined by the WPEA and MSPB regulation as follows:

> *Whistleblowing* is the making of a protected disclosure, that is, a formal or informal communication or transmission, but does not include a communication concerning policy decisions that lawfully exercise discretionary authority, unless the employee or applicant providing the disclosure reasonably believes that the disclosure evidences any violation of any law, rule, or regulation, gross mismanagement, a gross waste of funds, an abuse of authority, or a substantial and specific danger to public health or safety. It does not include a disclosure that is specifically prohibited by law or required by Executive order to be kept secret in the interest of national defense or foreign affairs, unless such information is disclosed to Congress, the Special Counsel, the Inspector General of an agency, or an employee designated by the head of the agency.[15]

13. For a more detailed analysis of the history behind the WPEA, see Jason Zuckerman, *Congress Strengthens Whistleblower Protections for Federal Employees*, American Bar Association (ABA) Labor and Employment Law Flash Newsletter, November–December 2012, https://www.zuckermanlaw.com/wp-content/uploads/2019/01/Whistleblower-Protection-Enhancement-Act.pdf.
14. *Supra* note 3 at 2302 (b). For more information on whistleblowing under the WPEA by the Office of Special Counsel (OSC), see ITB OSC, *Federal Whistleblower Rights and Protections*, YouTube (Jan. 27, 2013), https://www.youtube.com/watch?v=jzf2pboRaoQ.
15. Practices And Procedures For Appeals And Stay Requests Of Personnel Actions Allegedly Based On Whistleblowing Or Other Protected Activity, 5 C.F.R. 1209.4(b).

The WPEA only protects five categories of disclosures: (1) a violation of law, rule, or regulation;[16] (2) gross mismanagement;[17] (3) a gross waste of funds;[18] (4) an abuse of authority;[19] or (5) a substantial and specific danger to the public health and safety.[20]

If the employee discloses information that falls within one of the five categories above, they must also establish a "reasonable belief" that the disclosure was true. An employee can be inaccurate when making a whistleblower disclosure as long as the individual had a "reasonable belief" the allegations were true at the time of disclosure. The proper test for determining whether an employee had a reasonable belief is whether a disinterested observer with knowledge of the essential facts known to, and readily ascertainable by, the employee could reasonably conclude the actions evidenced at least one of the five categories of wrongdoing listed in the previous paragraph.[21]

An employee is not a whistleblower, however, if the information disclosed merely raises policy issues.[22] Further, an employee is not protected if they disclose information "specifically prohibited by law" or "required by executive order to be kept secret in the interest of national defense or the conduct of foreign affairs."[23]

When asserting a whistleblower reprisal claim, the employee bears the initial prima facie burden of establishing that (1) there was a disclosure or activity protected under the WPEA, as previously discussed;

16. The employee is not required to cite any specific law, rule, or regulation they reasonably believe was violated, where the employee's statements and the surrounding circumstances clearly implicate an identifiable law, rule, or regulation. *See Lane v. Department of Homeland Security*, 115 M.S.P.R. 342 (2010). There is no exception to that rule for a disclosure of a trivial or *de minimis* violation of a law, rule, or regulation. *Grubb v. Department of the Interior*, 96 M.S.P.R. 377 (2004).
17. "Gross mismanagement" is defined as "a management action or inaction which creates a substantial risk of significant adverse impact upon the agency's ability to accomplish its mission." *Francis v. Department of the Air Force,* 120 M.S.P.R. 138 (2013).
18. "Gross waste of funds" is defined as "a more than debatable expenditure that is significantly out of proportion to the benefit reasonably expected to accrue to the government." *McGowan v. Environmental Protection Agency*, 119 M.S.P.R. 9 (2012).
19. An "abuse of authority" is defined as "an arbitrary and capricious exercise of power by a federal official or employee that adversely affects the rights of any person or results in personal gain or advantage to herself or to other preferred persons." *Chavez v. Department of Veterans Affairs*, 120 M.S.P.R. 285 (2013).
20. "A substantial and specific danger to public health or safety" occurs when the disclosed danger is sufficiently substantial and specific to warrant protection under the WPA is guided by several factors, including: (1) the likelihood of harm resulting from the danger; (2) when the alleged harm may occur; and (3) the nature of the harm *(i.e.,* the potential consequences). *Chavez v. Department of Veterans Affairs,* 120 M.S.P.R. 285 (2013).
21. *See La Chance v. White*, 174 F.3d 1378, 1381 (Fed. Cir. 1999) *cert. denied*, 528 U.S. 1153 (2000).
22. *See Lachance v. White, 174 F.3d 1387; see also Hansen v. Merit Systems Protection Board*, 746 F. App'x 976, 979–80 (Fed. Cir. 2018) (*citing La Chance v. White*, 174 F.3d 1378, 1381 (Fed. Cir. 1999)) ("The WPA is not a weapon in arguments over policy. ..."); *Standley v. Merit Systems Protection Board*, 715 F. App'x 998, 1001–03 (Fed. Cir. 2017) (affirming a dismissal of an IRA appeal, where multiple disclosures consisted of a fairly debatable policy dispute); *O'Donnell v. Merit Systems Protection Board*, 561 F. App'x 926, 930 (Fed. Cir. 2014) (affirming dismissal of an IRA appeal, where the disclosures consisted of policy disputes over an agency's "discretionary authority"). "Mere differences of opinion between an employee's superiors as to the proper approach to a particular problem or the most appropriate course of action do not rise to the level of gross mismanagement." *White v. Department of Air Force*, 391 F.3d 1377, 1381 (Fed. Cir. 2004). "[W]here a dispute is in the nature of a policy dispute, 'gross mismanagement' requires that a claimed [federal contractor] error in the ... continued adherence to ... a policy be a matter that is not debatable among reasonable people." *White v. Department of Air Force*, 391 F.3d 1377, 1383 (Fed. Cir. 2004).
23. *See MacLean v. Department of Homeland Security*, 574 U.S. 373 (2015); 5 U.S.C. 2302(b)(8) (A)(ii).

(2) there was a personnel action authorized for relief under the WPEA; and (3) the protected disclosure or activity was a contributing factor to the personnel action.[24]

A "personnel action," as defined by the WPEA, is a predicate for a whistleblower retaliation appeal. Only upon proof of a qualifying personnel action may a claimant seek corrective action from the Board.[25] The WPEA defines the set of qualifying personnel actions at 5 U.S.C. § 2302(a)(2)(A). That section of the statute lists eleven specific personnel actions, including, for example, "an appointment," "a performance evaluation," and "a decision concerning pay"—followed by a catch-all provision: "any other significant change in duties, responsibilities, or working conditions."[26]

The employee may establish that the whistleblowing was a "contributing factor" behind the reasons for the adverse personnel action by presenting "circumstantial evidence, such as evidence that—(A) the official taking the personnel action knew of the disclosure or protected activity; and (B) the personnel action occurred within a period of time such that a reasonable person could conclude that the disclosure or protected activity was a contributing factor in the personnel action."[27] This is otherwise referred to as the "knowledge/timing test."[28] It is relatively easy to prove a prima face case of whistleblower retaliation.

Once an employee establishes a prima facie case by showing that a protected disclosure was a contributing factor in the agency's personnel action, the burden shifts to the agency to establish by "clear and convincing evidence that it would have taken the same personnel action in the absence of such disclosure."[29] As stated in *Duggan v. Department of Defense*, "Clear and convincing evidence is that measure or degree of proof that produces in the mind of the trier of fact a firm belief as to the allegations sought to be established."[30] This is a very high burden for the agency to meet.

Factors the Federal Circuit has identified—often referred to as the "*Carr* factors"—that are pertinent to this defense include

> the strength of the agency's evidence in support of its personnel action; the existence and strength of any motive to retaliate on the part of the agency officials who were

24. *Sistek v. Department of Veterans Affairs,* 955 F.3d 948, 953–54 (Fed. Cir. 2020) (citing *Piccolo v. Merit Systems Protection Board*, 869 F.3d 1369, 1371 (Fed. Cir. 2017)). The petitioner must prove these elements by a preponderance of the evidence. *Whitmore v. Dep't of Labor,* 680 F.3d 1353, 1367 (Fed. Cir. 2012). Once the petitioner has done so, the agency may rebut the petitioner's prima facie case of reprisal with "clear and convincing evidence that it would have taken 'the same personnel action in the absence of such disclosure.' *Whitmore v. Department of Labor*, 680 F.3d 1353, 1367 (Fed. Cir. 2012).

25. *See* Individual Right of Action in Certain Reprisal Cases, 5 U.S.C. § 1221(a).

26. *Id.* at § 2302(a)(2)(A)(i)–(xii); *Sistek v. Department of Veterans Affairs,* 955 F.3d 948, 953–54 (Fed. Cir. 2020) ("Noticeably absent from the list [of personnel actions] however, is any mention of a 'retaliatory investigation,' or indeed, any investigation at all. An investigation in and of itself, absent subsequent disciplinary action, was not a personnel action covered under the WPEA.")

27. *Delgado v. Department of Justice*, 979 F.3d 550, 554 (7th Cir. 2020) (referencing *Powers v. Department of the Navy*, 97 M.S.P.R. 554, 561 (2004)); *Grubb v. Department of the Interior*, 96 M.S.P.R. 377, 395 (2004); *Redschlag v. Department of the Army*, 89 M.S.P.R. 589, 634–35 (2001).

28. Id.

29. *Duggan v. Department of Defense,* 883 F.3d 845-46 (9th Cir. 2018); *see supra* note 25 (citing *Whitmore v. Department of Labor*, 680 F.3d 1353, 1367 (Fed. Cir. 2012)).

30. *Duggan v. Department of Defense,* 883 F.3d 845-46 (9th Cir. 2018) (quoting 5 C.F.R. § 1209.4(e)).

involved in the decision; and any evidence that the agency takes similar actions against employees who are not whistleblowers but who are otherwise similarly situated.[31]

It is not necessary to satisfy each of these factors; however, an administrative or federal court judge will carefully assess the totality of evidence for each of the factors, and the supervisor has a high burden to avoid a finding of retaliation.[32] For example, if a supervisor is considering taking a ten-day suspension against a whistleblower for refusing a direct order related to a work assignment, the supervisor should first carefully assess whether the evidence strongly supports the charge. If the evidence is clear that a direct order was provided by the supervisor and the employee knowingly refused to follow that order, the situation may satisfy one of the foregoing *Carr* factors. If the evidence is not clear or difficult to prove, the supervisor should probably opt to avoid taking this personnel action.

Even if the evidence of insubordination referenced in the example above is strong and easy to prove, the supervisor may be found to have retaliated against the employee if there are comparator employees, who are not whistleblowers, engaged in insubordination for similar behavior as the whistleblower but were not disciplined or received a lesser suspension or penalty than the whistleblower. See *Whitmore v. Department of Labor* for a discussion of the importance of examining the treatment of comparator employees.[33] The supervisor might be able to distinguish the comparator employees from the whistleblower because the harm caused by the whistleblower's insubordination was more serious, or perhaps, this is the third time the whistleblower was insubordinate, and the other comparators had no prior history of insubordination. However, the supervisor should carefully consider whether they can legitimately distinguish the treatment of the whistleblower as compared to the non-whistleblower before taking the suspension, even if the discipline or lack thereof was issued under different supervisors. Accordingly, a supervisor should carefully consult with legal counsel and the assigned employee relations specialist to gather all relevant evidence to support the charge against the whistleblower as well as that against the comparator employees. Taking these extra steps can help ensure the personnel action will satisfy the clear and convincing evidence standard.

The third *Carr* factor, "strength of any motive to retaliate on the part of the agency officials who were involved in the decision,"[34] must also be considered. Obviously, if the whistleblower's disclosure is criticizing a supervisor who subsequently takes a disciplinary action against the whistleblower, a finding of retaliation is more likely, absent clear evidence supporting the discipline and evidence of comparator, non-whistleblower employees who engaged in similar misconduct and received similar disciplinary actions. Another lesson learned from *Whitmore* is that even a supervisor who is not identified in any of the

31. *Marcato v. United States Agency for International Dev.*, 11 F.4th 781, 783 (D.C. Cir. 2021) (quoting *Carr v. Social Security Administration*, 185 F.3d 1318, 1323 (Fed. Cir. 1999)).

32. *See Murray v. Department of the Army*, No. 2021-1560, 2021 WL 3871964, at *2 (Fed. Cir. Aug. 31, 2021) ("*Carr* does not impose an affirmative burden on the agency to produce evidence with respect to each and every one of the three *Carr* factors to weigh them each individually in the agency's favor."); *see also Whitmore v. Department of Labor*, 680 F.3d 1353, 1374 (Fed. Cir. 2012) (Rather, "[t]he factors are merely appropriate and pertinent considerations for determining whether the agency carries its burden of proving by clear and convincing evidence that the same action would have been taken absent the whistleblowing." *Id.* The "absence of any evidence" relating to one factor "can effectively remove that factor from the analysis.").

33. *Whitmore v. Department of Labor*, 680 F.3d 1353, 1367 (Fed. Cir. 2012).

34. *Carr v. Social Security Administration*, 185 F.3d 1318, 1323 (Fed. Cir. 1999).

whistleblowing disclosures can be vulnerable under this factor if they are aware of the whistleblowing. In addition, a proposing official's strong motive for whistleblowing retaliation can be imputed to the deciding official.[35]

Further, in the refusal to perform a work assignment example discussed above, the supervisor should be aware that it would constitute a prohibited personnel practice for retaliating against an employee "for refusing to obey an order that would require the individual to violate a law, rule or regulation."[36]

Finally, the supervisor should avoid taking a personnel action directly due to the employee's whistleblowing. For example, a supervisor would be highly vulnerable to a finding of retaliation, if they expressly criticized the employee in a performance appraisal for disclosing information covered under the WPEA. This is an important lesson learned from *Department of Homeland Security v. MacLean.*[37] The supervisor should also avoid code words in emails or appraisals such as, "The whistleblower is not a team player" or "They need to learn how to get along with others." Such language may reasonably be construed as an intent to retaliate in response to the whistleblowing. Even if there is no apparent evidence of retaliatory animus like that described above, the supervisor should be aware that, whether through circumstantial evidence acquired during discovery, an investigation, or otherwise, the true motive behind the personnel action will most likely be revealed and whistleblower retaliation is a prohibited personnel practice that constitutes a serious offense.

Whistleblowing and Classified Information

An employee can lose their protected whistleblowing status if they disclose classified information to the press or another unauthorized source. The OSC and the Office of the Inspector General (IG), however, can receive classified information from employees. Accordingly, an employee who wishes to blow the whistle over a matter that requires the disclosure of classified information should raise the matter with the OSC or IG.[38]

35. *See supra* note 32 (For example, the Board has held that a "proposing official's strong motive to retaliate may be imputed to a deciding official" in some circumstances.); *Dwyne Chambers v. Department of Homeland Security*, 116 M.S.P.R. at 48 (citing *Miller v. Department of Veterans Affairs*, 92 M.S.P.R. 610, 619–20 (2002)).
36. Prohibited Personnel Practices, 5 U.S.C. 2302(b)(9)(D).
37. *Department of Homeland Security v. MacLean*, 574 U.S. 283 (2015). (Air Marshall was improperly fired for blowing the whistle on what he alleged was a substantial and specific danger to the public health and safety when he announced on MSNBC that there would be no Air Marshalls over Las Vegas air space, in violation of an agency rule prohibiting the release of Air Marshall schedules to the public.).
38. Inspector General Act of 1978, Pub. L. No. 95-452 (Oct. 12, 1978), 5 U.S.C. app. 3. The stated purpose of the IG Act is to create independent and objective units within each agency whose duty it is to combat waste, fraud, and abuse in the programs and operations of that agency. To this end, each IG is responsible, among other things, for conducting audits and investigations relating to the programs and operations of its agency. For a more detailed discussion on the role and responsibility of the IG, see Council of the Inspectors General and Integrity and Efficiency (CIGIE), The Inspector's General (July 14, 2014) https://ignet.gov/sites/default/files/files/IG_Authorities_Paper_-_Final_6-11-14.pdf. Each federal agency is assigned an Inspector General (IG). There were twelve original and are seventy-two current IGs.

The Whistleblower Appeals Processes

The MSPB has jurisdiction to adjudicate all whistleblowing retaliation claims that involve a personnel action and meet the standards set forth in the WPEA. The most obvious way of raising a whistleblower retaliation case before the MSPB is as an affirmative defense to a major adverse employment action (i.e., a fifteen-day suspension or more).[39] Such an appeal must be filed within thirty days of the effective date of the action.

Normally, the MSPB does not have jurisdiction over a suspension of fourteen days or fewer or a failure to promote, or an allegation challenging a performance appraisal. However, if the employee alleges such personnel actions were issued in retaliation for whistleblowing, the MSPB can have jurisdiction if the employee has exhausted administrative remedies prior to bringing the appeal to the MSPB. This appeal is referred to as an "individual right of action" (IRA) appeal to address whistleblowing retaliation. An IRA involves disciplinary actions less than fifteen days or other less severe personnel actions. The process first requires raising the whistleblowing retaliation allegation with the OSC and giving the OSC the opportunity to investigate it. OSC's primary mission is to safeguard the Merit System under 5 U.S.C. 2302 by protecting federal employees and applicants from prohibited personnel practices, including reprisal for whistleblowing.[40] Readers are encouraged to read the descriptions of all fourteen prohibited personnel practices.[41]

Upon receipt of a whistleblower retaliation allegation, the OSC will conduct an intake and investigation into the claim.[42] The OSC may request a stay of the personnel action before the MSPB, while the investigation is underway. The OSC can also reach agreement with the agency to stay the personnel action. If the OSC finds the allegations have merit, it may facilitate a settlement between the agency and employee. The OSC may also litigate the whistleblowing retaliation claim on behalf of the employee against the agency before the MSPB.

If the OSC determines the allegations lack merit, it will issue a letter to the complainant dismissing the complaint. The OSC letter of dismissal does not end the appeal rights of the employee, however. If the employee files their appeal within sixty-five (65) days of receipt of the OSC dismissal letter, they will have properly exhausted administrative remedies, and the MSPB will have jurisdiction to hear the case as an IRA

39. *Baca v. Department of the Army*, 983 F.3d 1131, 1137 (10th Cir. 2020) (The MSPB has jurisdiction of "major adverse employment action" under Cause and Procedure, 5 U.S.C. § 7513).
40. Office of Special Counsel, About OSC, https://osc.gov/Agency.
41. *See supra* note 3 at 2302 (b); For the OSC description of these prohibited personnel practices, see Office of Special Counsel, Prohibited Personnel Practices Overview, https://osc.gov/Services/Pages/PPP.aspx.
42. See Office of Special Counsel, What Happens When An Employee Files a Prohibited Personnel Practice Complaint, https://osc.gov/Services/Pages/PPP-Process.aspx.

appeal.[43] The employee, through private legal counsel or pro se, has the individual right to litigate the IRA appeal before the MSPB, even though the OSC determined the allegations lacked merit.

An employee can also file an IRA appeal if they first filed the whistleblower retaliation claim with the OSC and, after 120 days, OSC had not issued a letter accepting or dismissing the claim. The 120-day passage of time satisfies the exhaustion of administrative remedies requirement, and the MSPB will have jurisdiction to hear the IRA appeal.[44]

The IRA appeal may be resolved through the MSPB's mediation process. If the IRA appeal is filed directly with the MSPB without first filing the claim with the OSC, it will be dismissed by the MSPB for failure to exhaust administrative remedies. If the appeal is filed after sixty-five (65) days of receipt of the OSC dismissal letter, the MSPB will dismiss the appeal as untimely. Federal courts can exercise jurisdiction over cases appealed to and adjudicated by the MSPB.[45]

The IRA Appeal Process and Probationary Employees

The MSPB normally does not have jurisdiction to adjudicate a termination of a probationary employee. However, if the probationary employee asserts the termination is because of whistleblowing retaliation, the employee can file a complaint with the OSC and, after exhausting administrative remedies discussed in the previous section, file an IRA appeal with the MSPB over their termination. Under such a circumstance, the MSPB can have jurisdiction to adjudicate the termination of a probationary employee.[46]

There Are No Timeliness Requirements for Whistleblowing

An employee can blow the whistle any time. Further, unlike the federal Equal Employment Opportunity Commission (EEOC) complaint process, which requires an employee to file a complaint of discrimination within forty-five (45) days of being notified of a personnel action giving rise to the allegation of discrimination[47] (unless there is a continuing violation), there is no express timeliness requirement for when an employee must bring a whistleblower retaliation complaint before the OSC. Of course, if the employee does not bring the matter to the OSC until years after the personnel action occurred that gave rise to the

43. The IRA appeal process and the direct appeals process are not only applicable to *supra* note 3 at (b)(8) whistleblower retaliation allegations but also to allegations that the employee was retaliated against for engaging in certain protected activities covered under *supra* note 3 at 2302 (b)(9), including the following: the exercise of any appeal, complaint, or grievance right granted by any law, rule, or regulation—with regard to remedying a violation of paragraph (8); or other than with regard to remedying a violation of paragraph (8); testifying for or otherwise lawfully assisting any individual in the exercise of any right referred to in subparagraph (a)(i) or (ii); cooperating with or disclosing information to the Inspector General (or any other component responsible for internal investigation or review) of an agency or the Special Counsel, in accordance with applicable provisions of law; or refusing to obey an order that would require the individual to violate a law, rule, or regulation.
44. *See* Office of Special Counsel, OSC Fact Sheet for Whistleblowing Retaliation, https://osc.gov/Documents/PPP/OSC%27s%20Role/Fact%20Sheet%20for%20Whistleblower%20Retaliation.pdf.
45. Filing an Appeal and Responses to Appeals. 5 C.F.R. § 1201.22(b)(1).
46. *See Chavez v. Department of Veterans Affairs, 120* M.S.P.R. 285 (2013).
47. 29 C.F.R. § 1614.105(a)(1).

allegation, the OSC may determine that the employee has not set forth a prima facie case of whistleblower retaliation by failing to satisfy the "knowledge timing test" discussed previously. Again, employees who raise an appeal directly with the MSPB must do so within thirty (30) days of the major adverse action, in accordance with MSPB requirements.

In addition, most agencies have broad scope grievance procedures, permitting an employee to file a whistleblowing grievance over either a major adverse action or minor action, akin to an IRA. If the collective bargaining agreement permits, a whistleblower retaliation grievance can be litigated before an arbitrator.

Remedies Under the WPEA

A prevailing party may receive compensatory damages, which may include pain and suffering experienced because of the retaliation. Unlike the Civil Rights Act of 1991, which caps compensatory damages for pain and suffering in most EEO discrimination complaints against the federal government to $300,000, there is no cap on compensatory damages in a whistleblower retaliation complaint.

A prevailing party will be placed in the same position they would have been in had they not been retaliated against. Additionally, a prevailing party is entitled to back pay and attorney's fees.

Recent Updates to Whistleblower Law

In 2017, the Dr. Chris Kirkpatrick Whistleblower Protection Act was signed into law.[48] The Act provides that if a finding of whistleblower is made by the OSC, IG, MSPB, a judge of the United States, or the head of the agency, the agency must, at a minimum, propose a three-day suspension against the supervisor, and if such a finding occurs a second time, the agency must propose removal. The Act also created a new prohibited personnel practice for accessing medical records in furtherance of violating another prohibited personnel practice, and it required agencies to notify OSC if an agency employee committed suicide after making a protected disclosure and experiencing a personnel action by their agency in response. It also mandated certain training requirements regarding whistleblowing and prohibited personnel practices.[49]

In 2017, legislation reauthorizing OSC was signed. The legislation, included in the National Defense Authorization Act for Fiscal Year 2018, reauthorizes OSC through 2023. Section 1097 of the bill clarifies that when complying with OSC's information requests, federal agencies may not withhold information and documents from OSC by asserting common law privileges, such as attorney–client privilege. The reauthorization measure reasserts OSC's ability to obtain needed information and documents. The reauthorization also promotes greater efficiency and accountability within OSC, improves protections against retaliatory investigations and other forms of reprisal for whistleblowing, and requires managers across the federal government to respond appropriately to disclosures of waste, fraud, and abuse.[50]

48. *DeGrella v. Dep't of the Air Force*, No. SF-1221-19-0566-W-1, 2022 WL 17685969, at *3 (M.S.P.B. Dec. 14, 2022), citing the Dr. Chris Kirkpatrick Whistleblower Protection Act of 2017, Pub. L. No. 115-73, 131 Stat. 1235, 1236 (2017

49. *See supra* note 8 at 8.

50. *Id.*

In 2017, Congress passed the Follow the Rules Act,[51] which prohibits a federal agency from taking a personnel action against an employee for refusing to violate an order that would require the employee to violate a law, rule, or regulation. The Act was incorporated as a prohibited personnel practice under 2302(b)(9)(D) and protects federal employees when they are "refusing to obey an order that would require the individual to violate a law, rule or regulation." This Act overturned *Rainey v. MSPB*, which previously found it was a prohibited personnel practice only if the employee refused to violate a law.[52]

In 2018, Congress made permanent the All Circuits Review Act that allows federal whistleblowers to bring appeals of their cases from the MSPB beyond the federal circuit court of appeals to all circuit courts of appeals in the area they live or work.[53] Presidential Policy Directive 19 makes it unlawful for an agency to take any action affecting an employee's eligibility for access to classified information in reprisal for making a protected disclosure.[54]

The Enhancement of Contractor Protection from Reprisal for Disclosure of Certain Information was made law in 2013 and has been amended as recently as April of 2023.[55] Among other things, it protects employees of federal contractors, subcontractors, grantees, and personal service contractors from reprisal concerning protected disclosures about federal contracts or grants.[56] There is also current legislation under consideration by Congress: the Whistleblower Protection Improvement Act (WPIA).[57]

Nondisclosure Agreements: Special Requirements

Agencies often issue policies or enter settlement agreements that containing a non-disclosure agreement. The Whistleblower Protection Enhancement Act of 2012 prohibits agencies from issuing or enforcing nondisclosure agreements, policies, or forms that do not contain the following statement:

> These provisions are consistent with and do not supersede, conflict with, or otherwise alter the employee obligations, rights, or liabilities created by existing statute or Executive order relating to (1) classified information, (2) communications to Congress, (3) the reporting to an Inspector General of a violation of any law, rule, or regulation, or mismanagement, a gross waste of funds, an abuse of authority, or a substantial and specific danger to public health or safety, or (4) any other whistleblower protection.

51. Follow The Rules Act, H.R. 657 (2017–2018), https://www.congress.gov/115/crpt/hrpt67/CRPT-115hrpt67.pdf.
52. *Rainey v. MSPB*, 824 F.3d 1359 (Fed Cir. 2018).
53. An Act, Pub. L. 115–195, https://www.congress.gov/115/plaws/publ195/PLAW-115publ195.pdf.
54. See The OPM IG summarize the rights of whistleblowers including PPD-19. https://www.opm.gov/our-inspector-general/whistleblower-protection-information/.
55. Enhancement of Contractor Protection from Reprisal for Disclosure of Certain Information. 41 U.S.C. § 4712.
56. *See* Office of Personnel Management, Whistleblower Rights & Protections, https://oig.opm.gov/report-oig/whistleblower-rights-protections#:~:text=Federal%20whistleblower%20protection%20law%20provides,to%20public%20safety%20or%20health.
57. For a summary of this legislation, see Press Release on Government Accountability Project Applauds Introduction of Whistleblower Protection Improvement Act, May 3, 2021, https://whistleblower.org/whistleblower-profiles/government-accountability/press-release-government-accountability-project-applauds-introduction-of-whistleblower-protection-improvement-act/; *see also* Legal Alerts Blog Katz Marshall Banks, *House Considers Enhanced Protections from Federal Whistleblowers* 9 Nat. L. Rev., (2021), https://www.natlawreview.com/article/house-considers-enhanced-protections-federal-government-whistleblowers.

> The definitions, requirements, obligations, rights, sanctions, and liabilities created by controlling Executive orders and statutory provisions are incorporated into this agreement and are controlling.[58]

The issuance of a non-disclosure agreement without the foregoing language constitutes a prohibited personnel practice under 5 U.S.C. 2302(b)(13). Accordingly, agencies should take due care to ensure that any policy or settlement agreement with a non-disclosure provision containing the foregoing language.

Leadership in the Context of a Constitutional Government and Whistleblowing

The outstanding leader strives to create a culture that encourages the reporting of wrongdoing. To this end, the leader should encourage whistleblowers and support, not retaliate against, the whistleblower for making a protected disclosure. The leader does not have to agree with the employee's disclosure to recognize their right to express their views under the WPEA. Further, by encouraging whistleblowing, other disclosures of value to the agency or public may be forthcoming. By fostering an environment that encourages the disclosure of waste, fraud and abuse, the leader promotes a civil work environment dedicated to achieving the mission of the agency. Some organizations, such as the U.S. Nuclear Regulatory Commission (NRC), strive to create a "safety culture"; and encourage employees to report unsafe working conditions.[59] In this endeavor, the NRC has created "Open Door"[60] "Differing Professional Opinion"[61] Differing Professional Opinions Program, https://www.nrc.gov/docs/ML0417/ML041770431.pdf and "Nonconcurrence"[62] policies to encourage differing views. Employees who report information under these policies often qualify as whistleblowers (although a careful analysis of the WPEA must be applied to the facts of each case), and their disclosures can be critical to the agency as well as the protection of the public.

The effective leader embraces the wisdom of Martin Luther King, Jr., who said at Selma, "Our lives begin to end the day we become silent about things that matter."[63] A leader also heeds Dr. King's advice, "There comes a time when silence is a betrayal."[64] The effective leader is empathetic and understands that, oftentimes, whistleblowing requires real courage. Further, promoting internal whistleblowing is critical to creating an organizational culture that promotes ethical conduct.[65]

58. *Supra* note 3.
59. Safety culture, for example, is particularly important in the Nuclear industry. *See* U.S. Nuclear Regulatory Commission, Safety Culture (2021), https://www.nrc.gov/about-nrc/safety-culture.html.
60. U.S. Nuclear Regulatory Commission Management Directive, U.S. Nuclear Regulatory Commission Management Directive (MD): Open Door Policy, https://www.nrc.gov/docs/ML1521/ML15219A454.pdf.
61. U.S. Nuclear Regulatory Commission Management Directive, The NRC
62. U.S. Nuclear Regulatory Commission Management Directive: NRC Non-Concurrence Process, https://www.nrc.gov/docs/ML1317/ML13176A371.pdf
63. Martin Luther King, Speech Delivered in Selma, Alabama (Mar. 8, 1965).
64. Martin Luther King, Speech Delivered at Riverside Church (Apr. 4, 1967).
65. See Carl R. Oliver and Francis Daly, *Encouraging Ethical leadership (and More!)*, Markkula Center for Applied Ethics (June 1, 2007), https://www.scu.edu/ethics/focus-areas/business-ethics/resources/encouraging-internal-whistleblowing-and-more/

The connection between leadership and whistleblowing is further supported by the outstanding 1993 article by Dean Ludwig and Clinton Longnecker: "The Bathsheba Syndrome: The Ethical Failure of Successful Leaders."[66] Nathan, described by Ludwig and Longnecker as "the equivalent of a modern-day whistleblower," confronts King David over his cover-up of his unethical affair with Bathsheba and his abuse of power when he manipulated the battle plans of a war and sent Bathsheba's husband, Uriah, to the front lines, resulting in Uriah's death. The article, in discussing the "dark side of success"[67] provides advice to future leaders and emphasizes, among other things, the need to build an ethical team that can "challenge" the leader when needed.[68] The whistleblower, by challenging the leader or the efficiency or effectiveness of the government program they administer, can actually help the leader become more accountable to the staff and public.

This does not mean that a whistleblower is, per se, insulated from any disciplinary, performance-based action or other adverse personnel action. It does mean, however, given the clear and convincing evidence test, the supervisor must be able to clearly demonstrate that they would have taken the same action even if the employee had not been a whistleblower. Specifically, the supervisor should carefully consider the previously covered *Carr* factors when taking an action that could be subject to an allegation of whistleblower retaliation. If, for example, the whistleblower is treated less favorably than other non-whistleblower employees engaged in similar poor performance or misconduct, the evidence to support the adverse action is weak, or there is evidence of a strong motive to retaliate, the supervisor may not be able to support such a personnel action. The supervisor should understand that the failure to provide sufficient evidence to sustain such an action could have substantial adverse effects on the agency. Further, given the mandatory disciplinary action proposal requirements under the Dr. Chris Kirkpatrick Act, discussed previously, the failure to support such an action can substantially and adversely impact the supervisor's career.

Finally, whenever considering taking an adverse personnel action against a whistleblower, the supervisor should always keep in mind the closing words of *Whitmore v. Department of Labor*:

> Despite Robert Whitmore's highly unprofessional and intimidating conduct, which may well ultimately justify some adverse personnel action, he is nevertheless a bona fide whistleblower. Mr. Whitmore is ... entitled to the full scope of protection afforded by the Whistleblower Protection Act, which ensures for him and whistleblowers everywhere that they need not fear retribution for disclosing to the public such vital information concerning an agency or official as "a violation of any law, rule, or regulation, or

66. Dean Ludwig and Clinton Longnecker, *The Bathsheba Syndrome: The Ethical Failure of Successful Leaders*, J. Bus. Eth. (1992), http://ksuweb.kennesaw.edu/~uzimmerm/Notes/Ludwig+Longenecker,%20The%20Bathsheba%20Syndrome.pdf.

67. *See* Dan Stallard and Major Kurt Sanger, The Nathan Solution to the Bathsheba Syndrome, 98, 4 Mar. Corp. Gaz. (2014) ("Success often leads to privileged access to information, people, and objects; Success often leads to unrestrained control of organizational resources; Success can inflate a leader's belief in his personal ability to manipulate or control outcomes; Success often leads to privileged access to information, people, and objects; Personal and organizational success allows leaders to become complacent and lose strategic focus, diverting attention to things other than the management of their organizations.").

68. *See also* Mackubin Thomas Owens, *Petraeus's Bathsheba Syndrome* W. St, J., November 13, 2012, https://www.nationalreview.com/2012/11/petraeuss-bathsheba-syndrome-mackubin-thomas-owens/ (a discussion of the applicability of the Bathsheba Syndrome to a well-known military leader).

> gross mismanagement, a gross waste of funds, an abuse of authority, or a substantial and specific danger to public health or safety," 5 U.S.C. § 2302(b)(8). Congress decided that we as a people are better off knowing than not knowing about such violations and improper conduct, even if it means that an insubordinate employee like Mr. Whitmore becomes, via such disclosures, more difficult to discipline or terminate. Indeed, it is in the presence of such non-sympathetic employees that commitment to the clear and convincing evidence standard is most tested and is most in need of preservation.[69]

By proceeding with caution, seeking the advice of counsel before taking an adverse personnel action against a whistleblower, and ensuring the personnel action can be supported by clear and convincing evidence, the supervisor will heed the advice of *Whitmore* avoid violating the WPEA.

Cases and Review Questions

Directions: Use the provided links to access each noteworthy case. Then, provide complete and detailed responses to the questions and prompts about each case.

Department of Homeland Security v. MacLean, 574 U.S. 383 (2015)

https://supreme.justia.com/cases/federal/us/574/383/

1. Why was MacLean considered a whistleblower in this case?
2. If an employee violates an agency rule or regulation in the course of disclosing information, are they still a whistleblower?
3. What is meant by disclosing information that violates a law under the Whistleblower Protection Act?
4. Explain whether MacLean violated the law when he disclosed that air marshals would not be flying over Las Vegas airspace.
5. What are the consequences of this decision on the ability to discipline a whistleblower?
6. What could Congress or the President do to make it easier to discipline a whistleblower?

Whitmore v. Department of Labor, 680 F.2d 1353 (Fed Cir. 2012)

https://law.justia.com/cases/federal/appellate-courts/cafc/11-3084/11-3084-2012-05-30.html

1. What are the *Carr* factors?
2. What is the clear and convincing evidence standard, as it applies to a whistleblower case?
3. Why did the Court conclude that the government failed to prove that it would have taken the same action even if Mr. Whitmore was not a whistleblower?
4. What are the lessons learned in this decision about instituting a biased internal investigation into

69. *Whitmore v. Department of Labor*, 680 F.3d 1353, 1377 (Fed. Cir. 2012).

misconduct?

5. What impact do you see this decision having on managers considering disciplining an employee who is a whistleblower?
6. What can an employer do to encourage, rather than punish, a whistleblower?

Flynn v. United States Securities and Exchange Commission, 877 F.3d 200 (4th Cir. 2017)

https://caselaw.findlaw.com/us-4th-circuit/1882094.html

1. When a whistleblower asserts an agency is violating one of their rules, how is the word "rule" defined?
2. When the whistleblower disclosed that the SEC violated Rule 900(a) and Rule 900(b), why was a violation of Rule 900(b) considered whistleblowing but a violation of Rule 900(a) not?
3. How do you think this case will impact the way agencies draft rules in the future if they wish to insulate rules from whistleblower allegations?

Chapter 6

The Fourth Amendment

Introduction

This chapter provides a general overview of the Fourth Amendment, followed by its applicability to the government employer and employee in various circumstances, such as searching an employee's office, accessing computers and electronic devices, and drug testing. The chapter will also address leadership in the context of the Fourth Amendment followed by links to specific cases with follow-up questions to prompt classroom discussion.

General Overview of the Fourth Amendment and the Public

The Fourth Amendment provides the following:

> The right of the people to be secure in their persons, houses, papers, and effects, against unreasonable searches and seizures, shall not be violated, and no Warrants shall issue, but upon probable cause, supported by Oath or affirmation, and particularly describing the place to be searched, and the persons or things to be seized.[1]

The "goal" of the Fourth Amendment is "to protect people's right of privacy and freedom from unreasonable intrusions by the government."[2] Generally, it is applicable whenever the government seeks to search or seize a person and/or their property.

The Fourth Amendment provides that, with some exceptions, prior to conducting a search and/or seizure, the government must seek a warrant from an impartial judge or magistrate with sufficient detail to show there is "probable cause" that a crime was committed

1. U.S. Const. amend. IV.
2. *See* Legal Information Institute (LII) of Cornell Law School, Fourth Amendment (2017), https://www.law.cornell.edu/wex/fourth_amendment.

that justifies the search. Probable cause is a low evidentiary standard and has been defined as a "fair probability" that the object of the search may be found in the place to be searched."[3] In the context of an arrest warrant, probable cause has been defined as sufficient facts and circumstances to warrant "a reasonable [person] of reasonable caution in believing that the person arrested had committed an offense."[4]

There are well-known exceptions to the warrant requirement, including, but not limited to, consent to the search; a search incident to a lawful arrest; "exigent circumstances" that make the warrant impracticable, such as imminent danger; imminent destruction of evidence or imminent escape; or the objects to be searched being in plain view.[5] The Supreme Court has also recognized the right of the police, when they have less than probable cause but a "reasonable suspicion" that a criminal offense has been committed, to conduct a temporary investigatory "stop and frisk" search.[6]

Evidence obtained in violation of the Fourth Amendment, or otherwise in violation of the law, is subject to the "exclusionary rule"[7] and is not admissible as evidence, under the "fruit of the poisonous tree" doctrine: "In a nutshell, this doctrine counsels for the exclusion of evidence derived from information or items obtained in [an illegal] search."[8]

Fourth Amendment cases consistently balance an individual's privacy right against government intrusion, with the legitimate governmental interests at issue. For example, post-accident drug testing was upheld, despite the lack of reasonable suspicion evidence that the railway conductor in the case was under the influence of drugs while driving the train. In this case, the safety interests of the government were judged to have outweighed the privacy interests of the conductor.[9]

The courts also consider the degree to which the individual has a "reasonable expectation of privacy" and whether the search is "reasonable at its inception" and "reasonable in scope."[10] Accordingly, where and under what circumstances a search is conducted must be carefully considered on a case-by-case basis. For example, an individual has a very high expectation of privacy inside their home: "The law was clearly established at the time of entry that a warrantless entry into a private dwelling, absent exigent circumstances [or consent] is unlawful" and "presumptively unreasonable."[11] *On the other hand, in a school environment,* a warrant is not required before searching a student who is under the school's authority if it can be shown that the search is reasonable under all circumstances.[12]

Further, a warrantless search of an automobile is appropriate—given its inherent mobility and the

3. *United States v. Montgomery*, 527 F.3d 682, 686 (8th Cir. 2008) (in the context of an arrest warrant).
4. *Howlett v. Hack*, 794 F.3d 721, 727 (7th Cir. 2015).
5. Supra note 2.
6. *Terry v. Ohio,* 392 U.S. 1 (1968); See Constitution Annotated, Fourth Amendment, *Terry Stop and Frisks: Doctrine and Practice*, https://constitution.congress.gov/browse/essay/amdt4_4_4_1_1/.
7. *See Mapp v. Ohio,* 367 U.S. 643 (1961).
8. *See United States v. Elmore,* 18 F.4th 193 (6th Cir. 2021) (citing *Murray v. United States*, 487 U.S. 533, 536–37, 108 S. Ct. 2529, 101 L.Ed.2d 472 (1988)).
9. *Skinner v. Railway Labor Executives' Association*, 489 U.S. 602 (1989).
10. *City of Ontario v. Quon*, 560 U.S. 746 (2010).
11. *See Chamberlain Est. of Chamberlain v. City of White Plains*, 960 F.3d 100, 111 (2d Cir. 2020) (citing *Payton v. New York*, 445 U.S. 573, 586 (1980)).
12. *New Jersey v. TLO*, 469 U.S. 325 (1985).

diminished expectation of privacy—when it is reasonable to believe that the vehicle contains evidence of criminal activity. Once an officer has probable cause to search the vehicle under the automobile exception, they "may conduct a probing search of compartments and containers within the vehicle whose contents are not in plain view."[13] A recent and interesting development in Fourth Amendment law, however, involves the search of a vehicle based upon nothing more than the detection of an odor of marijuana, in a state where marijuana is legal. In these circumstances, some courts have found the search of the car unconstitutional.[14]

Further, it has always been presumed that the greatest expectation of privacy an individual has is in their home. However, in *Riley v. California*,[15] the Supreme Court unanimously held that the reasonable expectation of privacy in one's personal cell phone exceeds even the expectation of privacy in the home:

> In 1926, Learned Hand observed (in an opinion later quoted in *Chimel*) that it is "a totally different thing to search a man's pockets and use against him what they contain, from ransacking his house for everything which may incriminate him." *United States v. Kirschenblatt,* 16 F.2d 202, 203 (C.A.2). If his pockets contain a cell phone, however, that is no longer true. Indeed, a cell phone search would typically expose to the government far *more* than the most exhaustive search of a house: A phone not only contains in digital form many sensitive records previously found in the home; it also contains a broad array of private information never found in a home in any form—unless the phone is.[16]

Riley was initially stopped for a traffic violation and arrested when guns were found under the hood of his car. Riley was searched, incident to a lawful arrest. The subsequent search of his cell phone, without a warrant, revealed texts messages that documented his membership in a street gang and photographs that showed him standing by a car in a drive-by shooting. That evidence led to his conviction for murder and a fifteen-year prison sentence. The cell phone of the other arrested individual revealed a telephone call log that was traced and used to get a search warrant of a physical address. That search discovered, among other things, illegal drugs, which resulted in her conviction and a prison sentence.

In *Riley*, the Supreme Court examined *Chimel v. California*,[17] which allowed a police officer to perform a warrantless search within the area of immediate control of the individual arrested to preclude the potential destruction of evidence and to protect the safety of the arresting officer. It also examined *United States v. Robinson*,[18] which permitted a police officer, to search, incident to a lawful arrest, a cigarette pack found on the person of the individual arrested, which contained illegal drugs. In *Riley*, the Supreme Court distinguished such prior precedent when it came to searching a cell phone without a warrant. When

13. *See United States v. Ross,* 456 U.S. 798 (1982); *see also* United States Courts, What Does the Fourth Amendment Mean? https://www.uscourts.gov/about-federal-courts/educational-resources/about-educational-outreach/activity-resources/what-does-0.
14. *See People v. McKnight*, 446 P. 3d 997 (S. Ct. Col. 2021); *see also*, Caren Chesler, *A Whiff of Pot Alone no Longer Airtight Probable Cause for Police to Search Cars in Several States*, Wash. Post, June 26, 2021, https://www.washingtonpost.com/national-security/marijuana-police-probable-cause/2021/06/26/9d984f8e-d36c-11eb-a53a-3b5450fdca7a_story.html.
15. *Riley v. California*, 573 U.S. 373 (2014).
16. *Id.* at 396-97.
17. *Chimel v. California,* 395 U.S. 792 (1969).
18. *United States v. Robinson*, 414 U.S. 218 (1973).

balancing the government's interests, against the individual's privacy interests in the vast amount of private information contained in a cell phone, the Supreme Court held that the search of the individual's cell phone required a warrant:

> Modern cell phones are not just another technological convenience. With all they contain and all they may reveal, they hold for many Americans "the privacies of life ... ." The fact that technology now allows an individual to carry such information in his hand does not make the information any less worthy of the protection for which the Founders fought. Our answer to the question of what police must do before searching a cell phone seized incident to an arrest is accordingly simple—get a warrant.[19]

Another important case, *Carpenter v. United States*, extended *Riley*, and found that historical cell-site location information (CSLI) was protected by the Fourth Amendment.[20] Specifically, in *Carpenter*, the government requested the CSLI of various defendants from several wireless carriers, under the Stored Communication Act,[21] to prosecute them. They also used the records to prove the phones of defendants were within a two-mile radius of a Radio Shack store robbery. This evidence led to the defendants' convictions for aiding and abetting a robbery and the use or carriage of a firearm, in violation of the law. The Supreme Court overturned these convictions in a five-to-four decision and found that the government had violated the Fourth Amendment when it did not request a warrant prior to obtaining CSLI because an individual has a reasonable expectation of privacy in such cell phone tracking data. Chief Justice Roberts, who wrote for the majority, emphasized the comprehensive and ongoing nature of the surveillance which occurred in both public and private places. He went so far as to describe it as "near perfect surveillance, as if it had attached an ankle monitor to the phone's user."[22] *Carpenter* has been seen as an important case in protecting the privacy rights of the public in the digital age from such developing technologies as drones.[23]

One interesting and evolving area of Fourth Amendment law involves the warrantless search of cell phones and other electronic equipment, such as computers at the U.S. border, where the government interests are at their zenith. Although the Supreme Court has not expressly weighed in on this issue since *Riley*, the Congressional Research Service summarized the status of the law as follows:

> In sum, lower courts have generally agreed that [Custom and Border Protection] officers

19. *Id.* at 403.
20. *Carpenter v. United States*, 138 S. Ct. 2206 (2018).
21. Under the Stored Communications Act, the government may require the disclosure of telecommunications records when "specific and articulable facts show that there are reasonable grounds to believe" that the records sought "are relevant and material to an ongoing criminal investigation." Stored Communications Act, 18 U.S.C. § 2703(d).
22. *See supra* note 20 at 2218.
23. Laura Hecht-Felella, *The Fourth Amendment in the Digital Age: How Carpenter Can Protect Privacy Protections in the Digital Age*, Brennan Center for Justice, New York University School of Law, March 18, 2021, https://www.brennancenter.org/our-work/policy-solutions/fourth-amendment-digital-age.[/footnote] Many lawyers have been critical of the decision, and many courts have interpreted it narrowly.[footnote]*See* Matthew J. Tokson, *The Aftermath of Carpenter: An Empirical Study of Fourth Amendment Law, 2018-2021* Forthcoming Harv. L. Rev., University of Utah College of Law Research Paper No. 470, https://ssrn.com/abstract=3932015.

> may conduct relatively limited, manual searches of electronic devices at the border without a warrant or any particularized suspicion. But courts have disagreed about whether more intrusive, forensic searches [i.e., using software to copy the hard drive and analyze its contents, including deleted content] requires at least reasonable suspicion of a crime, and whether that reasonable suspicion must be tied to evidence of contraband within the device itself, or any evidence of potential criminal activity that may be taking place.[24]

Federal employees should, of course, refer to agency guidance and policy on this matter. Finally, Fourth Amendment law is continuously evolving as technology evolves:

> Today, we are at a jurisprudential inflection point as courts grapple with when and how the Fourth Amendment should apply to the data generated by technologies like cell phones, smart cars, and wearable devices. These technologies—which we rely on for enhanced communication, transportation, and entertainment—create detailed records about our private lives, potentially revealing not only where we have been but also our political viewpoints, consumer preferences, people with whom we have interacted, and more. The resulting trove of information is immensely valuable to law enforcement for use in investigations and prosecutions, and much of it is currently available without a warrant.[25]

Not surprisingly, it is important to carefully consult with legal counsel before authorizing or conducting a search.

The Fourth Amendment and the Government Employee

The Fourth Amendment also protects government employees against unreasonable searches and seizures. In *O'Connor v. Ortega*, involving the search of a government issued desk, the Supreme Court held: "Individuals do not lose Fourth Amendment rights merely because they work for the government instead of a private employer."[26] The search and seizure of private property of a government employee by the government, including the employee's supervisor, is protected by the Fourth Amendment.[27] A "search" occurs when a government actor infringes upon "an expectation of privacy that society is prepared to consider reasonable."[28] A "seizure" of property occurs "when there is some meaningful interference with an individual's possessory interests in that property."[29]

To invoke the protections of the Fourth Amendment, a government employee must first establish that

24. *See* Hillel R. Smith and Kelsey Y. Santamaria, *Searches and Seizures at the Border and the Fourth Amendment* 48 (2021), https://crsreports.congress.gov/product/pdf/R/R46601.
25. *Supra* note 20.
26. *See O'Connor v. Ortega*, 480 U.S. 709, 717 (1987).
27. *Id. at* 715 (1987).
28. *United States v. Jacobsen*, 466 U.S. 109, 113 (1984).
29. *Id.*

they have a reasonable expectation of privacy.[30] A government employee's expectation of privacy must by examined on a case-by-case basis, in the practical context of the employment relationship. An employee's reasonable expectation of privacy can be reduced by office policy, practice, and regulation, which serves to place the employee on advance notice that they may be subject to a search.[31] This applies not only to the search of an office desk or file cabinet but also to emails and computer searches, where, for example, there is often a banner warning that the computer may be subject to a search.[32] The government must also be prepared to show, as stated previously, that the search was reasonable at is inception and reasonable in scope.[33] This chapter examines the applicability of the Fourth Amendment in three common circumstances government employees may find themselves in during their career: the search of their government office, the search of their government computers and electronic devices, and drug testing.

The Search of the Contents of a Government Employee's Office

The search and seizure of the contents of a government employee's office is subject to a Fourth Amendment analysis, although the government will normally prevail, given the reduced expectation of privacy the employee has in their office:

> The employee's expectation of privacy must be assessed in the context of the employment relationship. An office is seldom a private enclave free from entry by supervisors, other employees, and business and personal invitees. Instead, in many cases offices are continually entered by fellow employees and other visitors during the workday for conferences, consultations, and other work-related visits. Simply put, it is the nature of government offices that others—such as fellow employees, supervisors, consensual visitors, and the general public—may have frequent access to an individual's office. We agree with Justice SCALIA that "[c]onstitutional protection against *unreasonable* searches by the government does not disappear merely because the government has the right to make reasonable intrusions in its capacity as employer," *post,* at 1505, but some government offices may be so open to fellow employees or the public that no expectation of privacy is reasonable. Cf. *Katz v. United States,* 389 U.S. 347, 351, 88 S.Ct. 507, 511, 19 L.Ed.2d 576 (1967) ("What a person knowingly exposes to the public, even in his own home or office, is not a subject of Fourth Amendment protection"). Given the great variety of work environments in the public sector, the question whether an employee has a reasonable expectation of privacy must be addressed on a case-by-case basis.[34]

30. *City of Ontario v. Quon*, 560 U.S. 746 (2010).
31. *James v. Hampton*, 592 F. App'x 449, 455–56 (6th Cir. 2015).
32. *United States v. Caputo,* No. 3:18-CR-00428-IM, 2019 WL 5788305, at *4 (D. Or. Nov. 6, 2019).
33. *Id.*
34. *O'Connor v. Ortega*, 480 U.S. 709, 718, (1987).

The search of a government desk for work-related reasons is normally entitled to a reduced expectation of privacy, especially when there are express office policies clearly communicated to employees that their workplace is subject to a search:

> The expectation of privacy in "offices, desks, and file cabinets ... may be reduced by virtue of actual office practice and procedures or by legitimate regulation." Put another way, "operational realities" may impact an employee's privacy expectations. *Von Raab*, 489 U.S. at 671, 109 S.Ct. 1384. Thus, "employer policies ... will of course shape the reasonable expectations of their employees, especially to the extent that such policies are clearly communicated."[35]

However, an employee may have a reasonable expectation of privacy for an item brought into an office that is not considered a part of the workplace context:

> Not everything that passes through the confines of the business address can be considered part of the workplace context, however. An employee may bring closed luggage to the office prior to leaving on a trip, or a handbag or briefcase each workday. While whatever expectation of privacy the employee has in the existence and the outward appearance of the luggage is affected by its presence in the workplace, the employee's expectation of privacy in the *contents* of the luggage is not affected in the same way. The appropriate standard for a workplace search does not necessarily apply to a piece of closed personal luggage, a handbag or a briefcase that happens to be within the employer's business address.[36]

A warrant is not required for the search of an office for non-investigatory, work-related purposes as well as for investigations of work-related misconduct. The Supreme Court has recognized a "special needs" exception in the government office environment, which renders the "warrant and probable-cause requirement impracticable." When conducting a search, the government will be judged by the standard of "reasonableness under all the circumstances" and must be prepared to establish that the search was reasonable at its inception and reasonable in scope.[37]

The Search of a Government Employee's Computer and Other Electronic Devices

The Fourth Amendment is also applicable to the search of a government computer or other government-owned electronic devices. In *Quon v. City of Ontario*,[38] the Supreme Court determined that the principles applicable to search of a physical office applied to the "electronic sphere"[39] and that a government

35. *Id.* at 760
36. *Id.* at 716, (1987)
37. *Id.*
38. *Supra* note 31.
39. *Id.* at 760.

employer's examination of text messages on a government-issued electronic device, a pager, was a search under the Fourth Amendment. The Supreme Court held that the search did not violate the Fourth Amendment because although the employee, a police officer, had some reasonable expectation of privacy in his text messages, the search was reasonable at its inception—to determine why his pager usage was so high—and reasonable in scope—limited only to a few years of unusually high pager activity. Accordingly, the Court upheld the removal of the employee, a police officer, for misusing the pager for personal reasons, to have an affair, rather than for work-related reasons.

In *Quon*, the Court clarified that "employer policies ... will of course shape the reasonable expectations of their employees, especially to the extent that such policies are clearly communicated."[40] Thus, in *United States v. Hamilton*,[41] the Fourth Circuit Court of Appeals determined that the defendant had no reasonable expectation of privacy, in light of the employer's computer usage policy, which advised that information received, accessed, or stored via the computer system was subject to inspection and monitoring. The Court elaborated that although there may be a reasonable expectation of privacy in e-mails on a government computer, the government employer adopted a computer usage policy that expressly provided that users had no expectation of privacy in their use of the computer system and that all information created, sent, received, accessed, or stored in the computer system was subject to inspection and monitoring at any time. Moreover, every employee had to acknowledge the policy every time they signed onto the computer.[42]

Similarly, in *United States v. Hill*, where a policy was issued by the Federal Bureau of Prisons (BOP) that placed a federal employee on notice that his government-issued phone and computer tablet were subject to being monitored and searched,[43] substantially diminished any reasonable expectation of privacy of the employee and permitted the Office of Inspector General to search and seize these devices in connection with a misconduct investigation. Further, in *Walker v. Coffey*, the search of the government computer without a warrant was permissible because the FBI had obtained consent from the employer, who exercised common authority over the workplace computer at issue.[44]

The Search of a Government Employee Through Drug Testing

Another context in which Fourth Amendment issues typically emerge is during drug testing. Mandatory drug testing when conducted by the government, is a search and seizure within the meaning of the Fourth Amendment.[45] Constitutional issues may arise in the context of random drug testing, post-accident drug testing, and reasonable suspicion drug testing.

Random drug testing has been upheld for government employees in "safety-sensitive" positions, such as those responsible for maintaining and operating trains, airplanes, and motor vehicles. It has also

40. *Id.* at 760.
41. 701 F.3d 404, 408–09 (4th Cir. 2012).
42. *Id.*
43. 319 F. Supp. 3d 44, 46 (D.D.C. 2018).
44. *Walker v. Coffey*, 905 F.3d 138, 149 (3d Cir. 2018).
45. *National Treasury Employees Union v. Von Raab*, 489 U.S. 656, 665 (1989); *Skinner v. Railway Labor Executives' Association*, 489 U.S. 602, 616–19 (1989).

applied to employees required to carry firearms in the performance of their duties and employees who inspect hazardous materials.[46] Random drug testing has also been authorized for employees with security clearances.[47] A full listing of positions subject to random testing in the federal government is set forth in the Department of Health and Human Services 2010 Updated Guidelines for Selection of Testing Designated Positions (TDPs).[48]

Post-accident drug testing is another basis for conducting a drug test for which the supervisor has a reasonable suspicion that the employee caused the accident.[49] A supervisor may also direct an employee to take a drug test when the supervisor has a reasonable suspicion the employee is under the influence of illegal drugs. Reasonable suspicion is a lesser standard than probable cause, both in terms of the content of the information provided and the required reliability of the source providing that information. It also permits a degree of uncertainty.[50] Reasonable suspicion is based on the factual information known to the agency at the time of its decision and does not take into account additional information that was subsequently disclosed or which could have been discovered through further inquiry.[51] Further, although reasonable suspicion drug testing does not require certainty, mere "hunches" are not sufficient to meet this standard.[52] The Model Plan for a Comprehensive Drug-Free Workplace provides the following criteria to consider to justify reasonable suspicion drug testing:

1. Observable phenomena, such as direct observation of drug use or possession and/or the physical symptoms of being under the influence of a drug;
2. A pattern of abnormal conduct or erratic behavior;
3. Arrest or conviction for a drug-related offense, or the identification of an employee as the focus of a criminal investigation into illegal drug possession, use, or trafficking;
4. Information provided either by reliable and credible sources or independently corroborated; or
5. Newly discovered evidence that the employee has tampered with a previous drug test.[53]

Clearly, any issues that arise involving drug testing should be referred to the agency drug testing office, the Human Resources department, and/or the Office of the General Counsel (OGC).

46. *National Federation of Federal Employees v. Vilsack, 681* F.3d 483, 490–91 (D.C. Cir. 2012).
47. *See Harmon v. Thornburgh,* 872, F.2d 484,491 (1989); *see also Hartness v. Bush,* 919 F.2d 170, 173 (1990).
48. Department of Health and Human Services, 2010 Guidance for Selection of Testing Designated Positions (TDPs) (2010), https://www.samhsa.gov/sites/default/files/workplace/2010%20Guidance%20for%20the%20Selection%20of%20TDPs%20Final%20Version%20April%205%202010%20508%20Compliant.pdf.
49. *See Holton v. Department of the Navy*, 884 F.3d 1142 (Fed. Cir. 2018) (It was reasonable for the Navy to suspect the employee, who was supervising team operating a crane, when the crane struck a building, could have caused, or contributed, to the accident, and thus, the supervisor's decision to administer a post-accident drug test on the employee met the applicable standard under the Fourth Amendment.).
50. *Alabama v. White*, 496 U.S. 325, 330 (1990).
51. *Garrison v. Department of Justice*, 67 M.S.P.R. 154, 162 (1995), *aff'd*, 72 F.3d 1566 (Fed. Cir. 1995).
52. *Id.* at 159.
53. SAMHSA, Federal Custody and Control Forms, HHS Guidelines, and Memos, 25, https://www.samhsa.gov/workplace/workplace-programs.

Leadership in the Context of the Fourth Amendment and Government Employment

The effective government leader must always be mindful of how their actions and directions affect the Fourth Amendment rights of employees and the public. The effective leader respects the privacy of employees and the public and avoids initiating or conducting unnecessary searches.

In the context of government employment, if a supervisor wants a work-related document they believe is stored in the employee's desk, the supervisor should first consider asking the employee for it, rather than initiating such a search without the employee knowing. The search may be permitted at its inception by the Fourth Amendment, but an unnecessary search could lead to the unnecessary disclosure of information that unexpectedly appears in plain view and adversely affect the supervisor's relationship with the employee.

If there is a search related to allegations of misconduct, it should be reasonable at its inception and reasonable in scope. In other words, the supervisor should be prepared to explain why the search was needed in the first instance and show how the scope of the search was justified. As previously discussed, in *Quon*, the Supreme Court noted that the review of the pager records was justified at its inception, since it was simply meant to determine the cause of such a high volume of pager use and that the search was reasonable in scope, as it was limited to only that period when pager use substantially increased. Similarly, the effective leader or supervisor should be thoughtful, discrete, and prepared to justify the reason for, and scope of, the search.

Further, if there is a need for a misconduct investigation, such as an inquiry into allegations of harassment, where documents and emails may be collected, the effective leader is sensitive to the potential Fourth Amendment and legal implications of such an inquiry and contacts the Office of Human Resources (OHR) or the OGC to make sure they are following agency policy. Most agencies assign someone from the OHR to conduct such an inquiry. Further, some types of misconduct might require notifying the Office of the Inspector General (OIG), so they, not the supervisor, can conduct the search.

The effective leader is transparent. In the context of the Fourth Amendment, this means providing advance notice to staff about clear agency policies stating that their work environment may be subject to a search. This notice may take the form of a banner on a government computer or a sign in a government garage notifying employees that those who park in the government garage are subject to random search. Supervisors may wish to invite someone to a staff meeting from the OHR or OGC to discuss, generically, such work environment searches. The effective leader exercises good judgment and discretion. For example, when referring an employee for reasonable suspicion drug testing, the supervisor should document the suspicious behavior and discuss what they observed with the OHR or OGC before directing an employee to take a drug test. By following the foregoing suggestions, the effective leader will be in the best position to balance the interests of the government with the privacy interests of the employee—while complying with the Fourth Amendment.

Cases and Review Questions

Directions: Use the provided links to access each noteworthy case. Then, provide complete and detailed responses to the questions and prompts about each case.

O'Connor v. Ortega, 480 U.S. 709 (1987)

https://www.law.cornell.edu/supremecourt/text/480/709

1. What were the reasons the government searched Dr. Ortega's office?
2. Was the search of the office protected by the Fourth Amendment?
3. Does the government employer always need a warrant prior to a search?
4. How does the Fourth Amendment apply to a government employee compared to a private citizen? What did the Court mean by "special needs" of the government workplace?
5. How do you determine whether an employee has a "reasonable expectation of privacy" and whether the government's search was reasonable at its inception and reasonable in its scope?
6. How does this case impact your office policies regarding search in a government office?

Quon v. City of Ontario, 560 U.S. 746 (2010)

https://www.law.cornell.edu/supct/pdf/08-1332P.ZO

1. What did the Court conclude about the applicability of the Fourth Amendment and the search of a government pager?
2. What did the government employer do to justify its search of the pager without first seeking a warrant?
3. How does this case impact government searches on government computers, government cell phones, or information technology devices?
4. What actions should the government take to ensure it can search a government computer, government cell phone, or government electronic device?

Riley v. California, 573 U.S. 373 (2014)

https://supreme.justia.com/cases/federal/us/573/373/

1. Does the Fourth Amendment apply to the search of a personal cell phone?
2. Does the government require a warrant prior to searching a personal cell phone?
3. How does the Supreme Court compare the reasonable expectation of privacy an individual has in their personal cell phone with the reasonable expectation an individual has in their home?
4. Are there exceptions to the warrant requirement of a personal cell phone?
5. How does this case impact the policies of your government agency regarding the search of a personal cell phone?

Carpenter v. United States, 138 S. Ct. 2206 (2018)

https://www.supremecourt.gov/opinions/17pdf/16-402_h315.pdf

1. In *Carpenter*, the government obtained, without a warrant, more than five months of historical cell phone location records for several different phone numbers from various wireless carriers.

The records had been transmitted though nearby cell phone towers, and the data led to the conviction of the defendants for robbery. Why did the Supreme Court reverse this conviction?

2. Does a citizen have a reasonable expectation of privacy in the location records for their cell phone?
3. How does this case differ from *Riley*?
4. What is the Stored Communications Act, and how does the Court examine its applicability in this case?
5. How did the Court address the fact that the cell phone owner, as a condition of using the phone, agreed to share the location data with the digital cell phone third-party provider?
6. What is the significance that the cell phone was used in a public place?
7. Does the fact that the cell phone records were shared with third-party providers affect the privacy rights of the cell phone owner?
8. How does this case impact a search by police of digital data maintained by Alexa or Google Assistant in the home or police drones in public places?
9. How could this case affect surveillance activities and warrantless searches of government agencies? How might the government avoid any potential violation of the Fourth Amendment under such circumstances?

Holton v. Department of Navy, 884, F.3d 1142 (4th Cir. 2018)

https://cafc.uscourts.gov/sites/default/files/opinions-orders/17-1430.Opinion.3-7-2018.1.PDF

1. Is a drug test ordered by the government a search under the Fourth Amendment?
2. Is a drug test ordered by a private employer a search under the Fourth Amendment?
3. What occurred in this case that led to a mandatory drug test of Mr. Holton?
4. What are the circumstances in which a government employer can order a mandatory drug test without a warrant?
5. How does this case impact your government employer's policy on post-accident testing?

Chapter 7

Religious Expression and the First Amendment

Introduction

This chapter covers religion and the Constitution, as they relate to the Free Exercise Clause and the Establishment Clause, the Religious Freedom Restoration Act (RFRA), and Title VII of the 1964 Civil Rights Act. The chapter covers what the meaning of religion is; the First Amendment's Free Exercise Clause and religious expression generally; the First Amendment and the limitations imposed on the government by the Establishment Clause; religion and reasonable accommodation in the workplace; religious accommodation and undue hardship; vaccine mandates and religious accommodations, practical guidance for federal government supervisors, addressing a broad array of religious rights issues in the federal workplace; leadership in the context of religious expression; and, finally, specific cases with questions for class discussion.

The First Amendment provides, in pertinent part:

> Congress shall make no law respecting an establishment of religion, or prohibiting the free exercise thereof ... .[1]

The clause prohibiting Congress from passing a law regarding the "establishment of religion" is generally referred to as the "Establishment Clause." The clause prohibiting Congress from passing a law prohibiting the "free exercise" of religion is referred to as the "Free Exercise Clause." Although the First Amendment expressly references Congress, these prohibitions have been interpreted broadly to apply to the federal, state, and local governments.[2] Thus, the government may not act in a matter that reflects it is either establishing a religion or prohibiting the free exercise of a religion.

1. U.S. Const. amend, I.

2. *See Cantwell v. Connecticut*, 310 U.S. 296 (1940).

What Is a Religion?

On January 12, 2021, the Equal Employment Opportunity Commission updated its guidance on religious discrimination.[3] This guidance defines religion very broadly:

> A belief is "religious" for Title VII purposes if it is "religious" in the person's "own scheme of things," i.e., it is a "sincere and meaningful" belief that "occupies a place in the life of its possessor parallel to that filled by ... God."[4]

The EEOC has further clarified that it is not for the court to examine the reasonableness of religious belief:

> The Supreme Court has made it clear that it is not a court's role to determine the reasonableness of an individual's religious beliefs, and that "religious beliefs need not be acceptable, logical, consistent, or comprehensible to others in order to merit First Amendment protection."[5] An employee's belief, observance, or practice can be "religious" under Title VII even if the employee is affiliated with a religious group that does not espouse or recognize that individual's belief, observance, or practice, or if few—or no—other people adhere to it.[6]

Religious belief must be sincerely held. It is normally not contested that a religious belief is sincerely held:

> The EEOC generally finds that the sincerity of an employee's stated religious belief is usually not in dispute and is "generally presumed or easily established."[7]

Thus, a supervisor should presume that a religious belief is sincerely held. In unusual circumstances, however, in which the sincerity of the religious belief is called into question, the EEOC has permitted questions based on a combination of the following four factors, which can serve to undermine the credibility of an employee:

> [1] whether the employee has behaved in a manner markedly inconsistent with the professed belief; [2] whether the accommodation sought is a particularly desirable benefit that is likely to be sought for secular reasons; [3] whether the timing of the request renders it suspect (e.g., it follows an earlier request by the employee for the same benefit for secular reasons); and [4] whether the employer otherwise has reason to believe the accommodation is not sought for religious reasons.[8]

3. *See* EEOC Directive No. 915.063, Chapter 12, *Religious Discrimination*, https://www.eeoc.gov/laws/guidance/section-12-religious-discrimination.
4. *See United States v. Seeger*, 380 U.S. 163, 166, 176 (1965). The EEOC and Courts have "consistently applied this standard" to define religion under Title VII. See Footnote 27, Chapter 12. *See Commission Guidelines*, 29 C.F.R. § 1605.1.
5. *See Thomas v. Review Board*, 450 U.S. 707, 714 (1981) (ruling that "religious beliefs need not be acceptable, logical, consistent, or comprehensible to others in order to merit First Amendment protection"); see Footnotes 19 and 22 of Chapter 12.
6. *See* Chapter 12, Footnote 23.
7. *See* Chapter 12, Footnote 40.
8. *See* Chapter 12, Footnotes 45-47.

The First Amendment's Free Exercise Clause and Religious Expression Generally

The Supreme Court has broadly held, "The door of the Free Exercise Clause stands tightly closed against any governmental regulation of religious *beliefs* ... ."[9] Up until 1990, the government had the burden to prove that any infringement upon religious expression was supported by a compelling state interest and narrowly tailored.

In 1990, however, the Supreme Court dramatically changed its analysis, finding that religious practice violated a valid neutral law. Specifically, in *Employment Division, Oregon Department of Human Services v. Smith,*[10] two drug counselors working for a private drug rehabilitation clinic ingested the hallucinogenic drug, peyote, in accordance with the religious practices of their Native American Church. After they were fired, the employees applied for unemployment compensation, but their application was denied under a neutral Oregon state law, which disqualified employees discharged for work-related misconduct. The employees argued that their First Amendment religious expression rights were violated. The Supreme Court disagreed and found that the "right of free exercise [of religion] does not relieve an individual of the obligation to comply with a valid and neutral law of general applicability."[11]

In 1993, Congress passed the Religious Freedom Restoration Act (RFFA) to reinstate the pre-*Smith* compelling-interest test by statute.[12] The RFRA authorizes courts to exempt a person from any law that imposes a substantial burden on sincere religious beliefs or actions, unless the government can show that the law is the "least restrictive means" of furthering a "compelling governmental interest."[13]

In 1997, the Supreme Court clarified that Congress only had the authority to apply the RFRA to the federal government but not to states and local governments.[14] Today, the RFRA still only applies to the federal government, although some states have passed specific-state RFRA statutes.

The interrelationship between Title VII of the 1964 Civil Rights Act, which, as amended, prohibits religious discrimination against federal employees, in part, and the RFRA is not absolutely clear. The EEOC has described the interaction between Title VII, the First Amendment, and the RFRA as "an evolving area of the law."[15] As a general rule, the Supreme Court held, in *Brown v. General Services Administration,*[16] that Title VII is the "exclusive, preemptive administrative and judicial scheme for the redress of federal employment discrimination." Certain courts have relied on *Brown* to mean that Title VII is the exclusive remedy for allegations of religious discrimination of federal employees, dismissing similar claims under the

9. *Sherbert v. Verner,* 374 U.S. 398, 402 (1963).
10. *Employment Division, Oregon Department of Human Services v. Smith*, 494 U.S. 872 (1990).
11. *Id.* at 879.
12. Religious Freedom Restoration Act, 42 U.S.C. § 2000bb.
13. *See* K. Novak Whitney, *Religious Freedom Restoration Act: A Primer*, Congressional Research Service, Apr. 3, 2020 (summarizing *Gonzales v. O Centro Espirita Beneficente Uniao do Vegetal*, 546 U.S. 418 (2006) (government had failed to demonstrate a compelling interest in applying the Controlled Substances Act to bar a church using a tea that contained hallucinogens regulated under that statute during religious services.)).
14. *See City of Boerne v. Flores*, 521 U.S. 507 (1997).
15. EEOC, Religious Discrimination, Chapter 12, § 3(c), (2021).
16. *Brown v. General Services Administration*, 425 U.S. 820, 829 (1976).

RFRA.[17] However, the Supreme Court has not clearly ruled on this issue, and the EEOC has determined, anyway, that eradicating discrimination would satisfy the compelling government interest requirement of the RFRA.[18]

The Supreme Court continues to strongly support and uphold religious expression in various forms.[19] *Fulton v. City of Philadelphia, Pennsylvania* is an important case because it cautions that a government program may lack neutrality, require strict scrutiny, and violate the Free Exercise Clause if the program "prohibits religious conduct, while permitting secular conduct that undermines the government's asserted interests in a similar way."[20] In *Fulton,* the Supreme Court found that the City of Philadelphia's foster care program was not neutral. On the one hand, the city had "sole discretion" to grant an exemption to its requirement that same sex couples be permitted to apply to the program, but on the other hand, Catholic Social Services (CSS) was prohibited from receiving such an exemption, even though its sincerely held

17. *Holly v. Jewell*, 196 Fed. Supp 3 1079 (2016).

18. *See* EEOC, Manual for Investigators, Chapter 12, footnote 122.

19. *See, e.g., Burwell v. Hobby Lobby Stores Inc.*, 573 U.S. 682 (2014) (Owners of three closely held for-profit corporations with sincere Christian beliefs that life begins at conception and that it would violate their religion to facilitate access to contraceptive drugs or devices that operate after that point were not required to comply with the contraception mandate of the Affordable Care Act); *Trinity Lutheran Church of Columbia, Inc. v. Comer*, 582 U.S. (2017) (Missouri violated the Free Exercise Clause when it denied a church a government grant to repaved roads with material made from recycled tires, based solely on the Church's status as a religious organization because, "To condition the availability of benefits ... upon [a recipient's] willingness to ... surrender his religiously impelled [status] effectively penalizes the free exercise of his constitutional liberties."); *Masterpiece Cakeshop, Ltd. v. Colorado Civil Rights Commission*, 584 U.S. (2018) (The decision of a bakery owner, who refused to design a custom wedding cake for a gay couple based on his religious beliefs, in violation of the Colorado Anti-Discrimination Act, was upheld on the narrow ground that the Colorado Civil Rights Commission did not employ religious neutrality when adjudicating the case); *Our Lady of Guadalupe School v. Morrissey-Berru*, 591 U.S. (2020) (upholding the "ministerial exception" to anti-discrimination laws that gives churches and similar religious organizations the power to remove certain important employees, including religious school teachers alleging violations of the Americans with Disabilities Act (Cancer) and Age Discrimination in Employment Act, even though the teachers lacked a distinctly religious job, primarily taught secular subjects, and did not practice the religion taught in the school); *Little Sisters of the Poor Saints Peter and Paul Home v. Pennsylvania*, 591 U.S. (2020) (The federal government had, under the Affordable Care Act (ACA) the discretion to exempt employers with religious and moral objections from the contraceptive-coverage health insurance mandate but did so without fully deciding the impact on the Religious Freedom Restoration Act.); *Espinoza v. Montana Dept. of Revenue*, 591 U.S. (2020) (Three low-income mothers in the state of Montana were improperly prohibited from using state scholarship money to attend a private religious school in violation of the Free Exercise Clause because even though states are not required to subsidize private education, if they do so, they cannot exclude religious schools from receiving those funds simply because they are religious.); *Uzuegbunam v. Preczewski,* 592 U.S. (2021) (Two evangelical Christian students (plaintiffs) had standing to raise a First Amendment Free Exercise claim when they were speaking in a free speech zone at Georgia Gwinnett College, told to stop, and threatened with discipline, based on student complaints of disturbing the peace, even though the university subsequently changed their policy, and the students made only a request for injunctive relief and nominal damages, where the plaintiff's claim is "based on a completed violation of a legal right."); *Fulton v. City of Philadelphia, Pennsylvania*, 593 U.S. ____ (2021) (The city's actions, in refusing to contract with state-licensed foster care organization affiliated with Roman Catholic Archdiocese unless the organization agreed to certify same-sex couples as foster parents, burdened the organization's religious exercise protected by the First Amendment, by putting it to the choice of curtailing its mission or approving relationships inconsistent with its beliefs that marriage was a sacred bond between a man and a woman and that the certification of prospective foster families was tantamount to endorsement of those families' relationships.).

20. *Fulton v. City of Philadelphia, Pennsylvania*, 141 S. Ct. 1868, *1877* (2021).

religious beliefs would not permit granting such applications. Accordingly, the government should take care to avoid policies that include a broad general exception because if that exception is applied to non-religious exemptions, and not to religious exceptions, the policy may be construed as lacking neutrality in violation of the First Amendment.

Another very important case affecting religious speech is *303 Creative LLC* v. *Elenis*, 600 U.S. 570 (2023). It involves the collision between free religious speech and sexual orientation rights. 303 Creative, a website designer in Colorado wanted to post a notice on her business website that because of her Christian faith she was unwilling to develop websites for same-sex marriages. Such a notice would violate the Colorado State Anti-discrimination laws that prevent businesses from discriminating based on a customer's sexual orientation. 303 Creative sued in Federal court to block enforcement of this state anti-discrimination statute. In a 6-3 decision, 303 Elenis prevailed. Justice Neil Gorsuch wrote the majority opinion and held that states cannot use public accommodation laws to limit the speech of business owners. Specifically, he wrote: "the better the artist ... the more easily his voice could be conscripted to disseminate the government's preferred message. That would not respect the First Amendment; more nearly it would spell its demise." Justice Sonia Sotomayer dissented finding Colorado's public accommodation law as requiring "equal dignity in the marketplace" and the Supreme Court decision undermines the LGBT right to such dignity. She explained the Constitution "contains no right to refuse service to a disfavored group." She feared the "symbolic effect of the decision is to mark gays and lesbians for second-class status."

The First Amendment and the Establishment Clause Generally

The Establishment Clause of the First Amendment provides that "Congress shall make no law respecting an establishment of religion."[21] Historically, most cases successfully evoking the Establishment Clause emphasize that government law, assistance, or action cannot be perceived to endorse a particular religion. Examples of government violating the establishment clause include Sunday closing laws[22] and the inclusion of religious symbols in government-sponsored holiday displays, in which the display had an overall religious, rather than secular, message.[23]

The Supreme Court's interpretation of the Establishment Clause has recently undergone a significant change. For many years, the Supreme Court found government law or action did not violate the Establishment Clause if it complied with the three-prong "*Lemon* Test" set forth in *Lemon v. Kurtzman*: For a government law, practice, or action to comply with the Establishment Clause, it (1) must have a secular purpose; (2) must have "a principal or primary effect" that "neither advances nor inhibits religion"; and (3) must not foster excessive government entanglement with religion.[24] However, the Supreme Court recently

21. U.S. Const. amend, I.

22. *McGowan v. Maryland*, 366 U.S. 420 (1961).

23. *Allegheny County v. Greater Pittsburgh* ACLU, 492 U.S. 573 (1989).

24. *Lemon v. Kurtzman*, 403 U.S. 602, 613 (1971).

overturned *Lemon*, in the case of *Kennedy v. Bremerton*.[25] In this case, the Supreme Court instead focused on "history, tradition, and original meaning"[26] to determine whether there had been a violation of the Establishment Clause.

Going forward, "the line that courts and governments must draw between the permissible and the impermissible has to accord with history and faithfully reflect the understanding of the Founding Fathers."[27] In *Kennedy*, the court held that a public high school football coach kneeling at midfield after three games to offer a quiet personal prayer did not cross any line separating protected private expression from impermissible government coercion of students to pray. Although several people saw the coach's religious exercise, and those close at hand might have heard him too, the majority of the Supreme Court justices found that his prayers were not publicly broadcast or recited to a captive audience. His plan was to wait to pray until the athletes were occupied. Students were not required or expected to participate, and none of the coach's students participated in any of the prayers.[28] While the government cannot act to "coerce" religious activity[29] nor "endorse" religious activity,[30] future Establishment Clause cases will likely carefully examine government activity through the lens of "history, tradition, and original meaning."[31] Other cases in which history and tradition have permitted a religious practice by the government include *Town of Greece v. Galloway*[32] and *American Legion v. American Humanist Association*.[33]

Religion and Reasonable Accommodation in the Workplace

Federal employees are entitled to religious accommodations for their religious beliefs under the U.S. Constitution and Title VII of the 1964 Civil Rights Act, as amended.[34] Typical examples of religious accommodation in the workplace cited by the Equal Employment Opportunity Commission (EEOC) in its guidance include, but are not limited to, the following:

- An employee needs an exception to the company's dress and grooming code for a religious practice (e.g., a Muslim woman who wears a religious headscarf [hijab] or a Jewish man who

25. *Kennedy v. Bremerton*, 142 S. Ct. 2407 (2022) (wherein a football coach did not violate the establishment clause when he prayed in midfield after a football game, joined by many of his players).
26. *Firewalker-Fields v. Lee,* 58 F.4th 104, 111 (4th Cir. 2023) (interpreting *supra* note 24).
27. *Sabra v. Maricopa County Community College, Dist.,* 44 F.4th 867, 888 (9th Cir. 2022) (citing *supra* note 24 at 2428).
28. *Kennedy v. Bremerton Sch. Dist.,* 142 S. Ct. 2407 (2022).
29. *Lee v. Weisman*, 505 U.S. 577 (1992).
30. *County of Allegheny v. American Civil Liberties Union, Greater Pittsburgh Chapter*, 492 U.S. 573, 592, (1989).
31. *Kennedy v. Bremerton School District,* 142 S. Ct. 2407 (2022).
32. *Town of Greece v. Galloway,* 572 U.S. 565, 571 (2014) (upholding the practice of opening a legislative session with a prayer in the town of Greece, N.Y. because it "fits within the tradition long followed in Congress and the state legislatures").
33. *American Legion v. American Humanist Association*, 139 S. Ct. 2067, 2079–80 (2019) (finding that the Bladensburg Peace Cross, a 32-foot Latin cross erected on government property in 1925 "as a tribute to 49 area soldiers who gave their lives in the First World War" did not violate the Establishment Clause, given its long established history in the community and the overall secular meaning of the monument.).
34. 1964 Civil Rights Act, Pub. L. 88-352, Title VII (The amended statute applies to government and private sector employees who work for employers with 15 or more employees.).

wears a yarmulke).

- A Catholic employee needs a schedule change, so he can attend church services on Good Friday.
- An atheist needs to be excused from the religious invocation offered at the beginning of staff meetings.
- An adherent to Native American spiritual beliefs needs unpaid leave to attend a ritual ceremony, or a Muslim employee needs a break schedule that will permit daily prayers at prescribed times.
- An employee needs accommodation of a religious belief that working on the Sabbath is prohibited.[35]

A religious accommodation need not be the perfect or the preferred accommodation of the employee, so long as the accommodation is reasonable.[36] If an employee cannot be reasonably accommodated in their current job, it is appropriate to consider reassigning them to a different position in which they can perform their essential functions within a setting that accommodates their religious requests.[37]

Religious Accommodation and Undue Hardship

An employer need not provide a reasonable accommodation if it will cause an undue hardship. Previously, under *Trans World Airlines Inc.* v. *Hardison*, 432 U.S. 63 (1977), an employer could, pursuant to Title VII of the 1964 Civil Rights Act, satisfy the undue hardship defense by establishing that a proposed accommodation posed "a more than de minimis" cost or burden on the employer. This was an easier standard to satisfy for an employer to meet than the undue hardship standard under the Americans with Disabilities Act (ADA) and the Rehabilitation Act of 1973, covering requests for reasonable accommodations by individuals with disabilities, unless it would cause an undue hardship, that is of "significant difficult or expense."[38] However, in *Groff* v. *DeJoy*, 600 U.S. 447 (2023), the Supreme Court unanimously established a more demanding undue hardship standard for the employer to satisfy before it could deny a religious accommodation. In this case, an Evangelical Christian, who believed for religious reasons that Sunday should be devoted to worship and rest, was required to work on Sundays after the U.S. Postal Service agreed to deliver mail for Amazon. His reasonable accommodation request, not to work on Sundays, was denied. He refused to work on Sundays, was subject to progressive discipline, and he eventually resigned. The Supreme Court remanded the case and held: "Title VII requires an employer that denies a religious accommodation to show that the burden of granting an accommodation would result in substantial increase in costs in relation to the conduct of its particular business."

35. U.S. Equal Employment Opportunity Commission, What You Should Know: Workplace Religious Accommodation (2014), https://www.eeoc.gov/laws/guidance/what-you-should-know-workplace-religious-accommodation.
36. EEOC, EEOC Investigative Manual, Question 34, Chapter 12, https://www.eeoc.gov/laws/guidance/section-12-religious-discrimination#h_12929403436951610749878556.
37. *Id.* at Question 35.
38. *See* EEOC, EEOC Guidance: Questions and Answers: Religious Discrimination in the Workplace, Question 6 (2008), https://www.eeoc.gov/laws/guidance/questions-and-answers-religious-discrimination-workplace.

Religious Accommodation, Undue Hardship, and Vaccine Mandates

When determining whether to grant or deny a religious accommodation to a vaccine mandate from the federal government, it is helpful to consider the EEOC's *What You Should Know About COVID-19 and the ADA, the Rehabilitation Act, and Other EEO Laws*, which provides essential criteria:

- Employees must request an exception to a COVID-19 vaccine requirement. Magic words are not required. EEOC has shared its own designated form for making such requests.[39]
- L.2.Generally, under Title VII, an employer should assume that a request for religious accommodation is based on sincerely held religious beliefs. However appropriate inquiry can be made, as discussed above and in Section L to assess whether the request for accommodation is based upon a sincerely held religious belief.
- The Supreme Court has held that requiring an employer to bear more than a "de minimis," or a minimal, cost to accommodate an employee's religious belief is an undue hardship. Costs to be considered include not only direct monetary costs but also the burden on the conduct of the employer's business—including, in this instance, the risk of the spread of COVID-19 to other employees or to the public.
- If there is more than one reasonable accommodation that would resolve the conflict between the vaccination requirement and the sincerely held religious belief without causing an undue hardship under Title VII, the employer may choose which accommodation to offer. If more than one accommodation would be effective at eliminating the religious conflict, the employer should consider the employee's preference but is not obligated to provide the reasonable accommodation preferred by the employee.[40]

Practical Guidance for Supervisors Addressing Religious Rights Issues in the Federal Government

On October 6, 2017, Attorney General Jeff Sessions of the Department of Justice issued a memorandum to all federal agencies, entitled "*Federal Law Protections on Religious Liberty,*"[41] which urged federal agencies to review and follow the "Guidelines on Religious Exercise and Religious Expression in the

39. EEOC, Religious Accommodation Request Form, https://www.eeoc.gov/sites/default/files/2021-10/EEOC%20Religious%20Accommodation%20Request%20Form%20-%20for%20web.pdf.
40. U.S. Equal Employment Opportunity Commission, What You Should Know About COVID-19 and the ADA, the Rehabilitation Act, and Other EEO Laws, Section L. (2022) (emphasis added), https://www.eeoc.gov/wysk/what-you-should-know-about-covid-19-and-ada-rehabilitation-act-and-other-eeo-laws#L.
41. Jeff Sessions, Attorney General, *Federal Law Protections of Religious Liberty,* October 6, 2017, https://www.justice.gov/opa/press-release/file/1001891/download.

Federal Workplace," which President Clinton issued on August 14, 1997.[42] These "Clinton Guidelines" provide an examination of the legal requirements as well as many practical examples for supervisors to consider when addressing a wide array of religious rights issues in the federal workplace. The following is a summary of the major points included in the "Clinton Guidelines":

- **Section 1 A. Religious Expression**. As a matter of law, agencies shall not restrict personal religious expression by employees in the federal workplace except where the employee's interest in the expression is outweighed by the government's interest in the efficient provision of public services or where the expression intrudes upon the legitimate rights of other employees or creates the appearance, to a reasonable observer, of an official endorsement of religion.
- **Section 1 (A)(1). Religious expression in private work areas is generally permissible**. A federal employee, for example, may keep a Bible or Koran on their private desk and read it during breaks.
- **Section 1(A)(2). Federal employees should be permitted to engage in religious expression with fellow employees**. Such expression may occur to the same extent that employees may engage in comparable nonreligious private expression, subject to reasonable and content-neutral standards and restrictions.
- **Section 1(A)(3). Employees are permitted to engage in religious expression directed at fellow employees**. But employees must refrain from such expression when a fellow employee asks that it stop or otherwise demonstrates that it is unwelcome.
- **Section 1(B)(1). Religious discrimination is prohibited.** No federal agency may promote, refuse to promote, hire, refuse to hire, or otherwise favor or disfavor, an employee or potential employee because of his or her religion, religious beliefs, or views concerning religion.
- **Section 1(B)(2). Coercion of an employee's participation or nonparticipation in religious activities by those with supervisory authority is prohibited.** A person holding **supervisory authority** over an employee may not, explicitly, or implicitly, insist that the employee participate in religious activities as a condition of continued employment, promotion, salary increases, preferred job assignments, or any other incidents of employment. Nor may a supervisor insist an employee refrains from participating in religious activities outside the workplace. Supervisors should be careful to ensure that their statements and actions are such that employees do not perceive any coercion of religious or nonreligious behavior (or respond as if such coercion is occurring), and should, where necessary, take appropriate steps to dispel such misperceptions.
- **Section 1(B)(3). Hostile work environment and religious harassment.**[43] Whether conduct gives rise to a hostile environment or constitutes religious harassment usually depends upon its

42. The White House, Office of the Press Secretary, Guidelines on Religious Exercise and Religious Expression in the Federal Workplace, Aug. 14, 1997, https://clintonwhitehouse4.archives.gov/WH/New/html/19970819-3275.html.

43. Since these "Clinton Guidelines" were issued, many federal agencies have issued anti-harassment policies that generally prohibit harassment based on a protected class, such as race, gender, national origin, age, disability, sexual orientation, and religion. Many agency policies have eliminated the "severe and pervasive" test from their definitions of "hostile environment harassment." Thus, a single incident of religious harassment could violate the agency's policy and subject the employee to potential discipline. Accordingly, federal employees should be careful that their conduct does not violate this agency anti-harassment policy.

frequency or repetitiveness as well as its severity. The use of derogatory language in an assaultive manner can constitute statutory religious harassment if it is severe or invoked repeatedly. A single incident, if sufficiently abusive, might also constitute statutory harassment. However, although employees should always be guided by general principles of civility and workplace efficiency, a hostile environment, under law, is not created by the bare expression of speech with which some employees might disagree.

- An agency should be prepared to grant a requested religious accommodation unless it would create an undue hardship, that is, the requested accommodation "creates a substantial increase in costs in relation to the conduct of its particular business.[44]
- **Section 1(D) Establishment of Religion.**[45] Federal employees are prohibited from engaging in activities or expression that a reasonable observer would interpret as government endorsement or denigration of religion a particular religion. Activities of employees need not be officially sanctioned to violate this principle; if, in all the circumstances, the activities would leave a reasonable observer with the impression that government was endorsing, sponsoring, or inhibiting religion generally or favoring or disfavoring a particular religion, they are not permissible. Section 1(D)(a) provides an example in which at the conclusion of each weekly staff meeting and before anyone leaves the room, an employee leads a prayer in which nearly all employees participate. All employees are required to attend the weekly meeting. The supervisor neither explicitly recognizes the prayer as an official function nor explicitly states that no one needs to participate in the prayer. This course of conduct is not permitted unless under all the circumstances, a reasonable observer would conclude the prayer was not officially endorsed.[46]

Office of the Press Secretary, Selections from "Guidelines On Religious Exercise And Religious Expression In The Federal Workplace," The White House, 1997.

Leadership in the Context of a Constitutional Government and Religious Expression

The effective leader is tolerant and respects the sincere religious beliefs of their employees and the public but is also careful not to give the appearance of endorsing a particular religion. The leader engages in a meaningful interactive dialogue with the employee who makes a request for reasonable accommodation of their religious beliefs and strives to meet their needs but also considers alternative accommodations that may prevent workplace disruption.

The effective leader follows the best practices described by the EEOC when addressing religious accommodations:

44. *See Groff v. DeJoy, supra.*
45. When the public has access to the federal workplace, all federal employees must be particularly sensitive to the Establishment Clause prohibition against creating the reasonable impression that the government is sponsoring, endorsing, or inhibiting religion, generally, or favoring or disfavoring a particular religion.
46. For additional updated guidance and examples, see EEOC, Technical Assistance Manual, § 12 (2021), https://www.eeoc.gov/laws/guidance/section-12-religious-discrimination.[/footnote]

- Informing employees and applicants that they will make reasonable efforts to accommodate religious practices.
- Training managers and supervisors how to recognize religious accommodation requests from employees.
- Developing internal procedures for processing religious accommodation requests.
- Assessing each individual request and avoiding assumptions or stereotypes about what constitutes a religious belief or practice or what type of accommodation is appropriate.
- Conferring fully and promptly to the extent needed to share any necessary information about the employee's religious needs and the available accommodation options.
- Considering the employee's proposed method of accommodation, and if it is denied because of more than one reasonable alternative, explaining to the employee the reasons the accommodation has not been granted.
- Considering alternative accommodations if the accommodation requested would pose an undue hardship.
- Consider offering alternative methods of accommodation on a temporary basis while a permanent accommodation is being explored and keeping the employee apprised of the status of the agency's efforts to implement a permanent accommodation.[footnote]*See* EEOC, Technical Assistance Manual, § 12.C.7 (2021), https://www.eeoc.gov/laws/guidance/section-12-religious-discrimination.

The effective leader also implements the best practices to prevent religious harassment, as described in section 12 of the EEOC's *Technical Assistance Manual*:

- Intervening proactively, with assistance from counsel, to discuss with the employee whether a particular religious expression is welcome if the manager believes the expression is likely to be construed as unwelcome to a reasonable person.
- Permitting religious expression among employees at least to the same extent that they allow other types of personal expression that are not harassing or disruptive to the operation of the agency.
- Cooperating with designated agency officials, once the supervisor is on notice that religious expression by an employee is unwelcome to another employee and taking appropriate steps to ensure the expression in question does not become sufficiently severe or pervasive as to create a hostile work environment.
- Taking appropriate corrective action if religious harassment has occurred.
- Avoiding any religious communication or action that may reasonably be perceived by subordinates as coercive, given the power and authority of the supervisor, even when not so intended.[47]

By following the foregoing guidance and seeking legal guidance, where appropriate, the government manger can be assured of complying with the First Amendment.

47. *Id.*

Cases and Review Questions

Directions: Use the provided links to access each noteworthy case. Then, provide complete and detailed responses to the questions and prompts about each case.

Peterson v. Hewlett Packard Co., 358 F.3d 599 (9th Cir. 2004)

https://caselaw.findlaw.com/us-9th-circuit/1423047.html

1. Why were Mr. Peterson's religious beliefs offended by the diversity policy of Hewlett Packard?
2. What actions did Mr. Peterson take to offend his coworkers?
3. What efforts did HP make to accommodate the religious beliefs of Mr. Peterson?
4. Was HP justified in firing Mr. Peterson?
5. What efforts can an employer make to reduce workplace harassment based on sexual orientation, religion, or any other protected basis?

Burwell, Secretary of Health and Human Services v. Hobby Lobby Stores, 573 U.S. 682 (2014)

https://www.law.cornell.edu/supremecourt/text/13-354

1. What were the circumstances in which Hobby Lobby was permitted by the Supreme Court not to comply with the Contraceptive Mandate under the Affordable Care Act?
2. What impact did the Religious Freedom Restoration Act (RFRA) have on the Supreme Court ruling on behalf of Hobby Lobby?
3. What burden must the federal government meet under the RFRA when it restricts the rights of a privately held corporation (the owner owns more than 50% of the stock) and the owner cannot comply with a government requirement because of sincerely held religious beliefs?
4. How can the federal government avoid violating the religious rights of privately held corporations in the future? What government controls would you put in place to ensure compliance with the First Amendment Free Exercise Clause and RFRA?

Masterpiece Cakeshop Ltd. v. Colorado Commission on Civil Rights, 584 U.S. 617 (2018)

https://www.supremecourt.gov/opinions/17pdf/16-111_j4el.pdf

1. Describe why the owner of Masterpiece Cakeshop was accused of violating Colorado Civil Rights Law when he refused to bake a same-sex couple a wedding cake?
2. Why was the Colorado Civil Service Commission deemed to lack neutrality in this case, and how could they have decided the case in a more neutral manner?
3. In an employment context, how do you address circumstances in which the religious beliefs of one employee interferes with the civil rights of another?

Fulton v. City of Philadelphia, Pennsylvania, 141 S. Ct. 1868 (2021)

https://www.supremecourt.gov/opinions/20pdf/19-123_g3bi.pdf

1. Why did the Supreme Court conclude that the refusal of Catholic Social Services (CSS) to certify same-sex couples as foster families could not be the city's reason for ending its long-held foster care placement contract with CSS?
2. How could the city have altered its Foster Care Funding program to appear more neutral?
3. How does the lack of a neutral state funding program effect the state's burden to prove it did not violate the Free Exercise Clause of the First Amendment?
4. What can federal, state, and local government do to be more neutral in addressing funding decisions involving religious institutions?

Kennedy v. Bremerton, 142 S. Ct. 2407 (2022)

https://www.law.cornell.edu/supremecourt/text/21-418#writing-21-418_OPINION_4

1. Describe the religious activity of Coach Kennedy in this case.
2. What was the *Lemon* test, and why did the Supreme Court overrule it?
3. How did the Supreme Court determine whether the Establishment Clause had been violated in this case?
4. What impact do you think *Kennedy* will have on future establishment clause cases?

303 Creative v. *Elenis*, 600 US 507 (June 30, 2023)

https://www.supremecourt.gov/opinions/22pdf/21-476_c185.pdf

1. Describe the religious speech at issue in this case.
2. Why was the Colorado Public Accommodation Law deemed unconstitutional?
3. What significance does the majority give to speech by an artist? Did that make a difference in this case? Is a web designer an artist?
4. What can states do after 303 Creative to ensure public accommodation laws continue to prohibit discrimination from businesses like that set forth in this case?

Groff v. Dejoy, 600 U.S. 447 (2023)

https://www.supremecourt.gov/opinions/22pdf/22-174_k536.pdf

1. How is the definition of undue hardship in religious accommodation cases changed after *Groff*?
2. What accommodation was Groff denied?
3. Are there circumstances where an employer can legally deny a request not to work on Sundays for religious reasons?
4. How will this case impact how employers process requests for religious based reasonable accommodation requests?

Chapter 8

Sovereign, Absolute, and Qualified Immunity for the President and Government Employees

Introduction

This chapter focuses on the application of "sovereign immunity" within the federal government as well as "absolute" and "qualified immunity" as those concepts apply to government officials. It addresses when the government can be sued, when a government employee can be sued personally—that is, in their individual capacity—and a 2022 Supreme Court decision that limits employee vulnerability to such individual lawsuits. The chapter proceeds to address the statutory right to have personal liability insurance paid for, in part; what to do if you are sued in your individual capacity; a discussion on leading in the context of a constitutional government and immunity; and, finally, an examination of cases with review questions for in-class discussion. The chapter also addresses recent Supreme Court precedent on the immunity of a President.

Sovereign Immunity Generally

"Sovereign immunity" refers to the notion that the government cannot be sued without its consent. Federal and state governments have the authority to waive their sovereign immunity. A waiver of sovereign immunity cannot be implied; it must be clear and unequivocally expressed.[1]

1. *El-Bey v. United States Postal Service*, 2022 WL 374406, at *3 (S.D. Ohio Feb. 8, 2022) (citing *United States v. White Mountain Apache Tribe*, 537 U.S. 465, 472 (2003) and *Mitchell v. United States*, 463 U.S. 206, 239 (1983)).

Sovereign Immunity and State Governments

Regarding state governments, "There are three exceptions to sovereign immunity: (1) when the state has waived immunity by consenting to the suit, (2) when Congress has expressly abrogated the states' sovereign immunity, and (3) when the doctrine set forth in *Ex Parte Young, 209 U.S. 123 (1908) applies."*[2] *Ex Parte Young* allows suits in federal courts for injunctions against officials acting on behalf of the states to proceed, despite the state's sovereign immunity, when the state is acting contrary to a federal law or the Constitution.[3] Moreover, the Eleventh Amendment of the U.S. Constitution bars lawsuits against states for monetary damages, unless the State has unequivocally consented to the suit or Congress has validly authorized the suit based on a federal constitutional provision.[4]

Sovereign Immunity and the Federal Government

A prime example in which the federal government has waived sovereign immunity is under the Federal Torts Claims Act (FTCA).[5] The U.S. House of Representatives website briefly summarizes the federal government's waiver of sovereign immunity under the FTCA as follows:

> Under the FTCA, the federal government acts as a self-insurer, and recognizes liability for the negligent or wrongful acts or omissions of its employees acting within the scope of their official duties. The United States is liable to the same extent an individual would be in like circumstances. The statute substitutes the United States as the defendant in such a suit and the United States—not the individual employee—bears any resulting liability.[6]

The FTCA waives sovereign immunity in part and allows the federal government to be sued for negligent acts committed by federal employees within the scope of the employee's job.[7] The FTCA waives immunity, however, only for nonintentional torts and does not cover independent contractors.[8]

> [T]he United States, as sovereign, is immune from suits save as it consents to be sued. Pursuant to the FTCA, Congress has waived sovereign immunity and has granted consent for the government to be sued for acts committed by any employee of the

2. *Boler v. Early*, 865, F.3d 391,410 (6th Cir. 2017)
3. *Whole Woman's Health v. Jackson*, 142 S. Ct. 522, 532 (2021)
4. *Daly v. Eagleson*, No. 1:19-CV-06020, 2021 WL 4439428, at *8 (N.D. Ill. Sept. 27, 2021) (citing *Green v. Mansour*, 474 U.S. 64, 68 (1985)); *Indiana Prot. & Advocacy Servs. v. Indiana Family & Soc. Servs. Admin.*, 603 F.3d 365, 374 (7th Cir. 2010); *see Will v. Michigan Dep't of State Police*, 491 U.S. 58, 66 (1989).
5. *See* Federal Torts Claims Act § 28 USC 1346.
6. U.S. House of Representatives, Federal Tort Claims Act, https://www.house.gov/doing-business-with-the-house/leases/federal-tort-claims-act. For a more detailed discussion of the FTCA, see Kenneth M. Lewis, Congressional Research Services Report: The Federal Torts Claims Act (FTCA): A Legal Overview, Nov. 20, 2019, https://sgp.fas.org/crs/misc/R45732.pdf.
7. *See* Definitions, 28 U.S.C. § 2671.
8. *See* Exceptions, 28 U.S.C. § 2680; *Nathan M. F. Charles v. United States of America* 2022 WL 558181, at 4 (D.D.C. Feb. 24, 2022) (citing *Gardner v. United States,* 213 F.3d 735, 737 n.1 (D.C. Cir. 2000)).

Government while acting within the scope of his office or employment. The FTCA, however, does not cover acts committed by independent contractors.[9]

For example, under the FTCA, the federal government has not waived sovereign immunity for a defamation claim. [10]

Another circumstance in which sovereign immunity arises is in the context of civil rights laws. For example, the Rehabilitation Act of 1973 does not waive the sovereign immunity of the United States for monetary claims arising from alleged disability discrimination "under any program or activity conducted by any Executive agency."[11] However, the federal government does, for example, expressly waive sovereign immunity and permit monetary damages for disability discrimination and reasonable accommodation employment complaints filed by federal employees,[12] including back pay and attorney fees. This is consistent with the waiver of sovereign immunity in discrimination employment complaints on a wide range of Federal civil rights statutes.[13]

Further, a federal employee may receive compensatory damages for past and future pecuniary losses (i.e., out-of-pocket expenses) and nonpecuniary losses (e.g., pain and suffering or mental anguish) as part of "make whole" relief for disability discrimination in accordance with the Civil Rights Act of 1991.[14] Congress also afforded the Commission the authority to award compensatory damages in the administrative process.[15]

Qualified Immunity and Absolute Immunity of Government Employees

In *Harlow v. Fitzgerald*, the Supreme Court addressed two forms of immunity afforded to government employees: qualified immunity and absolute immunity.[16] Most government employees have qualified immunity, which means they cannot be sued in their individual capacity if they act within the scope of their employment. In *Harlow,* the Supreme Court recognized the public policy interest in protecting government officials from individual personal lawsuits to ensure that they vigorously exercise their responsibilities. In other words, being subject to personal lawsuits would inhibit the exercise of discretion by a government employee. For example, a federal manager who supervises a poor performer is more likely to address the poor performance, and even remove the employee for unacceptable performance, if they know they have qualified immunity that protects them against personal civil lawsuits. Even if the unacceptable performance action is overturned, a personal civil lawsuit against the manager will likely be dismissed by the court.

9. *Creel v. United States,* 598 F.3d 210, 213 (5th Cir. 2010).
10. *See M. F. Charles v. United States of America* 2022 WL 558181, at 4 (D.D.C. Feb. 24, 2022) (citing *Gardner v. United States*, 213 F.3d 735, 737 n.1 (D.C. Cir. 2000)).
11. Rehabilitation Act of 1973, 29 U.S.C. 794 § 504; *see Lane v. Peña*, 518 U.S. 187, 191, 197 (1996).
12. *See Id.* § 501.
13. *See* EEOC.gov for a discussion of Federal laws enforced by the Equal Employment Opportunity Commission.
14. Civil Rights Act of 1991, 42 U.S.C. § 1981a(b)(3); *see West v. Gibson,* 527 U.S. 212 (1999).
15. *See Erik S., Complainant* EEOC DOC 2020004617, 2021 WL 6338637, at *3 (Dec. 13, 2021).
16. *Harlow v. Fitzgerald*, 457 U.S. 800 (1982).

Similarly, a police officer, is more likely to exercise their authority if they know they are immune from civil lawsuits.

Absolute immunity is a higher level of immunity and applies to very few positions, such as prosecutors, legislators, judges, and very high policy-making positions, including the President of the United States. For example, the President has absolute immunity from civil litigation for official acts.[17] However, the President does not have absolute immunity for acts that occurred before becoming President[18] and must comply with a state subpoena for documents sought related to a criminal prosecution.[19] Further, "a criminal prosecutor is fully protected by absolute immunity when performing the traditional functions of an advocate."[20] However, a prosecutor is entitled to only qualified immunity when they act outside of their traditional advocate responsibilities as a complaining witness by making sworn statements to the court in support of a criminal complaint.[21]

Lawsuits Filed Individually Against Government Employees for the Violation of a Constitutional Right

In *Bivens v. Six Unknown Named Agents*, the Supreme Court recognized a private right to sue individual police officers for violating a clearly established constitutional right.[22] Subsequently, lawsuits against government employees typically have been referred to as "*Bivens* actions" and pursued in accordance with 42 USC 1983. *Bivens* is a Fourth Amendment case involving warrantless searches and seizure. However, a *Bivens* action can apply to other Constitutional rights as well.[23]

However, to prevail in a *Bivens* action, the plaintiff must show more than a Constitutional violation; rather, the plaintiff must demonstrate a "clearly established" violation of the Constitution.[24] Furthermore, a plaintiff will not prevail in a *Bivens* action if there is a comprehensive remedial scheme established by Congress to remedy the alleged violation. For example, in *Bush v. Lucas*, the Supreme Court held that no *Bivens* remedy was available when a federal employer committed a First Amendment violation because Congress had passed legislation that included extensive statutory and administrative remedies in cases where federal government employees' First Amendment rights were violated while employed.[25]

17. *Nixon v. Fitzgerald*, 457 U.S. 731 (1982).
18. *Clinton v. Jones,* 520 U.S. 681 (1997).
19. *Trump v. Vance,* 140 S. Ct. 2412 (2020).
20. *Kalina v. Fletcher*, 522 U.S. 118 (1997).
21. *Id.*
22. *Bivens v. Six Unknown Named Agents*, 403 U.S. 388 (1971).
23. *See, e.g., Davis v. Passman*, 442 U.S. 228 (1979) (Fifth Amendment Equal Protection Clause violation based on gender discrimination of a public employee); *Carlson v. Green*, 446 U.S. 414 (1980) (Eighth Amendment violation related to inadequate prisoner medical care).
24. *Lane v. Franks*, 573 U.S. 228 (2014).
25. *Bush v. Lucas*, 462 U.S. 367 (1983); *see also United States v. Fausto*, 484 U.S. 439 (1988) (recognizing the Civil Service Reform Act as prohibiting a *Bivens* remedy in the context of its "new framework for evaluating adverse personnel actions" against federal employees).

Egbert v. Boule and Federal Employee Liability

Egbert v. Boule, an important 2022 Supreme Court decision, has substantially limited federal employees from individual liability.[26] The case involved a bed and breakfast, owned by Mr. Boule, situated a few feet from the U.S.–Canada border and aptly named the "Smuggler's Inn." Boule would sometimes act as a paid confidential informant for U.S. Border Patrol by providing the agency with information about persons of interest Boule was scheduled to lodge or transport. In 2014, Boule informed petitioner Erik Egbert, a U.S. Border Patrol agent, that a Turkish national, arriving in Seattle by way of New York, had scheduled transportation to Smuggler's Inn. When Agent Egbert observed one of Boule's vehicles returning to the inn, he suspected that the Turkish national was a passenger and followed the vehicle to the inn. Boule claimed he asked Egbert to leave, but Egbert refused, became violent, and threw Boule first against the vehicle and then to the ground. Egbert then checked the immigration paperwork for Boule's guest and left after finding everything in order. The Turkish guest unlawfully entered Canada later that evening. Boule filed a grievance with Agent Egbert's supervisors and an administrative claim with Border Patrol pursuant to the Federal Tort Claims Act (FTCA). Egbert allegedly retaliated against Boule by reporting Boule's "SMUGLER" license plate to the Washington Department of Licensing for referencing illegal activity and by contacting the Internal Revenue Service and prompting an audit of Boule's tax returns. Boule's FTCA claim was ultimately denied, and Border Patrol took no action against Egbert for his use of force or alleged acts of retaliation.

Boule then sued Egbert individually in Federal District Court, alleging a Fourth Amendment violation for excessive use of force and a First Amendment violation for unlawful retaliation. Invoking *Bivens*, Boule asked the District Court to recognize a damages action for each alleged constitutional violation. The District Court declined to extend *Bivens* as requested, but the Ninth Circuit Court of Appeals reversed. The Supreme Court rejected the Ninth Circuit's position that a *Bivens* claim could proceed for two reasons: (1) interfering with the conduct of border patrol agents has national security implications and (2) Congress has provided alternative remedies for aggrieved parties in Boule's position that independently foreclose a *Bivens* action here. The Court explained as follows:

> In *Hernández*, we declined to authorize a *Bivens* remedy, in part, because the Executive Branch already had investigated alleged misconduct by the defendant Border Patrol agent ... . And, by regulation, Border Patrol must investigate "[a]lleged violations of the standards for enforcement activities" and accept grievances from "[a]ny persons wishing to lodge a complaint." 8 C.F.R. §§ 287.10(a)–(b). As noted, Boule took advantage of this grievance procedure, prompting a year-long internal investigation into Agent Egbert's conduct.[27]

The Supreme Court did acknowledge that an individual "claiming to be the victim of an unlawful arrest and search could continue to bring a Fourth Amendment *Bivens* claim for damages against the responsible agents even though no federal statute authorized such a claim."[28] But extending *Bivens* is a "disfavored

26. *Egbert v. Boule*, 142 S. Ct 1793 (2022).

27. Id.

28. Id. (quoting *Hernández v. Mesa*, 140 S. Ct. 735, 741 (2020).

judicial activity."[29] The Supreme Court has extended *Bivens* only twice. First, it extended it in *Davis v. Passman* to imply a remedy under the Fifth Amendment when a congressman allegedly fired a female staffer on the basis of sex.[30] Second, it extended *Bivens* in *Carlson v. Green*, in which prison officials failed to provide proper medical care to the decedent in violation of the Eighth Amendment.[31] Since then, the Supreme Court has declined to extend *Bivens* on numerous occasions. The Court also laid out a new two-step inquiry required for a *Bivens* analysis:

> First, a court must determine whether a claim falls within the causes of action authorized under the Supreme Court's three *Bivens* cases—*Bivens, Davis*, and *Carlson*—or whether it "arises in a 'new context' or involves a 'new category of defendants.' A context is "new" when it is "different in a meaningful way from previous *Bivens* cases decided by [the] Court." If a court finds that a claim presents a "new context" different from the three *Bivens* cases, it must "proceed to the second step and ask whether there are any special factors that counsel hesitation about granting the extension" of *Bivens*. This "special factors" inquiry must focus on "separation-of-powers principles" and requires courts to ask whether judicial intrusion into a given field is appropriate.[32]

The Supreme Court emphasized, "If there is even a single 'reason to pause before applying *Bivens* in a new context,' a court may not recognize a *Bivens* remedy."[33] Based on the foregoing, it is evident that a federal employee, sued in their individual capacity, is highly likely to have such a complaint dismissed.

The Westfall Act and What a Federal Employee Should Do If Sued in Their Individual Capacity

The Westfall Act provides that if a federal employee is sued in their individual capacity for a tort committed while acting within the scope of their employment that the United States shall be substituted as the party defendant for the employee.[34] The Act also currently provides for federal agencies to reimburse qualified employees up to 50%—or up to $150—of their annual Federal Employee Professional Liability Insurance (FEPLI) premium.[35]

The Interests of United States in Pending Suits legislation authorizes DOJ attorneys to defend federal employees who are sued in their individual capacity if acting within the scope of their employment[36] in accordance with DOJ guidelines:

29. Id.

30. *Davis v. Passman*, 442 U.S. 228 (1979).

31. *Carlson v. Green*, 446 U.S. 14 (1980) (internal quotations omitted).

32. *Bulger v. Hurwitz*, 62 F.4th 127, 137 (4th Cir. 2023).

33. *Egbert v. Boule*, 142 S. Ct. 1793, 1803 (2022)

34. Westfall Act, 28 U.S.C. § 2679(b)(1).

35. See, e.g., Department of Homeland Security, Reimbursement For Professional Liability Insurance, No. 254-05 Rev. No. 01 Apr. 2, 2018, https://www.dhs.gov/sites/default/files/publications/mgmt/human-resources/mgmt-dir_254-05-reimbursement-professional-liability-insurance_rev-01.pdf.

36. Interests of United States in Pending Suits, 28 U.S.C. § 517.

> **(a)** Under the procedures set forth below, a federal employee (hereby defined to include present and former Federal officials and employees) may be provided representation in civil, criminal, and Congressional proceedings in which he is sued, subpoenaed, or charged in his individual capacity, not covered by § 15.1 of this chapter, when the actions for which representation is requested reasonably appear to have been performed within the scope of the employee's employment and the Attorney General or his designee determines that providing representation would otherwise be in the interest of the United States ... .[37]

Accordingly, if a federal employee is subject to a personal lawsuit, they will be served with a copy of the complaint filed in court by the complainant. The federal employee should immediately reach out to their Office of General Counsel (OGC) and provide a copy of the complaint. Typically, an official within the OGC will certify that the employee acted within the scope of their employment and contact a designated unit with the U.S. Department of Justice who handles government immunity issues.

Subsequently, an Assistant United States Attorney assigned to the case will file a motion to dismiss, asserting the employee is protected by qualified immunity, and will ask the court to substitute the name of the employee with the name of the head of the agency where the manager works. Such motions are routinely granted by the courts. The complainant will be permitted to pursue the case against the federal government but not against the federal employee.

Presidential Immunity

In *Trump v. United States*, 603 U.S. (2024), the Supreme Court granted the President unprecedented immunity from criminal prosecution. Specifically the Court held that the President is absolutely immune from criminal prosecution when exercising core constitutional powers, that is powers expressly provided by the Constitution itself. Those powers, referenced in Article II of the Constitution, include but are not limited to, the pardon power, appointing or removing Federal executives, appointing ambassadors and judges to the Supreme Court and powers related to serving as Commander in Chief. Thus, if the President violates the law when implementing these core powers, he or she is completely immune from criminal prosecution.

The Court also found that official acts within the outer perimeter of the President's official responsibilities are presumptively immune. The Court takes a broad view of what a President's official responsibilities are. Thus, if an action even touches on the President's official authority then the President enjoys a strong presumption of immunity from prosecution. The Court balanced two competing concerns: the interest in fair and effective enforcement of criminal laws, with a President making a difficult decision, not because it was the best decision but to avoid criminal prosecution. Thus, prosecutors will have the high burden to prove that prosecuting such charges would not adversely affect the functioning of the executive branch.

Unofficial acts would not enjoy any immunity from criminal prosecution. However, testimony and

37. Representation of Federal Officials and Employees by Department of Justice Attorneys or by Private Counsel Furnished by the Department in Civil, Criminal, and Congressional Proceedings in Which Federal Employees Are Sued, Subpoenaed, or Charged in Their Individual Capacities, 28 C.F.R. §50.15.

records of the President or the President's advisors pertaining to official acts may not be introduced as evidence when prosecuting other criminal acts pertaining to unofficial acts.

Leadership in the Context of a Constitutional Government and Immunity

The effective leader should always be mindful of their obligations and rights under the Constitution and federal law. It is critical to ask questions of legal counsel before acting and before potential Constitutional issues arise and *Bivens* lawsuits are filed. Although a federal employee is protected by qualified or absolute immunity, the employee's protections stem only from acting within the scope of employment. Moreover, even if an employee is immune from an individual lawsuit, they can still be disciplined, up through and including removal, for wrongdoing. The effective leader takes their oath to uphold the Constitution seriously, even if it means taking more time to ensure compliance with the Constitution. Ultimately, the greatest immunity any federal manager has from losing a lawsuit stems not from a Supreme Court decision limiting liability but from acting thoughtfully and carefully, seeking legal counsel where appropriate, and, perhaps most importantly, acting with integrity. As George Washington explained to Alexander Hamilton on August 28, 1788, in response to efforts to convince him to participate in the first presidential election: "Still I hope I shall possess firmness and virtue enough to maintain (what I consider the most enviable of all titles) the character of an honest man."[38]

Cases and Review Questions

Directions: Use the provided links to access each noteworthy case. Then, provide complete and detailed responses to the questions and prompts about each case.

Trump v. United States, 603 U.S. 593 (2024)

https://www.law.cornell.edu/supremecourt/text/23-939

1. When is the President immune?
2. Under what circumstances is the President absolutely immune or presumptively immune?
3. When can the president be criminally prosecuted?
4. What is the impact of this decision?

38. Letter from George Washington to Alexander Hamilton (Aug. 28, 1788), https://www.mountvernon.org/library/digitalhistory/past-projects/quotes/article/still-i-hope-i-shall-always-possess-firmness-and-virtue-enough-to-maintain-what-i-consider-the-most-enviable-of-all-titles-the-character-of-an-honest-man/.

Bivens v. Six Unknown Agents of the Federal Bureau of Narcotics, 403 U.S. 388 (1971)

https://www.law.cornell.edu/supremecourt/text/403/388

1. What did the federal agents do that violated the Constitution?
2. Do you believe it is appropriate that these agents can be sued in their individual capacity?
3. Do you believe the police and other government officials should be protected by qualified and absolute immunity?
4. What would the circumstances be without such immunity?

Wood v. Moss, 572 U.S. 744 (2014)

https://www.law.cornell.edu/supremecourt/text/13-115

1. What was the alleged constitutional violation that the Secret Service Agents violated?
2. Why did the Secret Service Agents prevail?
3. What does it mean to violate a "clearly established" constitutional right?
4. What would the consequences be if it were easier to personally sue a Secret Service Agent?
5. Would you propose any changes to the immunity laws to make it easier or more difficult to pierce qualified immunity?

Stewart Liff v. Office of the Inspector General, 156 F. Supp. 3d 1 (2016)

https://www.cadc.uscourts.gov/internet/opinions.nsf/57E67EBF550EDDAB8525822C005378F2/$file/16-5045-1716627.pdf

1. What did the Court of Appeals of the District of Columbia conclude about the current existing remedies under the Privacy Act affecting the right to bring a personal lawsuit against individual members of the Office of the Inspector General?
2. Do you believe an existing statutory remedy should trump a *Bivens* lawsuit?
3. Following the reasoning of this court, what can be done to limit future *Bivens* actions against government employees?

Egbert v. Boule, 596 U.S. 482 (2022)

https://www.supremecourt.gov/opinions/21pdf/21-147_g31h.pdf

1. What constitutional violations can someone bring against a federal employee after *Egbert*?
2. What impact did the agency's internal administrative grievance process have on protecting Erik Egbert from individual liability, and does your agency have such an administrative process? Should it?
3. Is the limitation on the application of *Bivens* in *Egbert* a good thing? Explain.
4. What potential impact will *Egbert* have on federal employee conduct?

Chapter 9

Nexus, Appropriate Penalty Analysis, and the Federal Disciplinary Action Process as Distinguished from the Unacceptable Performance Action Process

Introduction

Under Chapter 75[1] of the Civil Service Reform Act, an agency can only discipline an employee if it can prove by a preponderance of the evidence that the charged conduct occurred, there is a nexus between the charged conduct and the efficiency of the federal service, and that the penalty chosen because of the misconduct is reasonable (by applying the "*Douglas* factors," as set forth in *Douglas v. Veterans Administration*[2] *and subsequent cases relying*

1. 5 U.S.C 7501 et seq.
2. Douglas vs. Veterans Administration, 5 M.S.P.R. 280, 306–07 (1981).

on Douglas[3]). This chapter first addresses the nexus requirement in a disciplinary action and then the application of the Douglas factors when arriving at a reasonable penalty for the misconduct. This Chapter further explores the Unacceptable Performance Action process under Chapter 43 and how it differs from the Chapter 75 process. These sections are followed by a separate discussion on leadership in the context of a constitutional government and cases and review questions to enhance class participation.

Nexus

Under Chapter 75, a federal agency can take a disciplinary action against a federal employee "only for such cause as will promote the efficiency of the service."[4] A federal agency must establish a nexus between the misconduct and the efficiency of the service by showing a "clear and direct relationship between the articulated grounds for an adverse action and either the appellant's ability to accomplish his duties satisfactorily or some other legitimate government interest."[5]

An agency may show a nexus between an employee's off-duty misconduct and the efficiency of the service by one of three means: (1) a rebuttable presumption in certain egregious circumstances, (2) preponderant evidence that the misconduct adversely affects the employee's or coworkers' job performance or the agency's trust and confidence in the employee's job performance, or (3) preponderant evidence that the misconduct interfered with or adversely affected the agency's mission.[6]

Often, nexus is easy to prove, such as when an employee is absent without leave (AWOL) or fighting in the workplace. The connection between these disciplinary action charges and the efficiency of the government is readily apparent. The most challenging nexus questions often involve off-duty conduct. In either case, however, the nexus requirement protects the employee against arbitrary and capricious decision-making. For example, an agency official must establish more than moral outrage at the conduct of an employee to prove nexus. Although off-duty misconduct can satisfy the nexus requirement, it is not an open license to invade the private affairs and activity of government employees. For example, an employee

3. *See Pope v. U.S. Postal Service*, 114 F.3d 1144, 1147 (Fed. Cir. 1997). It is important to understand that the nexus and penalty assessment requirements are only applicable to Chapter 75 disciplinary and adverse action cases under the Civil Service Reform Act. Decisions taken for "unacceptable performance" in accordance with 5 U.S.C. § 4303 do not have to prove nexus or appropriateness of the penalty. Rather, all the agency must prove is that the employee's performance in one or more critical elements was unacceptable, the employee was given a reasonable opportunity to improve in accordance with a performance improvement plan (PIP) and that the employee's performance under the PIP did not rise to the minimum level required to be retained under the PIP. There is no need to show nexus, since there is a clear nexus between unacceptable performance and the efficiency of the Service. Further, unacceptable performance actions taken under Chapter 43 are not subject to a *Douglas* factor mitigation of penalty analysis in accordance with § 4303. *See Lisiecki v. Merit Systems Protection Board,* 769 F.2d 1558 (Fed. Cir. 1985).
4. Cause and Procedure, 5 U.S.C. § 7513 (a).
5. *See Hoofman v. Department of Army*, 118 MSPR 532,540 (2012), *aff'd sub nom. Hoofman v. Department of the Army,* 526 F. App'x 982 (Fed. Cir. 2013) (citing *Ellis v. Department of Defense*, 114 MSPR 407 (2010)). *See also Slayton v. Department of Agriculture*, 23 WL 2189529 (MSPB 2023).
6. *See Vestal v. Department of Treasury, 1 F 4th 1049 (Fed Cir. 2021) (*The Internal Revenue Service established a clear nexus when it fired an IRS agent who intentionally disclosed taxpayer information to an authorized person.); *Childress v. Department of the Interior*, 2023 WL 2657664 (MSPB March 27, 2023).

may engage in an affair with the married spouse of another individual, which may be contrary to the moral code of the proposing or deciding official considering a disciplinary action, but this, in and of itself, is insufficient to establish a nexus.

In *Doe v. Department of Justice*, for example, videotaping sexual encounters without the consent of the partners was in and of itself insufficient to establish a nexus, where there was no criminal law violation and no clear definition of what constitutes off-duty dishonesty because "misconduct that is private in nature and that does not implicate job performance in any direct and obvious way is often insufficient to justify removal from a civil service position."[7] If, however, an off-duty relationship directly affects the ability of an employee to perform their job, then a nexus can be established. For example, in *Brown v. Department of the Navy*, a nexus was properly established when a Program Manager for the Morale, Welfare, and Recreation Department of the Navy was removed for engaging in an affair with the spouse of a deployed soldier, since such off-duty conduct adversely affected the trust and confidence of his managers and those deployed and interfered with his ability to perform his job.[8]

Assessing the Appropriateness of a Penalty in a Disciplinary Action Taken Under Chapter 75 of the Civil Service Reform Act

An agency is required to consider the *Douglas* factors, set forth in *Douglas v. Veteran's Administration,*[9] to assess the appropriateness of the penalty, before taking a disciplinary action[10] or an adverse action[11] pursuant to the Civil Service Reform Act. The factors are as follows:

1. The nature and seriousness of the offense, and its relation to the employee's duties, position, and responsibilities ...;
2. the employee's job level and type of employment, including supervisory or fiduciary role, contacts with the public, and prominence of the position;
3. the employee's past disciplinary record;
4. the employee's past work record, including length of service, performance on the job, ability to get along with fellow workers, and dependability;
5. the effect of the offense upon the employee's ability to perform at a satisfactory level and its effect upon supervisors' confidence in the employee's ability to perform assigned duties;
6. consistency of the penalty with those imposed upon other employees for the same or similar offenses;
7. consistency of the penalty with any applicable agency table of penalties;
8. the notoriety of the offense or its impact upon the reputation of the agency;

7. *Doe v. Department of Justice*, 565 F.3d 1375 1379 (Fed. Cir. 2009).
8. *Brown v. Department of the Navy*, 229 F.3d 1356, 1358–61 (Fed. Cir. 2000).
9. *Douglas v. Veteran's Administration*, 5 M.S.P.R. 280, 332 (1981).
10. Civil Service Reform Act, 92 Stat. 1111 § 7503 (a suspension of up to fourteen days).
11. *Id.* at § 7513 (a fifteen-day suspension up to removal).

9. the clarity with which the employee was on notice of any rules that [were] violated ...;
10. potential for the employee's rehabilitation;
11. mitigating circumstances surrounding the offense ...; and

the adequacy and effectiveness of alternative sanctions to deter such conduct in the future by the employee or others.[12]

While not all the factors will be pertinent to every case, the board in *Douglas* explained that the agency must "consider the relevant factors" and "strike a responsible balance" in selecting a penalty[13]: "[A]n appropriate penalty must reflect a responsible balancing of the relevant factors."[14] The requirement to consider the *Douglas* factors is well established and intended to ensure that the agency does not impose an arbitrary and capricious penalty:

> This requirement that the *Douglas* factors be considered is consistent with the Supreme Court's decision in *Citizens to Preserve Overton Park, Inc. v. Volpe*, 401 U.S. 402, 91 S.Ct. 814, 28 L.Ed.2d 136 (1971), which held that, when reviewing whether an agency action was arbitrary or capricious under the Administrative Procedure Act, courts "must consider whether the decision was based on a consideration of the relevant factors and whether there has been a clear error of judgment." 401 U.S. at 416, 91 S.Ct. 814, *overruled on other grounds by Califano v. Sanders*, 430 U.S. 99, 97 S.Ct. 980, 51 L.Ed.2d 192 (1977).[15]

There is extensive caselaw defining each *Douglas* Factor. The Merit Systems Protection Board, arbitrators, and the federal courts carefully examine the *Douglas* factors in every disciplinary action case. Accordingly, it is critical for the manager to consult with the assigned Employee Relations Specialist (ERS) for specific guidance on the applicability of each factor. For example, when assessing *Douglas* factor (6), the ERS is expected to know whether other agency employees have been disciplined for comparable misconduct to avoid any disparate treatment. Moreover, the overall expertise of the ERS can help guide the manager. The ERS also ensures the manager complies with agency policy and legal requirements. As discussed in chapter 3, the due process requirements under the Fifth Amendment requires the proposed disciplinary action to identify the specific *Douglas* factors relied upon to arrive at the proposed penalty so that the employee has a chance to respond.[16] A deciding official cannot issue a penalty higher than the proposed penalty. It is therefore appropriate for the proposing official to consider the highest reasonable penalty warranted for the misconduct. The final agency decision must also include a careful *Douglas* factor analysis, wherein the deciding official considers whether to mitigate the penalty.

12. *See Connor v. Department of Veterans Affairs*, No. 21-1064 (Fed. Cir. 2021) (describing the Douglas factors); 5 M.S.P.R. 280, 332 (1981), *Douglas v. Veteran's Administration*.

13. *See id.* at 332–33.

14. *Connor v. Department of Veterans Affairs*, No. 21-1064 (Fed. Cir. 2021).

15. *Id.*

16. *See Ward v. U.S. Postal Service*, 634 F.3d 1274, 1282 (Fed. Cir. 2011).

The Performance Based Actions Under Chapter 43 and How They Differ Under Chapter 75

In an unacceptable performance case pursuant to 5 USC 4303, a Federal employee can only be removed for unacceptable performance, if it can show, by substantial evidence[17], that the agency has an approved Office of Personnel Management performance appraisal system, the agency communicated to the employee the performance standards and critical elements of his position, the performance standards are valid under 5 USC 4302 (b)(1), the agency warned the employee of the inadequacies of her performance during the appraisal period and gave her a reasonable opportunity to improve-typically referred to as a performance improvement plan (PIP), and the employee did not improve to the level required to be retained on the job.[18] In *Santos v. NASA*[19], the U.S. Court of Appeals for the Federal Circuit held that an agency is also required to justify its reason for putting the employee on a performance improvement plan in the first place.

Chapter 43 reductions in grade and removal are taken under 5 U.S.C. section 4303. Chapter 75 adverse actions are taken under 5 U.S.C. section 7513. An agency can take a performance-based action under either Chapter; however it must follow the requirements of the Chapter it relies upon. [20]

In taking a Chapter 43 action the agency has a lower burden of proof, substantial evidence as opposed to a preponderance of evidence. Further, once the agency can prove the employees was properly placed on a PIP and failed to raise her performance to level required to be retained on the job, the employee will be removed from the position, and that decision is not subject to a *Douglas factor* analysis because there is no mitigation of penalty in a 4303 case. In addition nexus is presumed in a Chapter 43 case. However, Chapter 43 actions can take longer and there are many procedural requirements that must be followed before taking such an action, which may bode for considering a Chapter 75 action instead. For example, a performance action under Chapter 75 does not require placing the employee on a PIP. Further there is no required examination of the adequacy of performance standards and critical elements. The supervisor should carefully consult with OCHCO and OGC to determine the appropriate approach given the facts of the case.[21]

Nexus and Penalty Assessment Decisions and Leadership in the Context of a Constitutional Government

The effective leader must always be careful to avoid imposing their morality on their colleagues and staff,

17. Pursuant to 5 CFR 1202.56 c)(1) substantial evidence is the " degree of relevant evidence that a reasonable person, considering the record as a whole, might accept as adequate to support a conclusion, even though other reasonable persons might disagree."
18. See *Santos v. NASA*, 990 F.3d 1355, (Fed. Cir. 2021).
19. See *Santos v. NASA*, 990 F.3d 1355, 1361 (Fed. Cir. 2021).
20. *Loveshin v. Department of the Navy*, 767 F.2d 826, 840 843 (1985).
21. For additional differences between Chapter 43 and Chapter 75 performance actions, see the Merit Systems Protection Board Guidance, Performance Based Actions under Chapters 43 and 75 of Title 5-Similarities and Differences. https://www.mspb.gov/studies/adverse_action_report/4_Performance-Based%20Actions.html

especially when considering taking a proposed or final disciplinary action. The effective leader should avoid acting reflexively and must take care to clearly identify the connection between the disciplinary action taken and efficiency of the government. In so doing, the leader avoids acting arbitrarily and capriciously, avoids unnecessarily intruding into the private off duty lives of their staff, and avoids depriving an employee of the property interests in their job, unless the supervisor can concretely show how the misconduct adversely affects the agency for which they are employed.

The effective leader does not, however, ignore misconduct that adversely affects the agency, whether it occurs on or off duty. Ignoring such misconduct can harm not only the agency but the trust and confidence staff may have in the leader. Some of the most difficult and complex nexus cases occur while an employee is off duty (e.g., posting comments on a personal social media account that may create a sexual or racial hostile work environment.) Accordingly, it is critical to carefully consult with the Human Resources department and legal counsel before taking a disciplinary action, especially when the misconduct occurs off duty.

Moreover, the effective leader strives to be fair, transparent and avoid arbitrary and capricious decisions. The *Douglas* factors provide the proposing and deciding officials with guidelines to help arrive at a fair, consistent, and well-reasoned decision. By considering such factors as the seriousness of the offense, progressive discipline (the employee's disciplinary history), consistency of the penalty, the employee's position, the notoriety of the offense, whether the employee was on notice of the wrongdoing, and the extent the employee may be rehabilitated, the manager has a roadmap to a well-reasoned and thoughtful decision. Further, because the relevant *Douglas* factors are expected to be considered in every disciplinary action case and addressed in the proposed and final decision, the responsible agency official engages in transparent decision-making, which balances the efficiency of the agency with the employee's property interests in their job.

Cases and Review Questions

Directions: Use the provided links to access each noteworthy case. Then, provide complete and detailed responses to the questions and prompts about each case.

Doe v. Department of Justice, 565 F.3d 1375 (Fed. Cir. 2009)

https://caselaw.findlaw.com/us-federal-circuit/1365251.html

1. What must an agency prove to establish a nexus between off duty conduct and the efficiency of the service?
2. Why did the Court not find a nexus in this case?
3. What can an agency do to establish clear guidance regarding the kinds of off-duty misconduct that may subject an employee to discipline?

Brown v. Department of the Navy, 229 F.3d 1356, 1358–61 (Fed. Cir. 2000)

https://caselaw.findlaw.com/us-federal-circuit/1203843.html

1. Why did the court find a nexus in this case, where an employee was having a personal off-duty affair with a married spouse?
2. How does this case differ from other conduct in which an employee engages in private activity that does not affect job performance?
3. What can an agency do to remind its managers that it is not to act like "moral police"?

Scheffler v. Department of the Army, 117 M.S.P.R. 499 (2012) aff'd 522 F.App'x 913 (Fed. Cir. 2013)

https://www.mspb.gov/decisions/precedential/
SCHEFFLER_RANDALL_AT_0752_10_1075_I_2_OPINION_AND_ORDER_699491.pdf

1. With what basis did the MSPB establish nexus in this case?
2. Explain why the reasons the MSPB found did not justify a nexus.
3. What can an agency do to ensure that its managers effectively consider nexus before rendering a disciplinary action decision?

LaChance v. Duvall, 178 F.3d 1246 (Fed. Cir. 1999)

https://caselaw.findlaw.com/us-federal-circuit/1142495.html

1. What kind of deference should the MSPB, and the Courts give to an agency's assessment of the penalty in a disciplinary action?
2. When can the MSPB exercise independent authority to mitigate the agency's penalty?
3. What happens to the agency's penalty assessment if the MSPB judge does not sustain all the charges against the employee?
4. What can the agency do to ensure that even if all the charges are not sustained, the agency's penalty assessment will still be sustained by the MSPB?

Douglas v. Veterans Administration, 5 M.S.P.R. 280 (1981)

https://www.mspb.gov/decisions/precedential/
DOUGLAS_CURTIS_ET_AL_AT075299006_OPINION_AND_ORDER_253434.pdf

1. What are the *Douglas* factors?
2. In what ways do the *Douglas* factors help a proposing or deciding official arrive at a reasonable penalty?
3. What can an agency do to ensure the *Douglas* factors are applied in a fair, consistent, and reasonable manner?

Santos v. NASA, 990 F.3d 1355 (Fed Cir 2021)

https://cafc.uscourts.gov/opinions-orders/19-2345.opinion.3-11-2021_1746433.pdf

1. What is the significance of Santos when taking an Unacceptable Performance Action Case?
2. What actions must a supervisor take to ensure compliance with *Santos* when taking a Chapter 43 unacceptable performance action?

Chapter 10

The Limited Power of the President and Article II Enumerated Authorities

This chapter identifies the specific enumerated authorities of the President to act in Article II of the U.S. Constitution and how most of those authorities are shared with Congress. The chapter discusses the important Supreme Court decision in *Youngstown Sheet & Tube Co. v. Sawyer*;[1] its impact on restricting the power of the President; and how the post-*Youngstown* Congress has expanded the power of the President, particularly when exercising emergency powers and serving as the Commander in Chief during wartime. The chapter ends by addressing leadership in the context of the limited authorities of the President along with the *Youngstown* case itself, followed by questions designed to stimulate class discussion.

The Enumerated Authorities of the President in Article II of the Constitution

Article II of the U.S. Constitution contains enumerated authorities of the President.[2] The most important in the first section are as follows:

- "The executive Power shall be vested in a President of the United States of America."
- "The 'Vesting' [C]lause establishes the President as the chief constitutional officer of the Executive Branch, entrusted with supervisory and policy responsibilities of utmost discretion and sensitivity ... including management of the Executive Branch."[3] This includes the power to remove executive officers of the United States whom the President has appointed by and with the advice and consent of the

1. *Youngstown Sheet & Tube Co. v. Sawyer*, 343 U.S. 579 (1952).
2. U.S. Const. art. II.
3. *Nixon v. Fitzgerald*, 457 U.S. 731, 749–50 (1982) (citing *Myers v. United States*, 272 U.S. 52, 134-135 (1926)).

Senate.[4] In *Morrison v. Olson*[5], however, the Supreme Court held that certain "inferior officers" such as an independent prosecutor under the Ethics in Government Act, could be appointed and removed without approval by the President.)[6]

Section 2 provides that the President

- "... shall be Commander in Chief [of the Armed Services.]"
- "... shall have Power, by and with the Advice and Consent of the Senate to make Treaties, provided two thirds of Senators present concur"
- "... shall nominate, and by and with the Advice and Consent of the Senate, shall appoint Ambassadors, other public Ministers and Consuls, Judges of the Supreme Court, and all other Officers of the United States whose Appointments are not herein otherwise provided for, and which shall be established by Law"
- "... shall have Power to fill up all Vacancies that may happen during the Recess of the Senate, by granting Commissions that shall expire at the End of their next session"[7]

As discussed in greater detail to follow, under the U.S. Constitution, the role of Congress is to declare war, and the role of the President, as Commander in Chief, is to implement it. The significance of the "Commander in Chief Clause" is to ensure that the military is ultimately under the control of a civilian and that this control is centralized under a single President, as opposed to decentralized to the states, as was previously set forth under the Articles of Confederation. Further, Congress may not delegate the ultimate command of the armed services to anyone other than the President.[8]
Section 3 provides that the President

- "... shall receive Ambassadors and other Public Ministers"
- "... shall take Care that the Laws be faithfully executed"
- "... shall Commission all the Officers of the United States"[9]

The "Take Care Clause" has been described as "a major source of presidential power because it seemingly invests the office with broad enforcement authority. Yet at the same time, the provision also

4. *Id.*
5. *Morrison v. Olson*, 487 U.S. 684 (1988)).
6. *Id.*
7. Const. art. II, § 2.
8. See Michael D. Ramsey and Steven I. Vladeck, *Commander in Chief Clause: Common Interpretation*, National Constitution Center, https://constitutioncenter.org/interactive-constitution/interpretation/article-ii/clauses/345.
9. Const. art. II, § 3.

serves as a major limitation on that power because it underscores that the executive is under a duty to faithfully execute the laws of Congress and not disregard them."[10]

Moreover, the critical responsibility of the President to "take [c]are" that the laws are faithfully executed requires assistance by all those in the executive branch:

> Article II provides that the President must "take Care that the Laws be faithfully executed." Art. II, § 3, c § 3. The entire "executive Power" belongs to the President alone. But because it would be "impossib[le]" for "one man" to "perform all the great business of the State," the Constitution assumes that lesser executive officers will "assist the supreme Magistrate in discharging the duties of his trust." 30 Writings of George Washington 334 (J. Fitzpatrick ed. 1939). These lesser officers must remain accountable to the President, whose authority they wield. *Bowsher*, 478 U.S., at 726, 106 S. Ct. 3181.[11]

Section 3 also provides that the President shall be empowered to "receive Ambassadors and other Public Ministers."[12] This has been referred to as the "Reception Clause" of the Constitution." This Supreme Court has been broadly interpreted the Reception Clause as providing the President with authority to recognize a foreign state: "It is a logical and proper inference, then, that a Clause directing the President alone to receive ambassadors would be understood to acknowledge his power to recognize other nations."[13] Moreover, the Court held the following: "[T]he power to recognize foreign states and governments and their territorial bounds is exclusive to the Presidency."[14] Although the President has formal recognition authority, Congress still maintains broad foreign affairs policy authority:

> Although the President alone effects the formal act of recognition, Congress' powers, and its central role in making laws, give it substantial authority regarding many of the policy determinations that precede and follow the act of recognition itself. If Congress disagrees with the President's recognition policy, there may be consequences. Formal recognition may seem a hollow act if it is not accompanied by the dispatch of an

10. *See* William P. Marshall, Saikrishna B. Prakash, and Paul G. Mahoney, *Article II, Section 3: Common Interpretation,* National Constitution Center, https://constitutioncenter.org/interactive-constitution/interpretation/article-ii/clauses/348#:~:text=The%20Take%20Care%20Clause%20has%20played%20a%20central,has%20a%20constitutional%20power%20to%20remove%20federal%20officers.
11. *Seila L. LLC v. Consumer Fin. Prot. Bureau*, 140 S. Ct. 2183, 2197, 207 L. Ed. 2d 494 (2020) (internal quotes omitted).
12. Const. art. II, § 3, cl. 2.
13. *Zivotofsky ex rel. Zivotofsky v. Kerry (Zivotofsky II),* 135 S. Ct. 2076, 2085 (2015) (Zivotofsky, a U.S. citizen born in Jerusalem, was prohibited from compelling the State Department to comply with a law that said it had to list Israel on his passport upon request. The purpose of this policy, at the time, was to refrain from acknowledging any foreign government's sovereign control over Jerusalem, especially given the dispute between Israel and Palestine. For more information on this case, see Jennifer K. Elsea, Congressional Research Service Report, *So, Now Can Menachem Zivotofsky Get His Passport Reissued to Say "Israel"?,* March 1, 2018, https://crsreports.congress.gov/product/pdf/LSB/LSB10088; *see also* Jennifer K. Elsea, *Congressional Research Service Report, Zivotofsky v. Kerry: The Jerusalem Passport Case and Its Potential Implications for Congress's Foreign Affairs Powers*, September 28, 2015, https://crsreports.congress.gov/product/pdf/R/R43773.
14. *Id.* at 2094.

> ambassador, the easing of trade restrictions, and the conclusion of treaties. And those decisions require action by the Senate or the whole Congress.[15]

Section 4 does not address the authorities of the President. Rather, it explains when the President can be removed from office. Specifically, the President, Vice President, and other civil Officers of the United States can be removed from office on impeachment for "Conviction of, Treason, Bribery, or other high Crimes and Misdemeanors."[16]

Most of the Enumerated Authorities of the President Are Shared with Congress

Most of the authorities of the President are shared with Congress. As explained by authors David M. Driesden and William C. Banks,

> [t]he Constitution shares practically all express authority between Congress and the President ... . The Constitution denies the President sole control over the executive and judicial branches by giving Congress a role in appointment and, through impeachment, in the power of removal. Thus, Article II authorizes the President to nominate "Officers of the United States," ambassadors, and federal judges, but these important officials only assume office if the Senate concurs.
>
> The Constitution also makes ... the power to make treaties, a shared power. It authorizes the President to negotiate treaties, but only allows them to take effect with the Senate's advice and consent.
>
> Congress has vast legislative authority, but the President may veto legislation (unless a supermajority overrides the veto). With respect to the war power, the Constitution authorizes only Congress to initiate war and allows it to regulate the armed forces, while making the President "Commander in Chief."
>
> Perhaps most importantly, the scope of the President's express authority to execute the law depends on the scope of congressional legislation. ...
>
> Finally, the Constitution authorizes Congress to enact laws "necessary and proper for carrying into execution" not only its own powers, but also powers exercised by "any ... Officer" of the government. This part of the Necessary and Proper Clause shows that Congress may shape presidential administration.[17]

The foregoing shared responsibilities between Congress and the President are intended to create a

15. *Id.* at 2087.

16. Const. art. II, § 4.

17. David M. Driesen and William C. Banks, *Implied Presidential and Congressional Powers*, 41, 4 Cordozo L. Rev. (2020) (footnotes omitted), http://law.syr.edu/uploads/docs/deans-faculty/Driesen.Banks.41.4.2_Online1.pdf.

government that secures liberty: "As we have explained on many prior occasions, the separation of powers is designed to preserve the liberty of all the people."[18]

Youngstown and the Constitutional Limitations on Presidential Authority

In *Youngstown Sheet & Tube Co. v. Sawyer,*[19] the Supreme Court held that President Truman, in his capacity as Commander in Chief during the Korean War, had no authority to seize the nation's private steel mills during a labor dispute. President Truman had issued Executive Order 10340 to seize certain private steel mills to avert an asserted national catastrophe which would result from a stoppage of steel production during a time of war. The Court found that the enumerated authorities in Article II did not expressly authorize such action and that absent an Act of Congress, the President had no such authority. Justice Jackson explained his concurring opinion in *Youngstown* regarding the authority of a President to act thusly:

> In considering claims of Presidential power this Court refers to Justice Jackson's familiar tripartite framework from *Youngstown Sheet & Tube Co. v. Sawyer* (concurring opinion). The framework divides exercises of Presidential power into three categories: First, when "the President acts pursuant to an express or implied authorization of Congress, his authority is at its maximum, for it includes all that he possesses in his own right plus all that Congress can delegate." Second, "in absence of either a congressional grant or denial of authority" there is a "zone of twilight in which he and Congress may have concurrent authority," and where "congressional inertia, indifference or quiescence may" invite the exercise of executive power. Finally, when "the President takes measures incompatible with the expressed or implied will of Congress ... he can rely only upon his own constitutional powers minus any constitutional powers of Congress over the matter." *Ibid.* To succeed in this third category, the President's asserted power must be both "exclusive" and "conclusive" on the issue.[20]

Thus, the President's authority is strongest when acting pursuant to an act of Congress and weakest when acting incompatible with the will of Congress.

Since *Youngstown*, Congress has passed legislation that provided the President with more expansive authority than that set forth in the Constitution. Two of those expansive authorities are set forth in the following sections.

18. *See Collins v. Yellen*, 141 S. Ct. 1761, 1780, 210 L. Ed. 2d 432 (2021) (citations omitted).

19. *Youngstown Sheet & Tube Co. v. Sawyer*, 343 U.S. 579 (1952).

20. *Zivotofsky ex rel. Zivotofsky v. Kerry*, 576 U.S. 1, 10, (2015) (citations omitted).

The Expansive Statutory Authority of the President During an Emergency

Congress has passed laws that authorize the President to act in times of emergency. For example, under the 1976 National Emergencies Act (NEA),[21] the President has very broad authority to declare and act during an emergency. This statute provides few restrictions on the President, since it does not even define what an emergency is. According to the Brennan Center, as of March 4, 2022, there are 136 statutory powers that become available upon the President's declaration of an emergency.[22]
https://www.brennancenter.org/our-work/research-reports/guide-emergency-powers-and-their-use.

The Expansive Statutory Authority of the President During War

Article I grants Congress the authority to declare war, and Article II provides the President, as "Commander in Chief of the Army and Navy," with the authority to conduct an authorized war.[23] The decision to share war powers was quite deliberate by our founding fathers, as James Madison explained in a letter to Thomas Jefferson:

> The [C]onstitution supposes, what the History of all Govts demonstrates, that the Ex. is the branch of power most interested in war, & most prone to it. It has accordingly with studied care, vested the question of war in the Legisl. [sic].[24]

Congress has passed two statutes authorizing Presidential war powers. The first was the *War Power Resolution*[25] in 1973 during the Vietnam War. Section 4(a)(1) requires the President to report to Congress, within forty-eight hours, any introduction of U.S. forces into hostilities or imminent hostilities.[26] Section 5(b) requires the use of force to be terminated within sixty days, with an additional thirty days to withdraw forces (for a total of ninety days), unless Congress authorizes such use or extends the time.[27] Section 3 of the law requires the President to consult with Congress wherever possible before introducing armed forces into any conflict.[28]

The second Presidential war powers authorization passed by Congress was the 2001 *Authorization for Use of Military Force*[29] (AUMF) bill to combat terrorism. Section 2(a) of the 2001 AUMF authorizes the President "to use all necessary and appropriate force against those nations, organizations, or persons

21. *See* National Emergencies Act (1976), 50 U.S.C. § 1601 *et seq.*
22. Brennan Center, *A Guide to Emergency Powers and Their Use,* March 4, 2022,
23. Const. art. I–II.
24. *See* Letter from James Madison to Thomas Jefferson (April 2, 1798), https://www.loc.gov/resource/mjm.06_0540_0542/?st=text.
25. *See* War Power Resolution (P.L. 93–148)
26. *Id.* at § 4(a)(1).
27. *Id.* at § 5(b).
28. *Id.* at § 3.
29. Authorization for Use of Military Force, Public Law 107–40 (2001–2002).

he determines planned, authorized, committed, or aided the terrorist attacks that occurred on September 11, 2001, or harbored such organizations or persons, in order to prevent any future acts of international terrorism against the United States."[30] It has been reported that the AUMF has been and continues to be used to justify military operations in 22 countries.[31] The AUMF has broadly expanded the authority of the President to combat terrorism and substantially diminished the role of Congress. Some have gone so far as to describe the relationship between Congress and the President under the AUMF as follows: "Under this AUMF, Congress relinquished its constitutionally assigned war powers in the fight against 'terrorism,' ceding to the president its responsibility to decide whether, when, and where the United States chooses war."[32]

Leadership in the Context of A Constitutional Government and the Limited Authorities of the President and the Executive Branch

The Constitution itself does not discuss leadership:

> The Constitution says almost nothing about leadership. It does not identify a leader of the country, a head of state, or even a head of government. By vesting the executive power in the president, it implies that the president is leader of the executive branch, but not that he is the leader of the country or the government.[33]
>
> https://direct.mit.edu/daed/article/145/3/35/27107/Presidential-Leadership-amp-the-Separation-of.

The Constitution requires leadership in the context of a government where power is defused, by creating a separation of powers between three branches of government. Often, this involves shared responsibilities between the federal government and state and local governments, commonly referred to as "Federalism," as Justice Jackson explained:

> While the Constitution *diffuses power the better to secure liberty*, it also contemplates that practice will integrate the dispersed powers into a workable government. It enjoins upon its branches separateness but interdependence, autonomy but reciprocity. Presidential powers are not fixed but fluctuate, depending upon their disjunction or conjunction with those of Congress.[34]

30. *Id.* at § 2(a).
31. See Stephanie Savell, *The 2001 Authorization for Use of Military Force: A Comprehensive Look at Where and How it Has Been Used,* Dec. 14, 2021, https://watson.brown.edu/costsofwar/files/cow/imce/papers/2021/Costs%20of%20War_2001%20AUMF.pdf.
32. *See id.*; *see also* Heather Brandon-Smith, *The President's War Powers: Article II War Powers and the Authorizations for Use of Military Force.* Friends Committee on National Legislation, Feb. 10, 2021, https://www.fcnl.org/warpowers.
33. *See* Eric A. Posner, *Presidential Leadership & the Separation of Powers* (abstract), 145, 3 Daedalus 35–43 (2016),
34. *Youngstown Sheet & Tube Co. v. Sawyer,* 343 U.S. 579, 635, 72 S. Ct. 863, 96 L. Ed. 1153 (1952) (emphasis added).

By defusing power, the President's ability to influence others and develop coalitions is paramount:

> Presidents who are judged great leaders overcome entrenched resistance to implement policies that advance the public interest; they do so usually by knitting together a coalition of groups whose trust they have managed to win.[35]

Successful Presidents typically lead by demonstrating that "[they share] the group's interests and will keep [their] promises."[36]

Supervisors can learn a great deal about the Constitution and how leadership in an environment of diffused power promotes liberty. Supervisors in the federal government have various authorities, including to assign work, appraise employees, and hire and fire employees, just to name a few.[37] None of these basic responsibilities necessarily require coalition building or diffusion of power. However, to facilitate meaningful change in federal government policies and practices, the supervisor as successful leader must be capable of influencing others; building trust and meaningful coalitions amongst staff, clients, and higher-level management; as well as building trust and meaningful coalitions amongst Congress, state and local governments, and the public. The successful supervisor or leader does not act as a monarch or authoritarian but, rather, defuses their authority and liberates the ingenuity of their staff by, among other things, empowering their employees to be creative and develop new ideas. In so doing, the successful leader creates not a democracy but a culture of innovation, which is critical to a successful organization.[38] Of course nothing herein should be construed to limit the authority of the supervisor to exercise final decision-making authority.

Cases and Review Questions

Directions: Use the provided links to access each noteworthy case. Then, provide complete and detailed responses to the questions and prompts about each case.

Youngstown Sheet & Tube Co. v. Sawyer, 343 U.S. 579 (1952)

https://www.law.cornell.edu/supremecourt/text/343/579

1. Why did the President order the takeover of the steel mills?
2. Why was the President prohibited from taking over the steel mills?
3. What could Congress have done to help the President take over the steel mills?
4. What impact does *Youngstown* have on the authority of the President to act?
5. What does *Youngstown* say about separation of powers under the Constitution?

35. *Id.*
36. *Id.* For an outline of additional factors that make a successful President, see *supra* note 32 at footnote 15.
37. *See* Management Rights, 5 USC 7106 (a).
38. *See* Slalom Consulting Team, *Risk and Reward: A Framework for Federal Innovation,* Partnership of Public Service (2019), https://ourpublicservice.org/wp-content/uploads/2019/10/Risk-and-Reward-Report.pdf (for more detailed discussion on developing a culture of leadership in the federal government).

6. What is the significance of Justice Jackson's concurring opinion? When is the President's authority to act at its highest and lowest level?

U.S. v. Nixon, 418 U.S. 683 (1974)

https://www.law.cornell.edu/supremecourt/text/418/683

1. What is executive privilege?
2. What is the exception to executive privilege discussed in this case?
3. Do you believe the case was properly reasoned? Why, or why not?
4. What actions can a President make to ensure their communication is protected from discovery in the future?

Hamdi v. Rumsfeld, 542 U.S. 507 (2004)

https://supreme.justia.com/cases/federal/us/542/507/

1. Can the Government detain a U.S. citizen as an "enemy combatant" without access to legal counsel?
2. What rights does a U.S. citizen have when being detained as an enemy combatant?
3. What do you think of the Court's reasoning that "a state of war is not a blank check for the President when it comes to the rights of the Nation's citizens?"

Chapter 11

Investigatory Interviews and the Constitution: Miranda, Kalkines, Garrity Warnings and Weingarten Rights

Introduction

This chapter focuses on the Fifth Amendment right against self-incrimination and the Sixth Amendment right to counsel and the progeny of cases addressing the rights and obligations of employees in federal investigatory interviews. The chapter discusses *Miranda* warnings, stemming from the Supreme Court case *Miranda v. Arizona*;[1] *Kalkines* warnings, stemming from the court of claims decision *Kalkines v. United States*;[2] *Garrity* warnings, stemming from the Supreme Court case *Garrity v. New Jersey*;[3] and *Weingarten* rights, stemming from the case *National Labor Relations Board v. J. Weingarten*.[4] The chapter concludes with a section on leadership in the context of a constitutional government followed by court decisions with questions to stimulate class discussion.

Miranda Warnings

In *Miranda v. Arizona*, the Supreme Court recognized a defendant's constitutional Fifth Amendment right against self-incrimination and the right to counsel, in the context of the inherently coercive nature of custodial interrogation by the police.[5] Thus, under *Miranda*, "the prosecution may not use statements, whether exculpatory or inculpatory, stemming

1. *Miranda v. Arizona*, 384 U.S. 436 (1966),
2. *Kalkines v. United States*, 473 F.2d 1391 (Fed. Cl. 1973),
3. *Garrity v. New Jersey*, 385 U.S. 493 (1967)
4. *National Labor Relations Board v. J. Weingarten*, 420 U.S. 251 (1975).
5. *Supra* note 1.

from custodial interrogation of the defendant unless it demonstrates the use of procedural safeguards effective to secure the privilege against self-incrimination."[6] The police are, therefore, required to provide the following Miranda Warnings to the detained defendant:

> You have the right to remain silent. Anything you say can and will be used against you in a court of law. You have the right to an attorney. If you cannot afford an attorney, one will be provided for you. Do you understand the rights I have just read to you? With these rights in mind, do you wish to speak to me?[7]

Miranda and the privilege against self-incrimination have been extended to federal administrative investigatory interviews by the Office of the Inspector General and other federal agency officials, in the case that the federal employee is in a custodial interrogation and reasonably believes their testimony may be used against them in a criminal proceeding.[8] Statements made during such an interrogation without *Miranda* warnings may not be used in a Merit Systems Protection Board proceeding.[9]

Miranda applies only to custodial interrogations.[10] Whether an interrogation is custodial is determined by an objective standard, the totality of the circumstances—how a reasonable person would understand the situation—not on the subjective beliefs of the law enforcement officers or the person being questioned.[11]

In an important case, *Vega v. Tekoh*,[12] the Supreme Court held that the government was not liable to pay a civil penalty when it failed to provide a *Miranda warning.* The Court held the only remedy for the failure to provide *Miranda* warnings is suppression of a confession or other evidence at trial. Specifically, in *Vega*, during a custodial interrogation regarding sexual assault allegations at the workplace, a Deputy Sherriff did not give the plaintiff Miranda warnings, yet received from him a handwritten apology for inappropriately touching the complainant. The handwritten apology was inadmissible during a criminal prosecution for sexual assault. Subsequently, the plaintiff sued the government for civil damages under 42 U.S.C. 1983[13] for violating his Fifth Amendment right against self-incrimination when it failed to provide him *Miranda* warnings. The Supreme Court ruled for the government, characterizing *Miranda* warnings not as a Constitutional right but merely a "prophylactic rule" that the Court found to be necessary to protect the

6. *California v. Prysock,* 453 U.S. 355, 359 (1981).
7. *Supra* note 1.
8. *Modrowski v. Department of Veterans Affairs*, 252 F.3d 1344, 1350 (Fed. Cir. 2001) (citing *Kastigar v. United States*, 406 U.S. 441, 444–45 (1972); *Weston v. U.S. Department of Housing and Urban Development,* 724 F.2d 943, 947–48 (Fed. Cir. 1983); *Tannehill v. Department of the Air Force*, 58 MSPR 219, 222 (1993).
9. *Cooper v. U.S. Postal Service*, 42 M.S.P.R. 174, 178 (1989) (an employee's pre-removal statement, given during custodial detention to agency investigators, may be used against the employee in Board proceedings only if the employee waived their Fifth Amendment rights), *aff'd*, 904 F.2d 46 (Fed.Cir.1990)).
10. *See Sher v. Department of Veteran's Affairs,* 97 MSPR 232 (2004).
11. *See Berkemer v. McCarty*, 468 U.S. 420, 442 (1984).
12. *Vega v. Tekoh*, 142 S. Ct. 2095, (2022).
13. Civil Action for Deprivation of Rights, 42 U.S. Code § 1983.

Fifth Amendment right against compelled self-incrimination.[14] Thus, the lawsuit, filed under 42 U.S.C. 1983 was dismissed. This case will certainly limit future civil litigation for violation of *Miranda* rights.

Kalkines Warnings

If an OIG agent or other law enforcement officer or federal official, wishes to compel the testimony of the federal employee witness, they must first inform the employee that their statements will not be used in future criminal prosecution but only for administrative purposes. By offering the employee immunity from criminal prosecution, the agency is permitted to discipline the employee up to and including removal for failure to answer questions and cooperate in the investigation. This is referred to as a *Kalkines* warning.[15] An example of a *Kalkines* warning used by the Department of Homeland Security is as follows:

> The *Kalkines* form utilized by DHS (INV FORM–26) states:
>
> You are going to be asked a number of specific questions concerning the performance of your official duties. You have a duty to answer these questions. U.S. Department of Homeland Security disciplinary proceedings resulting in your discharge may be initiated as a result of your answers. Neither your answers nor any information or evidence which is gained by reason of such statements can be used against you in any criminal proceedings except a prosecution for false statements made during this interview. You are subject to discipline, including dismissal, if you refuse to answer or fail to respond truthfully to any questions. You are subject to criminal prosecution if you make false statements or give false answers during this interview.[16]

Consultation with the U.S. Attorney's office is strongly advised before offering a *Kalkines* warning because the employee is being offered use immunity against using their statements in future criminal prosecution.

Garrity Warnings

Another warning that may be used in an investigatory interview, in both the federal and public sectors is referred to as a *Garrity* warning.[17] A *Garrity* warning informs the employee they are not in custody, not compelled to testify, can refuse to answer questions if they think their answers will incriminate them, their answers are strictly voluntary, and refusal to answer the questions will not result in removal or lesser discipline but could result in criminal prosecution or administrative discipline. An example of a *Garrity* warning offered by a federal agency, the U.S. Fish and Wildlife Service, is as follows:

14. *Supra* note 12; *See Fosnight v. Jones*, 41 F. 4th 916, 923 (7th Cir. 2022) (relying on *Vega*, the Court of Appeals held "the mere failure to give *Miranda* warnings is not a constitutional violation.")(citations omitted).
15. *Supra* note 2.
16. *Abdallah v. Napolitano*, 909 F. Supp. 2d 196, 201, footnote 5 (W.D.N.Y. 2012)
17. *Supra* note 3.

You are being contacted/interviewed to solicit your cooperation in an inquiry regarding information pertaining to allegations of misconduct or improper performance of official duties. You are advised the authority to conduct this interview is contained in Title 50, Code of Federal Regulations, Subchapter A, Section 1.2, and Title 43, Code of Federal Regulations, Section 1466. This interview is confidential. The matter under investigation could also constitute a violation of law which could result in criminal prosecution of responsible individuals. You have the right to remain silent. If you do decide to answer questions or make a statement, you may stop answering at any time. Although you would normally be expected to answer questions regarding your official duties, in this instance you are not required to do so. Your refusal to answer on the ground that the answers may tend to incriminate you will not subject you to disciplinary action by FWS or the Department of the Interior. Any statement you furnish may be used as evidence against you in any future criminal proceeding or agency disciplinary proceeding or both.[18]

Summarizing the Differences between Kalkines and Garrity Warnings.

The difference between *Kalkines* and *Garrity* warnings in an administrative investigation is as follows: the investigator provides *Kalkines* warnings to compel an employee's testimony under threat of removal if the employee refuses to answer by ensuring the employee's statements will not be used in future criminal prosecution. *Garrity* warnings, on the other hand, apply when the testimony is not compelled by the government but is voluntary and the employee is free not to answer questions under the threat of discipline. The Merit Systems Protection Board summarizes the difference between *Miranda*, *Kalkines*, and *Garrity* warnings as follows:

> *Miranda v. Arizona,* 384 U.S. 436 (1968) (holding that, prior to police questioning, detainees must be advised of their constitutional right to an attorney and against self-incrimination); *see also Kalkines v. United States,* 473 F.2d 1391 (Ct.Cl.1973) (discussing *Kalkines* warnings, which are provided when an employee is warned that he or she may be removed for failing to answer questions in an investigation, but his or her responses may not be used in a future criminal prosecution); *Garrity v. New Jersey,* 385 U.S. 493, 499–500 (1967) (explaining that *Garrity* warnings involve situations when public employees are told that they have the right to remain silent in an investigation, and any statements made could subject them to administrative or criminal liability).[19]

18. U.S. Fish & Wildlife Service, *Professional Responsibility Unit and Allegations of Service*, LE Misconduct, 441 FW 5 (2007), https://www.fws.gov/policy/441fw5.html.
19. Dorsey-*Williams v. Department of Air Force*, No. SF-0752-16-0034-I-1, 2016 WL 4771515 (M.S.P.B. Sept. 12, 2016) (non-precedential decision but cited for its persuasiveness).

Weingarten Rights

Another right, afforded only to bargaining unit employees who are represented by a federal union, based not on the Constitution but on private, public, and federal labor laws are *Weingarten* rights, named after the Supreme Court case *National Labor Relations Board v. J. Weingarten*.[20] Weingarten rights refer to the right of a bargaining unit employee to request union representation in an employer investigatory interview. Although the *Weingarten* case involves a private sector union employee, Congress incorporated *Weingarten* rights as a part of Chapter 71 of the Civil Service Reform Act:

> **(2)** An exclusive representative of an appropriate unit in an agency shall be given the opportunity to be represented at—
>
> ...
>
> **(B)** any examination of an employee in the unit by a representative of the agency in connection with an investigation if—
>
> **(i)** the employee reasonably believes that the examination may result in disciplinary action against the employee; and
>
> **(ii)** the employee requests representation.[21]

Federal agencies provide an annual notice to their bargaining unit employees of their *Weingarten* rights.[22] The Federal Labor Relations Authority has held that *Weingarten* rights are triggered when four elements are present:

> (1) the meeting at issue must be an examination of an employee by a representative of the agency; (2) the examination must be in connection with an investigation; (3) the employee must reasonably believe that the examination may result in disciplinary action against the employee; and (4) the employee must request representation. The determination of whether an employee's belief that disciplinary action may result is reasonable rests on objective factors.[23]

It is well established that *Weingarten* rights do not apply during performance counseling meetings with an employee; they are designed only to apply in an investigatory interview that could result in disciplinary action.[24]

20. *National Labor Relations Board v. J. Weingarten*, 420 U.S. 251 (1975).
21. Civil Service Reform Act, 5 U.S.C. 7114 (a)(2)(B).
22. *See, e.g.*, Forest Service, U.S. Department of Agriculture, Annual Weingarten Notice, (May 27, 2022), https://www.fs.usda.gov/inside-fs/mail-call/annual-weingarten-notice.
23. United States Department of the Interior Bureau of Land Mgmt. Eugene Dist. Portland, Oregon (Agency) & American Federation of Government Employees Local 1911 (Union), 68 F.L.R.A. 178, 181 (2015) (citations omitted).
24. Internal Revenue Service, Detroit, Michigan, and National Treasury Employees Union, 5 FLRA 421 (1981).

Leadership in the Context of a Constitutional Government and the Fifth Amendment Right Against Self-Incrimination

The U.S. Supreme Court has long recognized the coercive nature of being interrogated while in custody. Effective leadership includes not taking advantage of employees when in such coercive conditions. When a manager wishes to set up an investigative interview upon suspicion of employee misconduct, the manager should consult with legal counsel and the Human Resources department to assess whether the matter should be referred to the Office of the Inspector General (OIG). The OIG agent is best positioned to assess whether *Miranda*, *Kalkines*, or *Garrity* may be applicable. Further, the OIG also has the relationship with the Assistant United States Attorney to ensure that immunity from prosecution can be offered as part of a *Kalkines* warning if that is appropriate. When the manager believes an investigatory interview of a bargaining unit employee is needed to assess whether an employee engaged in misconduct, the manager should be mindful of potential *Weingarten* rights and, again, seek the assistance of the agency's labor relations counsel or the labor relations specialist in advance of the interview. By recognizing the foregoing rights, the manager can ensure that the constitutional and legal rights of their staff will not be violated.

Cases and Review Questions

Directions: Use the provided links to access each noteworthy case. Then, provide complete and detailed responses to the questions and prompts about each case.

Vega v. Tekoh, 142 S. Ct. 2095 (2022)

https://www.supremecourt.gov/opinions/21pdf/21-499_gfbh.pdf

1. Why was the plaintiff in custody?
2. What were the ramifications for failing to provide the plaintiff with *Miranda* warnings yet accepting an apology for inappropriately touching a coworker?
3. How did the Supreme Court characterize a violation of *Miranda* rights? Do you agree with this characterization?
4. What can agency employers do to ensure that all the rights of employees during an investigatory interview are protected?

Modrowski v. Department of Veteran's Affairs (2001), 252 F.2d 1344 (2001)

https://law.justia.com/cases/federal/appellate-courts/F3/252/1344/499970/

1. When, according to the Court, do *Miranda* rights apply in an administrative investigatory interview?
2. Why were the plaintiff's *Miranda* rights violated?
3. What can an agency do to ensure that *Miranda*, *Kalkines*, and *Garrity* warnings are appropriately and clearly communicated to a witness?

National Aeronautics and Space Administration v. Federal Labor Relations Authority, 527 U.S. 229 (1999)

https://supreme.justia.com/cases/federal/us/527/229/

1. What were the circumstances that led to the investigative interview in this case?
2. Was the Inspector General required to give *Weingarten* rights to a federal employee? If so, what was the Court's rationale?
3. What can an agency do to ensure its employees are aware of their rights during an investigative interview?

Miranda v Arizona, 384 U.S. 436 (1966)

https://supreme.justia.com/cases/federal/us/384/436/

1. What are *Miranda* warnings and why does failure to provide such warnings violate the 5th or 14th Amendment?
2. What are *Kalkines* warnings and what are the circumstances when they are most likely to be provided in the government workplace?
3. What are *Garrtity* warnings and how do they differ from *Miranda* and *Kalkines* warnings?

Chapter 12

An Overview of Administrative Law

Administrative rulemaking is an important means by which the President and the Executive Branch fulfills its Article II, Section 3 obligation to "take care that the laws be faithfully executed."[1] This chapter sets forth the purpose of rulemaking, the rulemaking process, judicial review, and the authority of the courts to overturn arbitrary and capricious rules and agency decisions. It also examines recent Supreme Court case law that held that agency interpretations of the law are not entitled to judicial deference and the recent emergence of the "Major Questions Doctrine" as discussed in *West Virginia v. Environmental Protection Agency.*[2] Finally, the chapter includes specific administrative law cases with discussion questions and a discussion on leadership in the context of a constitutional government.

The Purpose of Rulemaking

When Congress passes a law, it typically grants a federal agency the authority to issue rules and regulations to implement that law. The Administrative Procedure Act (APA) is the central statute governing federal government rulemaking.[3] A "rule" is broadly defined under the APA as any "agency statement of general or particular applicability and future effect designed to implement, interpret, or prescribe law or policy or describing the organization, procedure, or practice requirements of an agency."[4] The rulemaking process is generally designed to ensure

- the public is informed of rules before they take effect;

1. U.S. Const. art. II, § 3.
2. *West Virginia v. Environmental Protection Agency*, 597 U.S. ___ (2022).
3. Administrative Procedure Act, 5 U.S.C. § 551 *et seq.*; This chapter does not address other important administrative procedure laws. *See, e.g.*, Regulatory Flexibility Act, 5 U.S.C. ch. 6 § 601 *et seq.*; Paperwork Reduction Act, 44 U.S.C. ch. 1 § 101, 44 U.S.C. ch. 35, subch. I § 3501 *et seq.*; Unfunded Mandates Reform Act, Pub. L. 104-4; Information Quality Act, Pub. L. 106-554 § 515.
4. Administrative Procedure Act, *5 U.S.C.* § 551(4).

- the public can comment on proposed rules and provide additional data to the agency;
- the public can access the rulemaking record and analyze data and analysis behind a proposed rule;
- the agency analyzes and responds to the public's comments;
- the agency creates a permanent record of its analysis and the rulemaking process; and
- the agency's actions can be reviewed by appropriate officials to ensure the correct procedure was followed.[5]

The Rulemaking Process

Federal agency rules can be created through "formal rulemaking" or "informal rulemaking." Formal rulemaking, which is rare, requires the consideration of a proposed rule during a trial-like hearing process. Most federal rules are created under informal notice and comment rulemaking.[6] In informal rulemaking, the APA generally requires federal agencies to publish a notice of proposed rulemaking (NPRM) in the *Federal Register*. The Congressional Research Service (CRS) explains the process as follows:

> The notice must contain (1) a statement of the time, place, and nature of public rulemaking proceedings; (2) reference to the legal authority under which the rule is proposed; and (3) either the terms or substance of the proposed rule or a description of the subjects and issues involved. After giving "interested persons" an opportunity to comment on the proposed rule, and after considering the public comments, the agency may then publish the final rule, incorporating a general statement of its basis and purpose. Although the APA does not specify the length of this public comment period, agencies commonly allow at least 30 days. Public comments as well as other supporting materials (e.g., hearing records or agency regulatory studies but generally not internal memoranda) are placed in a rulemaking "docket" which must be available for public inspection. Finally, the APA states that the final rule cannot become effective until at least 30 days after its publication unless (1) the rule grants or recognizes an exemption or relieves a restriction, (2) the rule is an interpretative rule or a statement of policy, or (3) the agency determines that the rule should take effect sooner for good cause and publishes that determination with the rule.[7]

See the website of Office of the *Federal Register*[8] and the Federal Communication Commission[9] for a detailed and simple-to-understand step-by-step analysis of the federal rulemaking process.

5. Office of Directives Management, *Rulemaking*, U.S. Department of State, https://www.state.gov/rulemaking/.
6. For information on other forms of Rulemaking, including "formal," "hybrid," and "direct final," see A Brief Overview of Rulemaking and Judicial Review, CRS Report No. R41546 (January 4, 2011–March 27, 2017), https://www.everycrsreport.com/reports/R41546.html.
7. *Id.*
8. Office of the Federal Register, A Guide to the Rulemaking Process, https://www.federalregister.gov/uploads/2011/01/the_rulemaking_process.pdf.
9. Federal Communications Commission, Rulemaking Process of the FCC, https://www.fcc.gov/about-fcc/rulemaking-process.

Recognized exceptions to the foregoing informal notice and comment procedures include

> when an agency finds, for "good cause," that those procedures are "impracticable, unnecessary, or contrary to the public interest." When agencies use the good cause exception, the act requires that they explicitly say so and provide a rationale for the exception's use when the rule is published in the *Federal Register*. The APA also provides explicit exceptions to the NPRM requirement for certain categories of regulatory actions, such as rules dealing with military or foreign affairs; agency management or personnel; or public property, loans, grants, benefits, or contracts. Further, the APA says that the NPRM requirements do not apply to interpretative rules; general statements of policy; or rules of agency organization, procedure, or practice. However, these rules do have to be published in the *Federal Register*.[10]

Further, Congress may overturn a "major" rule under the Congressional Review Act (CRA).[11] The CRA requires federal agencies to report their "major" rulemaking[12] activities to Congress, so it may consider legislation to overturn these rules (which it has done over 20 times) before they go into effect. Such rules must first be coordinated with the Office of Information and regulatory Affairs (OIRA) and the Office of Management and Budget (OMB). The Congressional Research Service has an outstanding discussion of the CRA.[13]

Adjudication is another way an agency can address issues within its statutory jurisdiction. Agency adjudications "typically resolve a claim or dispute between specific individuals in a specific case." Rulemaking, on the other hand, involves "forward-looking actions that affect the rights of broad classes of unspecified individuals."[14] Formal adjudication is required by statute, which typically involves an adversarial trial, whereas informal adjudication, provides the Agency flexibility to resolve the dispute without regard to

10. *Id.*; see also Kyle Schneider, *Judicial Review of Good Cause Determinations Under the Administration Procedure Act*, 73 *Stanford L. Rev.* (2021) for an excellent discussion of the "good cause" exception for the APA, https://review.law.stanford.edu/wp-content/uploads/sites/3/2021/01/Schneider-73-Stan.-L.-Rev.-237.pdf#:~:text=Stanford%20Law%20Review%20Volume%2073%20January%202021%20NOTE,notice-%20and-comment%20procedures%20when%20justified%20by%20%E2%80%9Cgood%20cause.%E2%80%9D.
11. Congressional Review Act (CRA), 5 U.S.C.§ 801 (a) (1) (A)).
12. In accordance with 5 U.S.C. § 804(2), a "major rule" is defined as "(A) an annual effect on the economy of $100,000,000 or more; (B) a major increase in costs or prices for consumers, individual industries, Federal, State, or local government agencies, or geographic regions; or (C) significant adverse effects on competition, employment, investment, productivity, innovation, or on the ability of United States-based enterprises to compete with foreign-based enterprises in domestic and export markets." *See* Memorandum from Russell T. Vaught, Acting Director, Office of Management and Budget to All Federal Agency Heads, Guidance on Compliance with the Congressional Review Act (April 11, 2019), https://www.whitehouse.gov/wp-content/uploads/2019/04/M-19-14.pdf.
13. Congressional Research Service, *The Congressional Review Act (CRA): Frequently Asked Questions* (Nov. 12, 2021), https://sgp.fas.org/crs/misc/R43992.pdf.
14. Ben Harrington, Legislative Attorney, and Daniel J. Sheffner, *Informal Administrative Adjudication: An Overview*, Congressional Research Service (October 1, 2021), https://crsreports.congress.gov/product/pdf/R/R46930#:~:text=%E2%80%9CFormal%20adjudication%E2%80%9D%20describes%20adjudicative%20proceedings%20that%20are%20governed,a%20residual%20term%20for%20all%20other%20adjudicative%20proceedings.

formal trial procedures. Courts typically defer to an agency's decision to address issues through rulemaking or adjudication.[15]

Judicial Review and the Authority of the Courts to Overturn Arbitrary and Capricious Rules

Most agency rulemaking or adjudicatory decisions are subject to judicial review unless otherwise precluded by statute: "The presumption favoring judicial review of administrative action ... may be overcome by specific language or specific legislative history that is a reliable indicator of congressional intent."[16] With respect to judicial review, "[t]he APA requires courts to set aside rules that are 'arbitrary and capricious, an abuse of discretion, or otherwise not in accordance with law.'"[17]

Such a review is narrow and requires that an agency "examine the relevant data and articulate a satisfactory explanation for its action."[18] Specifically, the agency's explanation must show a rational connection between the facts found and the choice made: "If the agency has exercised its reasoned judgment, a reviewing court is not to substitute its judgment for that of the agency."[19] A court should invalidate agency determinations as arbitrary and capricious "if the agency has relied on factors which Congress has not intended it to consider entirely, failed to consider an important aspect of the problem, offered an explanation for its decision that runs counter to the evidence before the agency, or is so implausible that it could not be ascribed to a difference in view or the product of agency expertise."[20]

Examples of arbitrary and capricious decision-making that have been overturned by the courts include the following: the U.S. Bureau of Census deciding to include a citizenship question in the Census, where the reason given to justify adding the question was "improved citizenship data to better enforce the Voting Rights Act," which was not supported by the record and seemed "contrived"[21]; the Department of Homeland Security deciding to rescind the Deferred Action for Childhood Arrivals (DACA) policy, which was overturned because the DHS did not explain why it was terminating the forbearance policy, which was at the heart of DACA and was especially justified for young people brought to the United States as children that "only know this country as home"[22]; the Environmental Protection Agency deciding not to regulate greenhouse gases under the Clean Air Act (CAA) upon receipt of a petition for rulemaking by 19 private organizations, which was overturned and deemed arbitrary and capricious, as the agency "offered no reasoned explanation for its refusal to decide whether greenhouse gases cause or contribute to climate change" and the rationale was contrary to the statutory text of the CAA.[23]

15. *National Labor Relations Board v. Bell Aerospace Company*, 416 U.S. 267 (1974).
16. *Bowen v. Michigan Academy of Family Physicians*, 476 U.S. 667, 670 (1986).
17. *See* Scope of Review, 5 U.S.C. § 706(2)(A).
18. *FCC v. Fox Television Stations, Inc.*, 509 U.S. 502, 513 (2009).
19. *Motor Vehicle Manufacturers Association of U.S., Inc. v. State Farm Mutual Auto. Insurance Co.*, 463 U.S. 29, 43 (1983).
20. Id. at 43.
21. *Department of Commerce v. New York*, 139 S. Ct. 2551 (2019).
22. *Department of Homeland Security v. Regents, of the University of California*, 140 S. Ct. 1891 (2020).
23. *Massachusetts v. Environmental Protection Agency*, 549 U.S. 497 (2007).

Loper Bright Enterprises v. Raimondo[24] and the End of Deference to an Agency's Interpretation of a Law It Administers

In *Loper Bright*, the Supreme Court overturned 40 years of precedence and eliminated the deference courts gave to a federal agency's interpretation of the law that the agency administers. The doctrine that was overturned was referred to as *Chevron deference* based on the Supreme Court decision *Chevron U.S.A., Inc. v. Natural Resources Defense Council.*[25] *Under Chevron,* if the law is either "silent" or "ambiguous," the court will defer to the agency's reasonable interpretation of the law it administers and uphold the regulation if it "is based on a permissible construction of the statute."[26] Under *Chevron,* the Court acknowledged the technical expertise of the agency and determined it would not substitute its interpretation of the law for the reasonable interpretation of the agency. Further, an agency's interpretation of its own regulations was given "controlling weight unless it is plainly erroneous or inconsistent with the regulation."[27] This doctrine, of deferring to an agency's reasonable interpretation of its own regulations, is commonly referred to as "*Auer* deference." Some have predicted the demise of the *Auer* doctrine after *Loper Bright.*[28]

In *Loper Bright*, the Supreme Court carefully examined the Magnus-Stevens Fishery Conservation and Management Act, (heretofore the Act) which permitted fishing vessels to carry Federal monitors to limit the amount of fishing the vessel could perform. The Act permitted paying the cost of monitors in herring fisheries in the Pacific but did not expressly reference paying for monitors of Atlantic herring fisheries. The National Marine Fisheries Service (NMFS) passed a rule in 2020 that required the Atlantic fisheries to pay for monitoring on their ships. This rule was challenged and overturned in *Loper Bright Enterprises v. Raimondo*, 603 U.S. (2024). The Court found that the rule was inconsistent with the Act. Further, the Court overturned *Chevron* and determined that it would not provide any deference to the NMFS, finding that the Administrative Procedures Act required the Federal courts to interpret the laws, and did not authorize providing deference to Federal agency interpretations of a law. *Loper Bright* requires a court to render independent judgment regarding the interpretation of a law, even if the law is silent or ambiguous on the subject of the litigation, but a court is still permitted to agree with the agency's interpretation. The impact of the *Loper Bright* case is expected to be quite significant. It has been referred to as "the end of an era in administrative law."[29] It is expected to significantly increase litigation challenging agency rules and regulations. *Loper Bright* may also impact agency decisions to issue certain regulations that are not clearly authorized by the law, even if the law is silent or ambiguous and it in the public interest to do so. "In a world without *Chevron*, one would expect judges to find it harder to separate their judging from their politics."[30]

24. Loper Bright v. Raimondo, 603 U.S. 369 (2024)
25. *Chevron U.S.A., Inc. v. Natural Resources Defense Council,* 467 U.S. 837, 842–843 (1984).
26. *Id.*
27. *Auer v. Robbins*, 519 U.S. 452, 461 (1997).
28. *Chevron Deference's Demise Suggests Auer Won't Last Much Longer* by Sean Lyness, Bloomberg Law, July 10, 2024
29. "What *Loper Bright Enterprises v. Raimondo* Means for the Future of Chevron Deference" by Christopher J. Walker, *Yale Journal on Regulation* (June 28, 2024)
30. Id.

While *Loper Bright* requires a court to exercise its independent judgment when considering an agency's interpretation of an ambiguous statute, it does not require the court to disagree with the agency. Courts in the exercise of their own judgment may still conclude that the agency has the best reading of an ambiguous statute.

West Virginia v. EPA[31] and the Major Questions Doctrine

The Supreme Court has always acknowledged that "Congress ... does not alter the fundamental details of a regulatory scheme in vague terms or ancillary provisions—it does not, one might say, hide elephants in mouseholes."[32]

In *West Virginia v. Environmental Protection Agency*[33], the Supreme Court substantially weakened *Chevron,*[34] *before it was officially overturned by Loper Bright.*[35] In their ruling, the Court found that the EPA was not authorized by Congress in Section 111(d) of the Clean Air Act to issue regulations which would restructure the Nation's overall mix of electricity and diminish the use of coal from 38% to 27% by 2030. The Court held that the regulatory initiative had to satisfy the **"major questions doctrine"** which provides that, in certain "extraordinary cases," federal agencies must have "clear congressional authorization" to regulate changes of great "economic and political significance." The majority held there was not clear congressional authorization for the EPA to issue such a generational shifting clean energy plan.[36] Accordingly, the regulations designed to combat global warming were struck down.

Under the major questions doctrine, Courts will not defer to agency discretion to regulate major agency initiatives of great economic and political significance unless Congress clearly and expressly delegates that specific regulatory authority to the agency. *West Virginia v. EPA* applies not only to environmental regulation but to any regulation, by any federal agency, that seeks to regulate a major question under the enabling statute. The impact of the major questions doctrine is significant because it will likely limit the reach and breadth of federal regulators in the future. Accordingly, caselaw interpreting this doctrine should be carefully monitored.

In *Biden v. Nebraska*, 600 U.S. 477 (2023) the Supreme Court ruled that the federal government overstepped its authority when it announced it would cancel up to $20,000 in individual student loans totaling up to 400 billion dollars affecting approximately 43 million Americans. The Biden Administration relied on the HEROES Act, which permits the government during a national emergency to "waive or modify" any statutory or regulatory provision involving student loans. Roberts concluded that the HEROES Act should not be interpreted to eliminate such an extensive debt without more express intent by Congress. Roberts relied on the Major Questions Doctrine to conclude that if Congress had wanted to give the Federal government such express authority to waive student loans of such a vast economic significance it

31. 142 S.Ct. 2587 (2022).
32. *Whitman v. Am. Trucking Associations*, 531 U.S. 457, 468 (2001).
33. 142 S.Ct. 2587 (2022).
34. *Supra* note 3.
35. *Loper Bright v. Raimondo*, 603 U.S. (2024)
36. *Supra* note 3.

would have clearly stated so. The foregoing words "waive or modify" were not sufficiently clear to give the Executive Branch such authority.

Leadership in the Context of a Constitutional Government and Administrative Law

The effective leader is accountable to the public and considers differing views in approaching and addressing problems and issues within the agency's jurisdiction. The federal agency rulemaking process is designed, in part, to make the government accountable to its citizenry. The notice and comment period for proposed rules informs the public of the reason and purpose of the rules and requires the federal government to consider differing views and perspectives prior to finalizing them. Thus, federal rulemaking, which is often complex, requiring regulatory analysis, internal and interagency reviews, and opportunities for public comments, can be quite challenging, time-consuming, and exhausting. However, it is, all the same, critical to an effective, transparent, and responsive government. As James Madison explained, "We may define a republic to be ... a government which derives all its powers directly or indirectly from the great body of the people and is administered by persons holding their offices during pleasure for a limited time, or during good behavior."[37] Rulemaking is a means by which the federal government is responsive to the "great body of the people," and it should be embraced by the public, federal employees, and leaders alike.

The federal government must also take care that its rules and actions are justified and not arbitrary and capricious. The insistence of well justified and well supported decision-making in accordance with the terms and conditions set forth in the statutory text, is another means by which the federal government is accountable to the public and aligns with the will of the Founding Fathers that the Executive Branch abide by Article II, Section 3 to "take care that the laws be fully executed."[38] Effective federal leaders embrace the responsibility and challenge of thoughtful decision-making, bound by reason, common sense, and the rule of law, and in doing so, they honor the will and vision of the Founding Fathers. Finally, in this era of the emergence of the Major Questions Doctrine, an additional burden will be placed on the Legislative Branch to be clear and comprehensive. To the extent that Congress fails to meet this legislative burden, the federal government will be unduly restricted in its ability to regulate and address changing circumstances. In such an environment, the need for effective leadership, including the ability to listen, learn, and bridge differences, will become more important and more valuable than ever.

Cases and Review Questions

Directions: Use the provided links to access each noteworthy case. Then, provide complete and detailed responses to the questions and prompts about each case.

37. https://founders.archives.gov/documents/Madison/01-10-02-0234
38. U.S. Const. art. II, § 3.

Massachusetts v. Environmental Protection Agency, 549 U.S. 497 (2007)

https://supreme.justia.com/cases/federal/us/549/497/

1. What was the EPA's explanation for not regulating greenhouse gases?
2. What was the petitioner's explanation for why the Clean Air Act compelled regulation of greenhouse gases?
3. Why did the Court rule the EPA's rationale for not legislating to be "arbitrary and capricious?
4. What can you and your agency do to avoid making decisions that may be characterized as arbitrary and capricious?

Loper Bright Enterprises v. Raimondo, 603 U.S. 369 (2024)

https://www.law.cornell.edu/supremecourt/text/22-451

1. *What law was reviewed by the Supreme Court in this case and why did the Court not grant deference to the agency's interpretation of that law?*
2. *Why did the Supreme Court overturn Chevron?*
3. *Why did the Supreme Court not apply stare decisis in this case?*
4. *What do you believe the impact of this decision will be on the Federal government?*

West Virginia v. Environmental Protection Agency, 142 S. Ct. 2587 (2022)

https://www.law.cornell.edu/supremecourt/text/20-1530

1. What is the major questions doctrine, and what impact will it have on rulemaking?
2. Can you identify any rules or regulations in your agency that may not be granted deference, if challenged in the courts?
3. What can an agency do to ensure their regulations will be granted deference by the courts in light of this case?

Biden v. *Nebraska*, 600 U.S. 477 (2023)

https://www.supremecourt.gov/opinions/22pdf/22-506_nmip.pdf

1. What role did the Major Questions Doctrine have in overturning Biden's Student Loan Forgiveness Program?
2. Why were the HEROES Act terms "waive" and "modify" insufficient to justify waiver of student loans? What if the amount of the student loan forgiveness program was substantially smaller, would the government be authorized to waive the loans? Are they authorized to delay the repayment of the loans?
3. What would Congress have to have stated in the HEROES Act to have provided the President with the authority to waive over 400 billion dollars in student loans?
4. What must Congress do, when passing legislation, to ensure it is authorizing the government to

act?

Chapter 13

An Overview of the Equal Protection Clause and Civil Rights Laws

This chapter provides a general overview of the Equal Protection Clause; describes how it impacts marriage, college admissions, and employment; and examines the impact of *Adarand v. Pena* and civil right laws on hiring in the federal government. Finally, there is a section addressing the analytical framework for determining whether an employee has been subjected to disparate treatment discrimination under civil rights law and examples of the kinds of decisions managers make that can make a manager vulnerable to an allegation of discrimination. The chapter concludes with a section on leadership in the context of a constitutional government followed by cases with review questions to promote class discussion.

The Equal Protection Clause

General Overview of the Equal Protection Clause

The Equal Protection Clause of the Fourteenth Amendment, applicable to the states, provides that "[n]o State shall ... deny to any person within its jurisdiction the equal protection of the laws. ... The central purpose of the Equal Protection Clause of the Fourteenth Amendment is the prevention of official conduct discriminating on the basis of race."[1] However, it applies to other forms of arbitrary government discrimination as well: "The purpose of the equal protection clause of the Fourteenth Amendment is to secure every person within the State's jurisdiction against intentional and arbitrary discrimination, whether occasioned by express terms of a statute or by its improper execution through duly constituted agents."[2]

1. *Washington v. Davis*, 426 U.S. 229, 239 (1976).
2. *Village of Willowbrook v. Olech*, 528 U.S. 562, 564 (2000) (quoting *Sioux City Bridge Co. v. Dakota County*, 260 U.S. 441, 445 (1923)).

Unlike the Fourteenth Amendment, the Fifth Amendment, which applies to the federal government, does not contain an express equal protection clause. However, the Supreme Court has applied the same equal protection analysis under the Fifth Amendment to the federal government as it has to the states under the Fourteenth Amendment.[3]

Strict Scrutiny, Intermediate Scrutiny, and Rational Basis in Equal Protection Claims

Any government action will be subject to one of three tiers of scrutiny by a court under the Equal Protection Clause. Those three tiers are Strict Scrutiny, Intermediate Scrutiny, and Rational Basis Scrutiny, and are discussed below.

Strict Scrutiny

Government decision-making is subject to tiers of scrutiny under the Equal Protection Clause as described below. If the challenged action involves a "suspect" class based upon race, alienage, national origin, or it infringes on a fundamental constitutional right, the "strict scrutiny" standard applies.[4] Under strict scrutiny, the action will be sustained only if the government can establish a "compelling interest" for its actions and the means chosen to achieve the interest are "narrowly tailored" to achieve the goal. Under strict scrutiny, the Supreme Court struck down race-based "set-asides" in government contracting[5] and race-based quotas in college admissions[6] but allowed race to be considered as a "plus" factor in college admissions.[7]

Intermediate Scrutiny

"Intermediate scrutiny," which is less demanding than strict scrutiny and is applicable to quasi-suspect classes, including gender and illegitimacy,[8] requires the government to show an "important interest" for its actions and the means chosen for achieving the interest to be "substantially related" to the important governmental objective.[9] Government entities "may not exclude qualified individuals based on 'fixed

3. *Adarand Constructors, Inc. v. Pena,* 515 U.S. 200. 214–18 (1995).
4. *Supra note 3.*
5. *Supra note 3.*
6. *Gratz v. Bollinger,* 539 U.S. 244 (2003).
7. *Grutter v. Bollinger,* 539 U.S. 306 (2003).
8. *United States v. Virginia (VMI),* 518 U.S. 515, 532–33, 116 S. Ct. 2264, 135 L. Ed. 2d 735 (1996); *Mississippi Univ. for Women v. Hogan*, 458 U.S. 718, 724, 102 S. Ct. 3331, 73 L. Ed. 2d 1090 (1982); *Craig v. Boren*, 429 U.S. 190, 197, 97 S. Ct. 451, 50 L. Ed. 2d 397 (1976); *Frontiero v. Richardson*, 411 U.S. 677, 682, 93 S. Ct. 1764, 36 L. Ed. 2d 583 (1973) (plurality opinion).
9. *Clark* v. Jeter, 486 U.S. 456, 461 (1988).

notions concerning the roles and abilities of males and females.'"[10] They may not, for example, arbitrarily make gender-based decisions regarding the drinking age of young adults.[11]

Rational Basis

If the government action does not burden a fundamental right or target a suspect class or quasi-suspect class as discussed in the preceding subsections, it will be upheld if there is a "legitimate" governmental objective for the action and the means of achieving it is "rationally related" to the objective.[12] This "rational basis" review is a very deferential standard, and governmental action is routinely upheld under it.[13]

Marriage and the Equal Protection Clause

In *Loving v. Virginia*, the Supreme Court held that Virginia's Racial Integrity Act of 1924, which prohibited interracial marriage, was intended to promote "White Supremacy."[14] The Court held that "restricting the freedom to marry solely because of racial classifications violates the central purpose of the Equal Protection Clause."[15] The case also established marriage as a fundamental right and overturned the 1924 law as violating substantive due process. *Loving* was subsequently cited in *Obergefell v. Hodges*,[16] to support same-sex marriage. To further support the right to marry, Congress passed the Respect for Marriage Act[17] on December 13, 2022. The bill, as summarized by the Congressional Research Service is as follows:

[The Respect for Marriage Act provides] statutory authority for same-sex and interracial marriages. Specifically, the bill replaces provisions that define, for purposes of federal law, marriage as between a man and a woman and spouse as a person of the opposite sex with provisions that recognize any marriage between two individuals that is valid under state law. (The Supreme Court held that the current provisions were unconstitutional in *United States v. Windsor* in 2013.) The Act also replaces provisions that do not require states to recognize same-sex marriages from other states with provisions that prohibit the denial of full faith and credit or any right or claim relating to out-of-state marriages on the basis of sex, race, ethnicity, or national origin. (The Supreme Court held that state laws barring same-sex marriages were unconstitutional in *Obergefell v. Hodges* in 2015; the Court held that state laws barring interracial marriages were unconstitutional in *Loving v. Virginia* in 1967.) The bill allows the Department of Justice to bring a civil action and establishes a private right of action for violations. The bill does not (1) affect religious

10. *United States v. Virginia*, 518 U.S. 515, 541–42, (1996) (Virginia Military Institute (VMI) could not explain or justify why female candidates were prohibited from attending the military.).
11. *Craig v. Boren*, 429 U.S. 190, 197 (1976) (heightened drinking age of men as compared to women could not be justified where there was insufficient statistical or antidotal evidence that younger males were more prone to the charge of driving while intoxicated than women).
12. *FCC v. Beach Communications, Inc.*, 508 U.S. 307, 313, 113 S. Ct. 2096, 124 L. Ed. 2d 211 (1993).
13. *But see City of Cleburne v. Cleburne Living Center*, 473 U.S. 432 (1985) (where the City of Cleburne, Texas could not even satisfy the rational basis standard when it denied a permit to a group home of residents with intellectual disabilities).
14. *Loving v. Virginia*, 388 U.S. 1 (1967).
15. *Id.* at 12.
16. *Obergefell v. Hodges*, 576 U.S. 644 (2015).
17. Respect for Marriage Act, H.R. 8404, https://www.govtrack.us/congress/bills/117/hr8404/text.

liberties or conscience protections that are available under the Constitution or federal law, (2) require religious organizations to provide goods or services to formally recognize or celebrate a marriage, (3) affect any benefits or rights that do not arise from a marriage, or (4) recognize under federal law any marriage between more than two individuals.[18]

College Admissions and the Equal Protection Clause

In two landmark 2003 Supreme Court cases, *Grutter v. Bollinger* and *Gratz v. Bollinger*, the U.S. the Supreme Court held that government funded universities considering race in college admissions are subject to strict scrutiny.[19] The Court, citing *Regents of the University of California v. Bakke,*[20] acknowledged in both cases that creating a diverse student body is a compelling reason to permit the consideration of race; however, it reached divergent results when examining whether the specific admissions processes of the different universities were "narrowly tailored" to achieve its goal of a diverse class. In *Grutter*, an admissions policy that considered race merely as a "plus factor" amongst many other weighted factors when evaluating each individual applicant, as opposed to awarding points to achieve a racial quota, survived the "narrowly tailored" test and strict scrutiny. In *Gratz*, however, the Court struck down an admissions policy as not narrowly tailored that gave specific points to applicants due to their race, which was akin to creating an unfair advantage and establishing a racial quota. This has been the law of the land for decades.[21]

On June 29, 2023, however, the Supreme Court, held in *Students for Fair Admissions* v. *President and Fellows of Harvard College*[22] that here was not a compelling reason to consider race as a plus factor in college admissions, and in so doing undermined affirmative action previously used by universities to increase diversity in their student body. Justice Roberts explained: "Both programs [Harvard and University of North Carolina] lack sufficiently focused and measurable objectives warranting the use of race, unavoidably employ race in a negative manner, involve racial stereotyping and lack meaningful end points." Justice Roberts did explain that an applicant's discussion of how race affected his or her life is permitted "so long as the discussion is concretely tied to a quality of character or unique ability that the particular applicant can contribute to the university." Justice Ketanji Brown Jackson, in her dissent stated: "With let-them-eat-cake obliviousness, today, the majority pulls the ripcord and announces 'colorblindness for all' by legal fiat. But deeming race irrelevant in law does not make it so in life."

18. Id.
19. *See supra* note 6; *see also supra* note 7.
20. *Regents of Univ. of California v. Bakke*, 438 U.S. 265 (1978).
21. *See, e.g.*, *Fisher v. University of Texas*, 579 U.S. 365 (2016).
22. *Students for Fair Admissions* v. *President and Fellows of Harvard College*, 600 U.S. 381 (2023) https://www.supremecourt.gov/opinions/22pdf/20-1199_hgdj.pdf.

Federal Employment and the Equal Protection Clause and the Impact of *Adarand v. Pena*

In *Adarand v. Pena,*[23] a case overturning race-based and national-origin-based "set-asides" for federal government contracting under the Fifth Amendment, the Supreme Court held that strict scrutiny is the standard of constitutional review for federal affirmative action programs that use racial or ethnic classifications as the basis for all federal government decision-making. *Adarand* relied, in part, on *City of Richmond v. J.A. Croson Co.*[24] and *Wygant v. Jackson Board of Education.*[25]

Adarand has been interpreted by the U.S. Department of Justice to require strict scrutiny in all race-based and national origin-based hiring and other employment decisions by the federal government.[26] The EEOC's Directive 715 (MD-715)[27] instructs agencies to refer to the foregoing Department of Justice "Post Adarand Guidance" in addressing *Adarand (hereinafter the DOJ Schmidt Memo)* and the legal limits on affirmative action.[28] This guidance does not endorse the consideration of race or other protected group status as a "plus factor" when making selections.

In accordance with the *DOJ Schmidt Memo,* a selecting official making a merit-based decision to hire or promote, should select the best qualified candidate, and not consider the race or ethnicity of the applicants. The very rare exception to this rule only applies when the agency can show (1) it intends to remedy the past effects of discrimination by the agency or (2) where the agency can establish a specific "operational need" to justify consideration of the applicant's race, ethnicity, gender, or other protected

23. *Supra* note 3.
24. *City of Richmond v. J. A. Croson Co.*, 488 U.S. 469 (1989) (overturning race- and national-origin-based set-asides in state and local government contracting under the Equal Protection Clause of the Fourteenth Amendment).
25. *Wygant v. Jackson Board of Education*, 476 U.S. 267 (1968) (a race-based layoff program agreed to by a local government school board and the teachers' union violated the Equal Protection Clause of the Fourteenth Amendment, where the government could not satisfy the demanding strict scrutiny standard).
26. *See* Walter Dellinger, *Legal Guidance on the Implications of the Supreme Court's Decision in Adarand Constructors, Inc. v. Peña*, 19 Office of Legal Counsel Opinions, 171, 177 (1995), https://www.justice.gov/sites/default/files/olc/opinions/1995/06/31/op-olc-v019-p0171_0.pdf; Memorandum from John Schmidt, Office of the Associate Attorney General, to all Federal Government Attorney Generals, Re: Post-*Adarand* Guidance on Affirmative Action in Federal Employment (Feb. 29, 1996) (heretofore referred to as the DOJ Schmidt Memo).
27. Foster B., Complainant, EEOC DOC 2019005682, 2021 WL 1925576, at *9 (Apr. 12, 2021) explains: "The Commission's MD-715 is the policy guidance which the Commission provides to federal agencies for their use in establishing and maintaining effective programs of equal employment opportunity under Title VII and the Rehabilitation Act. MD-715 provides a roadmap for ensuring that all employees and applicants for employment enjoy equality of opportunity in the federal workplace regardless of race, sex, national origin, color, religion, disability, or reprisal for engaging in prior protected EEO activity. Compliance with MD-715 is mandatory for all Executive agencies." See MD-715 ("Responsibilities") ("Agency Heads are responsible for the following: 1. Ensuring compliance with this Directive and those implementing instructions issued by EEOC in accordance with existing law and authority."). See also 29 C.F.R. § 1614.103(b)(2) ("This part applies to ... Executive agencies as defined in 5 U.S.C. 105 ..."); and 29 C.F.R. § 1614.102(e) ("Agency [EEO] programs *shall* comply with this part and the Management Directives and Bulletins that the Commission issues.") (emphasis added)."
28. EEOC, Frequently Asked Questions About Management Directive-715, Question 10, https://www.eeoc.gov/federal-sector/management-directive/frequently-asked-questions-about-management-directive-715.

civil rights category.[29] The decision regarding whether these exceptions apply will be made at the agency level after careful consultation by legal counsel, the agency Human Resources office (commonly referred to as OCHCO), and the agency Civil Rights office. A supervisor should never independently decide to apply these exceptions and should seek out legal counsel before considering anything other than selecting the best-qualified candidate. This equal protection analysis applies to all personnel decisions, from reassignment to removal—not just merit staffing.[30] An agency is, however, legally permitted to work with Human Resources and develop strategies to expand the pools of applicants.

The Analytical Framework for Determining Whether an Employee Has Been Subjected to Discrimination

A manager who must defend a personnel action against an allegation of discrimination should be aware of the analytical framework for processing a complaint of disparate treatment (intentional discrimination). The traditional analysis for evaluating a discrimination claim, where there is no direct evidence of discrimination (e.g., a statement or admission that the manager intentionally discriminated) is found in *McDonnell Douglas Corp. v. Green*.[31] Disparate treatment occurs when an employer treats some individuals in the workplace less favorably than others because of their membership in a protected group covered by a civil rights statute.[32] In a nonselection case, where no direct evidence of discrimination exists, the complainant must initially show, as part of a *prima facie case,* that the complainant is a member of a protected group; applied and was qualified for the position at issue; was not selected; and an individual outside of complainant's protected group was selected.[33] The *prima facie* case is not rigid but varies in different factual contexts; essentially, a complainant must show actions taken by an employer, which, if unexplained, show that the employment decision was made based on discrimination.[34] The *McDonnell Douglas* analytical framework is designed to bring the litigants "expeditiously and fairly" to the ultimate question of whether the employer intentionally discriminated against the complainant. [35] Under *McDonnell Douglas*, the employer has the

29. *See also* DOJ Schmidt Memo at 5–10.
30. Some federal courts have dismissed Equal Protection Clause claims, holding that Title VII and its prohibition against discrimination "preempts" such constitutional allegations. *See Kaswatuka v. United States Dep't of Homeland Security,* 7 F.4th 327, 330–31 (5th Cir. 2021) (citing *Brown v. General Services Administration*, 425 U.S. 820, 835 (1976)) ("to the extent that allegations of constitutional violations 'arise out of the same facts' as employment discrimination allegations, they are preempted by Title VII." (emphasis added). Moreover, Equal Employment Opportunity Commission Administrative judges do not accept jurisdiction over such claims, addressing only the underlying statutory allegations of discrimination. *See, e.g., Martin Bettwieser, Complainant,* EEOC DOC 01A05107, 2001 WL 309362, at *2 (Mar. 20, 2001). Some courts, however, have accepted jurisdiction over Equal Protection Clause claims raised by federal employees through 42 USC 1983. *See Henley v. Brown,* 686 F.3d 634, 642 (8th Cir. 2012) ("while Title VII provides the exclusive remedy for employment discrimination claims created by its own terms, its exclusivity ceases when the employer's conduct also amounts to a violation of a right secured by the Constitution").
31. *McDonnell Douglas Corp. v. Green*, 411 U.S. 792 (1973).
32. *International Brotherhood of Teamsters v. United States,* 431 U.S. 324, 335 & n.15 (1977).
33. *McDonnell Douglas Corp. v. Green,* 411 U.S. 792 at 803.
34. *Furnco Construction Corp. v. Waters,* 438 U.S. 567 (1978).
35. *Texas Department of Community Affairs v. Burdine*, *450 U.S. 248, 253 (1981).*

burden of production, as opposed to persuasion, to identify a legitimate nondiscriminatory reason for its actions. In a nonselection case, this reason is almost always that the selectee was the best qualified candidate. Although this burden is easily met, an agency will not meet this burden if it fails to produce sworn affidavits in the investigative file justifying the nonselection.[36] Thus, the federal manager should take care to fully respond to an EEO investigator's questions.

The complainant then has the ultimate burden of persuasion to prove by a preponderance of evidence that is it is more likely than not that the reason articulated by the employer is merely a *pretext* for discrimination. It is worth noting that the complainant always has the burden to prove discrimination, as declared by the Supreme Court.[37]

> The factfinder's disbelief of the reasons put forward by the defendant (particularly if disbelief is accompanied by a suspicion of mendacity) may, together with the elements of the prima facie case, suffice to show intentional discrimination. Thus, rejection of the defendant's proffered reasons will *permit* the trier of fact to infer the ultimate fact of intentional discrimination ... .[38]

In other words, if the legitimate nondiscriminatory reason articulated by the manager does not make sense, the trier of fact is legally permitted to infer discrimination. To avoid an inference of discrimination, therefore, the federal manager should take care to ensure that their proffered reasons for taking the personnel action are credible and legitimate. For example, in a nonselection case, an inference of discrimination can derive from a finding that the complainant was "plainly superior" to the selectee.[39] A complainant/plaintiff is plainly superior to a selectee if the "differences in qualifications ... are of such weight and significance that no reasonable person in the exercise of impartial judgment could have chosen the candidate selected over the plaintiff for the job in question."[40]

Application of "procedural irregularities" may also constitute evidence of discrimination. For example, when an employer inconsistently applies its RIF criteria, or there are other procedural irregularities in the RIF process, the court considers the inconsistency to be evidence of discrimination.[41] Highly subjective reasons proffered by the employer, lack of documentation to support the decision, or evidence that contradicts the reasons articulated by the agency can support an inference of discrimination. As the DC Circuit explained, "To sum up, then, we believe that, when taken together, the evidence of a significant disparity in the candidates' qualifications, the highly subjective nature of the Secretary's proffered nondiscriminatory explanation, and the absence of any contemporaneous documentation supporting that explanation could lead a reasonable jury to disbelieve the Secretary and to reach a verdict in Hamilton's

36. *Toshia F., Complainant,* EEOC DOC 0120160388, 2018 WL 1255359, at *3 (2018) (enforced by EEOC DOC 2019004336, 2020 WL 634828, at *2 (2020)).

37. *St. Mary's Honor Center v. Hicks*, 509 U.S. 502, 511 (1993).

38. *Id.*

39. *See Billy L., Complainant*, EEOC DOC 2022001307, 2022 WL 16848697, at *4 (Oct. 31, 2022) (citing *Bauer v. Bailar*, 647 F.2d 1037, 1048 (10th Cir. 1981)).

40. *Celestine v. Petroleos de Venezuela SA*, 266 F.3d 343, 347 (5th Cir. 2001).

41. *Sanders v. Southwestern Bell Tel., L.P.*, 544 F.3d 1101, 1106–07 (10th Cir. 2008).

favor."[42] Or as the EEOC explained before finding discrimination in a nonselection case, "In sum, the record is bereft as to how the Selecting Official identified the five candidates he decided to interview, and how he ultimately came to select the Selectee rather than Complainant."[43]

Another factor to be considered that may raise questions of pretext is if the reasons articulated by the agency are inconsistent with the requirements of the position as posted on the vacancy announcement. Thus, the EEOC explained, "[C]omparing the agency's stated reasons with the duties and responsibilities of the position, as listed in the vacancy announcement, we find that the agency's reasons are not fully substantiated by the evidence on record."[44] But in another case, the EEOC found no discrimination where the reason for selecting selectee was social media experience, which was not listed in the vacancy announcement but was listed in the position description of the public affairs specialist position.[45]

A determination that the supervisor's testimony lacks credibility may also lead to a finding of discrimination:

> In finding that S3 was not credible when he testified that SE had better KSA responses, better communication skills, and better references, the AJ relied on the applicants' KSA responses, the absence of interviews during the selection process, Complainant's 2009 performance appraisal, and the applicants' references. In finding that S3 was not credible when he testified at the hearing that his first-hand knowledge of Complainant's performance deficiencies impacted his selection decision, the AJ relied on the differences between his affidavit testimony and his hearing testimony; he did not mention it [performance deficiencies] as a consideration in his affidavit testimony but did in his hearing testimony.[46]

In the foregoing case, the supervisor's reliance on the complainant's performance deficiencies, which were not previously raised in his sworn affidavit, made his testimony appear as if it were an **after–the–fact justification** for his nonselection. A supervisor never wants their testimony to appear like they are raising arguments for the first time just to win the case. As the Equal Employment Opportunity Commission has explained,

> The Commission notes that the credibility of the Agency's explanation is key and must be judged in light of all the evidence obtained. *See EEOC Compliance Manual Section 15. "Race and Color Discrimination."*, EEOC Notice No. 915.003, § V.A.2 (Apr. 19, 2006). A witness's credibility will be undermined if his or her explanation is unsupported by or contrary to the balance of the facts. *See id*. Similarly, the credibility of the witness's explanation can be called into question if it is unduly vague, appears to be an after-

42. *Hamilton v. Geithner*, 666 F.3d 1344, 1357 (D.C. Cir. 2012).
43. *William G., Complainant v. Mattis, Secretary of Defense*, EEOC DOC 0120160837, 2018 WL 1109732, at *3.
44. *Solidelle Wasser, Appellant*, EEOC DOC 01930995, 1993 WL 1506479, at *4 (1993).
45. *William C. Winter, Complainant*, EEOC DOC 0120122544, 2012 WL 5426936, at *5 (2012).
46. *Neil M., Complainant*, EEOC DOC 0720140005, 2016 WL 7433311, at *6 (2016).

the-fact justification or otherwise appears fabricated (e.g., the explanation shifts, or inconsistent reasons are given).[47]

Accordingly, a manager should take care that their EEO affidavit is full, fair, and responsive to the questions posed to them and that their testimony at trial is consistent with that affidavit. Further, to make a fair decision that minimizes the chances of a finding of discrimination, the federal manager and Human Resources department should ensure that the reasons taken to support the personnel action are credible, well documented, and supported by the record; the hiring procedures used are applied equitably and consistently; the vacancy announcement reflects all the relevant evaluation factors needed to perform the job successfully; and the overall merit staffing process, including the selection decision, appears fair, reasonable, and explainable.

Leadership in the Context of a Constitutional Government and Equal Protection and Civil Rights Law

As previously discussed, the Fifth and Fourteenth Amendments to the Constitution require equal protection of the laws in the federal workplace, and civil rights laws prohibit discrimination. The model manager must, of course, be careful to abide by these legal requirements and strive to treat staff equally. In the federal workplace, an effective leader is mindful that each employee is equal under the law of the workplace and entitled to equal treatment in the application of rules, policies, and practices under their supervision. Further, a model manager is careful to take a personnel action only for legitimate and well-documented reasons because failure to do so could render the supervisor vulnerable to a finding of discrimination and a violation of civil rights law as well as undermine the supervisor's status as a fair and impartial leader.

The supervisor should communicate with, listen to, and address the concerns of staff. The model supervisor is constantly in a state of self-awareness and self-examination. If staff employees are represented by a union, the supervisor should first seek out a labor relations specialist to ensure any future actions or consultations with staff are in accordance with federal labor law. Consultation with Human Resources is always wise before a vacancy announcement is issued to assess whether there are opportunities to expand the pool of potential applicants and diversify the office. Consultation with legal counsel is always advisable before making any decision that could render the supervisor vulnerable to a complaint of discrimination.

The model manager is a mindful leader who thinks before they act and seeks out timely and effective advice before making a personnel decision. The model manager embraces the principles of equality set forth in the Equal Protection Clause by the Founding Fathers and civil rights laws passed by Congress and seeks to create a model workplace. In so doing, the supervisor creates a more productive work environment that attracts the best and brightest staff and provides outstanding leadership in the context of a constitutional government.

47. *Owen L., Complainant*, EEOC DOC 2020000990, 2021 WL 3419340, at *15 (2021).

Cases and Review Questions

Directions: Use the provided links to access each noteworthy case. Then, provide complete and detailed responses to the questions and prompts about each case.

Loving v. Virginia, 388 U.S. 1 (1967)

https://supreme.justia.com/cases/federal/us/388/1/

1. What level of scrutiny did the Court apply to interracial marriage under the Equal Protection Clause?
2. How did the Court handle Virginia's argument that the state law at issue did not violate the Equal Protection Clause because it equally prohibited both Whites and Blacks from interracial marriage?
3. How did the Court address marriage under substantive due process?
4. What relationship did the Virginia Law prohibiting interracial marriage have with laws that permitted slavery?
5. What impact did *Loving v. Virginia* have on the right to marry?

Obergefell v. Hodges, 576 U.S. 644 (2015)

https://www.law.cornell.edu/supct/pdf/14-556.pdf

1. How did the Court address same-sex marriage under the Equal Protection Clause?
2. How did the Court address same-sex marriage under substantive due process?
3. Why did the Court grant certiorari to hear the case in the first place after the 6th Circuit ruled against same-sex marriage?
4. What was the Significance of *Loving v. Virginia* in this Case?
5. Why did Congress find it necessary to pass the Respect for Marriage Act in 2022?

United States v. Virginia, 518 U.S. 515 (1996)

https://www.law.cornell.edu/supct/html/94-1941.ZO.html

1. What was Virginia's argument to support its policy of excluding women from the Virginia Military Institute?
2. Why was the exclusionary policy found to have violated the Equal Protection Clause?
3. What level of scrutiny was applied in the case?
4. How did the Court address Virginia's offer to create a separate but equal Virginia Military Institute for Women?

Craig v. Boren, 429 U.S. 190 (1976)

https://supreme.justia.com/cases/federal/us/388/1/

1. What was the rationale for the law that permitted women to purchase beer at the age of 18 but required men to wait until they were 21?
2. What level of scrutiny did the Court apply to this case?
3. Why was the law struck down under the Equal Protection Clause?
4. What does this case instruct future policymakers on the facts and justification required to support a law or governmental policy?

St. Mary's Honor Center v. Hicks, 509 U.S. 502 (1993)

https://www.law.cornell.edu/supremecourt/text/509/502

1. What are the facts and holding in this Title VII discrimination case?
2. Who has the burden of proof in a disparate treatment discrimination case?
3. How does a complainant meet this burden of proof?
4. How can a complainant show a pretext for discrimination?
5. How does this case impact how a supervisor should justify and document a personnel decision?

Students For Fair Representation v. *Fellows of Harvard College*, 600 U.S. 181 (2023)

https://www.supremecourt.gov/opinions/22pdf/20-1199_hgdj.pdf

1. Why did the Supreme Court no longer permit universities to consider race as a plus factor in college admissions?
2. Can an applicant's race been considered at all?
3. What impact will this case have on affirmative action in college admissions?
4. What strategies can a university legally employ to ensure a diverse student body?

Adarand Constructors, Inc. v. Peña, 515 U.S. 200 (1995)

https://www.law.cornell.edu/supremecourt/text/515/200

1. What does *Adarand* hold regarding minority contracting in the federal government?
2. What impact does *Adarand* have on affirmative action hiring in the federal government?
3. What can a government employer do or not do after *Adarand* to promote affirmative action hiring?

Bostock v. Clayton County, Georgia, 140 S. Ct. 1731 (2020)

https://www.law.cornell.edu/supct/pdf/17-1618.pdf

1. What are the facts and holding in this case?
2. How did the Supreme Court justify same-sex employment discrimination being prohibited under Title VII?
3. How did the Supreme Court justify transgender employment discrimination being prohibited under Title VII?
4. What is the significance of this case regarding employer policies on harassment and other forms of anti-discrimination policies?

Chapter 14

An Overview of Substantive Due Process

Introduction

This Chapter focuses on the meaning of substantive due process. It also examines the decision in *Dobbs v. Jackson Women's Health Organization*[1] and how the current Supreme Court has substantially restricted its application in future cases.

An Overview of Substantive Due Process

Substantive due process protects certain fundamental rights from government intrusion absent narrowly tailored and compelling reasons. Procedural due process, set forth in Chapter 3, focuses on whether sufficient procedures, such as notice or a hearing, were given before the deprivation of that right. Substantive due process has been applied to enumerated and unenumerated rights in the Constitution. Substantive due process is rooted in the Fifth and Fourteen amendment's prohibition against unreasonably depriving an individual of "life, liberty and property." Some Supreme Court decisions have emphasized that the word "liberty"[2] prohibits the government from taking away certain fundament freedoms. Some decisions have found that substantive due process stems from a "penumbra"[3] of rights set forth in the Bill of Rights. The Supreme Court recently held, as discussed in more detail below, that an unenumerated right must only be upheld if it is "deeply rooted in the nation's history and tradition" (*Dobbs*).

Substantive due process has been applied, but not limited, to the following cases involving unenumerated rights:

1. 597 U.S. 215 (2022)
2. *Cruzan v. Director, Missouri Department of Health,* 497 U.S. 261 (1990)
3. *Griswold v. Connecticut, 380 U,S. 479 (1965)*

The right to control the education of a child voiding state laws mandating students to attend public school.[4]

The right of custody of one's children.[5]

The right of privacy which permits a married couple to use contraception.[6]

The right of unmarried individuals to use contraception.[7]

The right to interracial marriage[8]

The right to share a home with one's extended family.[9]

The right to refuse medical treatment.[10]

The right to same-sex intimacy.[11]

The right to same-sex marriage.[12]

In *San Antonio Independent School District v. Rodriguez*[13] plaintiff argued he had a fundamental right to an education and that wealth-based discrimination led to uneven distribution of funding of schools. The Supreme Court found there was no fundamental right to an education and wealth-based funding of schools was not subject to strict scrutiny analysis.

In Washington v. Glucksberg[14] *the Supreme Court found that aiding or abetting suicide was not a substantive due process right. The Court found that unenumerated rights could only be protected if they were "deeply rooted in the nation's history." The Court also noted that 49 of 50 states prohibited such activity. This decision was a minority opinion and was not followed, for example, in Lawrence v. Texas and Obergefell v. Hodges, until recently, when the Supreme Court issued its decision in Dobbs v. Jackson Women's Health Organization.*[15]

Substantive Due Process and the Right to an Abortion

In *Roe v. Wade,*[16] *the S*upreme Court recognized the right of privacy as it pertains to a woman's right to an

4. *Pierce v. Society of Sisters, 2*68 U.S. 510 (1925).
5. *Stanley v. Illinois,* 405 U.S. 465 (1972).
6. *Griswold v. Connecticut, 380 U,S. 479 (1965)*
7. *Eisenstadt v. Baird*, 405 U.S. 438 (1972)
8. *Loving v. Virginia, 3*80 U.S. 1 (1967)
9. *Moore v. City of East Cleveland,* 431 U.S. 494 (1977)
10. *Cruzan v. Director, Missouri Department of Health,* 497 U.S. 261 (1990)
11. *Lawrence v. Texas,* 539 U.S. 569 (2003)
12. *Obergefell v. Hodges, 576 U.S. 644 (2015).*
13. *San Antonio Independent School District v. Rodriguez,* 411 U.S. 1 (1973)
14. *Washington v. Glucksberg, 5*21 U.S. 702 (1997*)*
15. 597 U,S. 215 (2022).
16. 410 U.S. 113 (1973)

abortion. It found that states could not intervene in a person's decision to have an abortion during the first trimester of a pregnancy, states could regulate but not prohibit an abortion during the second trimester, and states could regulate and prohibit abortions after viability during the third trimester, unless necessary to save the life of the mother. Thus, the state's right to regulate an abortion increased as the period of pregnancy lengthened.

In *Planned Parenthood v. Casey,*[17] the Supreme Court upheld *Roe v. Wade's* holding that there was a fundamental right of privacy to have an abortion. However, it overturned Roe's trimester analysis, in favor of a viability analysis. The Supreme Court also altered Roe's strict scrutiny analysis with an undue burden analysis. This permitted a state to regulate an abortion even during the first trimester, unless it would create an undue burden on the right of a woman to have an abortion. *Casey* found that an undue burden occurred when a statute creates a substantial obstacle to the right to an abortion. Under this new standard the Supreme Court upheld four provisions of a Pennsylvania law,[18] but overturned the requirement to spousal notification prior to the abortion.

Both *Roe v. Wade* and *Planned Parenthood v. Casey* were overturned *by Dobbs v. Jackson Women's Health Organization.*[19] *Dobbs u*pheld a Mississippi law that bans almost all abortions after the fifteenth week of pregnancy, unless there was a medical emergency, or a severe fetal abnormality. The law did not make exceptions for rape or incest.

Dobbs found there was no fundamental right to an abortion. Thus, abortion rights were up to individual states, and state laws were subject to the lowest standard of review, rational basis. The decision cites *Washington v. Glucksberg f*or the proposition that rights unenumerated in the Constitution, will only be found if those rights are "deeply rooted in this Nation's history and tradition." The Court found that prior to the 20th century the right to an abortion did not exist in American law. The Court found that the *Roe* and *Casey* decisions were so poorly reasoned that they were not entitled to be followed under the well-established principal *stare decisis.*

The *Dobbs* decision elevates the *Washington v. Glucksberg* analysis for determining whether there was a substantive due process fundamental right. Many legal scholars have expressed concern that *Dobbs* could roll back other fundamental rights, like the right to same sex intimacy or marriage[20] Further, how are the courts expected to ascertain what the history and tradition was hundreds of years ago and why should the courts be controlled by a history and tradition that could perpetuate inequality as it were centuries ago?

17. 505 U.S. 833 (1992)
18. The Supreme Court upheld Pennsylvania's requirement that: a minor seeking an abortion would have to obtain parental consent, unless a court authorized the abortion; a woman would have to be given informed consent and provided certain information 24 hours before the abortion was performed; compliance with the foregoing would be exempted in the case of a medical emergency; and certain reporting requirements were imposed on the facility providing abortions.
19. 597 U.S. 215 (2022)
20. See *After the Supreme Court's Abortion Ruling, What Could Happen to Other Unwritten Rights?* By Kenji Yoshino, Washington Post Magazine, November 30, 2022. https://www.washingtonpost.com/magazine/interactive/2022/substantive-due-process-dobbs/

Leadership in the Context of a Constitutional Government and Substantive Due Process Rights

The government must be careful to act in a manner that does not violate the fundamental rights of its citizens. Those rights are more ambiguous after *Dobbs*. An effective leader will carefully consult with legal counsel before taking any action that could violate these rights. Moreover, when creating and implementing policy, a leader should carefully consider the adverse impact created by such a policy and minimize such an impact.

Cases and Review Questions

Directions: Use the provided links to access each noteworthy case. Then, provide complete and detailed responses to the questions and prompts about each case.

Dobbs v. Jackson Women's Health Organization, 597 U.S. 215 (2022)

https://www.supremecourt.gov/opinions/21pdf/19-1392_6j37.pdf

1. How does *Dobbs* reach its conclusion that there is not a fundamental right to an abortion?
2. How does the Court determine that fundamental rights should be "deeply rooted in our history and tradition?"
3. What impact does the Dobbs decision have on rights, in addition to abortion rights?

Griswold v. Connecticut, 381 U.S. 479 (1965)

https://www.law.cornell.edu/supremecourt/text/381/479

1. How does the Supreme Court reach its conclusion that a married couple has the right to use contraceptives?
2. How does the Supreme Courts understanding of substantive due process differ from the Court's decision in *Dobbs?*
3. Which case analysis do you agree with and why?

San Antonio Independent School District v. Rodriguez, 411 U.S. 1 (1973)

https://supreme.justia.com/cases/federal/us/411/1/

1. What does the Court rule regarding the Constitutional right to an education and how does it reach its conclusion?
2. What does the Court rule regarding whether wealth-based discrimination is subject to strict scrutiny and how does it reach its decision?
3. Do you agree with the Courts decision and why do you agree or disagree with it?

Appendix A

The Constitution of the United States: A Transcription

The Constitution of the United States of America, 1789.

We the People of the United States, in Order to form a more perfect Union, establish Justice, insure domestic Tranquility, provide for the common defence, promote the general Welfare, and secure the Blessings of Liberty to ourselves and our Posterity, do ordain and establish this Constitution for the United States of America.

Article. I.

Section. 1.

All legislative Powers herein granted shall be vested in a Congress of the United States, which shall consist of a Senate and House of Representatives.

Section. 2.

The House of Representatives shall be composed of Members chosen every second Year by the People of the several States, and the Electors in each State shall have the Qualifications requisite for Electors of the most numerous Branch of the State Legislature.

No Person shall be a Representative who shall not have attained to the Age of twenty five Years, and been seven Years a Citizen of the United States, and who shall not, when elected, be an Inhabitant of that State in which he shall be chosen.

Representatives and direct Taxes shall be apportioned among the several States which may be included within this Union, according to their respective Numbers, which shall be determined by adding to the whole Number of free Persons, including those bound to Service for a Term of Years, and excluding Indians not taxed, three fifths of all other Persons. The actual Enumeration shall be made within three Years after the first Meeting of the Congress of the United States, and within every subsequent Term of ten Years, in such Manner as they shall by Law direct. The Number of Representatives shall not exceed one for every thirty Thousand, but each State shall have at Least one Representative; and until such enumeration shall be made, the State of New Hampshire shall be entitled to chuse three, Massachusetts eight, Rhode-Island and Providence Plantations one, Connecticut five, New-York six, New Jersey four, Pennsylvania eight, Delaware one, Maryland six, Virginia ten, North Carolina five, South Carolina five, and Georgia three.

When vacancies happen in the Representation from any State, the Executive Authority thereof shall issue Writs of Election to fill such Vacancies.

The House of Representatives shall chuse their Speaker and other Officers; and shall have the sole Power of Impeachment.

Section. 3.

The Senate of the United States shall be composed of two Senators from each State, chosen by the Legislature thereof, for six Years; and each Senator shall have one Vote.

Immediately after they shall be assembled in Consequence of the first Election, they shall be divided as equally as may be into three Classes. The Seats of the Senators of the first Class shall be vacated at the Expiration of the second Year, of the second Class at the Expiration of the fourth Year, and of the third Class at the Expiration of the sixth Year, so that one third may be chosen every second Year; and if Vacancies happen by Resignation, or otherwise, during the Recess of the Legislature of any State, the Executive thereof may make temporary Appointments until the next Meeting of the Legislature, which shall then fill such Vacancies.

No Person shall be a Senator who shall not have attained to the Age of thirty Years, and been nine Years a Citizen of the United States, and who shall not, when elected, be an Inhabitant of that State for which he shall be chosen.

The Vice President of the United States shall be President of the Senate, but shall have no Vote, unless they be equally divided.

The Senate shall chuse their other Officers, and also a President pro tempore, in the Absence of the Vice President, or when he shall exercise the Office of President of the United States.

The Senate shall have the sole Power to try all Impeachments. When sitting for that Purpose, they shall be on Oath or Affirmation. When the President of the United States is tried, the Chief Justice shall preside: And no Person shall be convicted without the Concurrence of two thirds of the Members present.

Judgment in Cases of Impeachment shall not extend further than to removal from Office, and disqualification to hold and enjoy any Office of honor, Trust or Profit under the United States: but the Party convicted shall nevertheless be liable and subject to Indictment, Trial, Judgment and Punishment, according to Law.

Section. 4.

The Times, Places and Manner of holding Elections for Senators and Representatives, shall be prescribed in each State by the Legislature thereof; but the Congress may at any time by Law make or alter such Regulations, except as to the Places of chusing Senators.

The Congress shall assemble at least once in every Year, and such Meeting shall be on the first Monday in December, unless they shall by Law appoint a different Day.

Section. 5.

Each House shall be the Judge of the Elections, Returns and Qualifications of its own Members, and a Majority of each shall constitute a Quorum to do Business; but a smaller Number may adjourn from day to day, and may be authorized to compel the Attendance of absent Members, in such Manner, and under such Penalties as each House may provide.

Each House may determine the Rules of its Proceedings, punish its Members for disorderly Behaviour, and, with the Concurrence of two thirds, expel a Member.

Each House shall keep a Journal of its Proceedings, and from time to time publish the same, excepting such Parts as may in their Judgment require Secrecy; and the Yeas and Nays of the Members of either House on any question shall, at the Desire of one fifth of those Present, be entered on the Journal.

Neither House, during the Session of Congress, shall, without the Consent of the other, adjourn for more than three days, nor to any other Place than that in which the two Houses shall be sitting.

Section. 6.

The Senators and Representatives shall receive a Compensation for their Services, to be ascertained by Law, and paid out of the Treasury of the United States. They shall in all Cases, except Treason, Felony and Breach of the Peace, be privileged from Arrest during their Attendance at the Session of their respective Houses, and in going to and returning from the same; and for any Speech or Debate in either House, they shall not be questioned in any other Place.

No Senator or Representative shall, during the Time for which he was elected, be appointed to any civil Office under the Authority of the United States, which shall have been created, or the Emoluments whereof shall have been encreased during such time; and no Person holding any Office under the United States, shall be a Member of either House during his Continuance in Office.

Section. 7.

All Bills for raising Revenue shall originate in the House of Representatives; but the Senate may propose or concur with Amendments as on other Bills.

Every Bill which shall have passed the House of Representatives and the Senate, shall, before it become a Law, be presented to the President of the United States; If he approve he shall sign it, but if not he shall return it, with his Objections to that House in which it shall have originated, who shall enter the Objections at large on their Journal, and proceed to reconsider it. If after such Reconsideration two thirds of that House shall agree to pass the Bill, it shall be sent, together with the Objections, to the other House, by which it shall likewise be reconsidered, and if approved by two thirds of that House, it shall become a Law. But in all such Cases the Votes of both Houses shall be determined by yeas and Nays, and the Names of the Persons voting for and against the Bill shall be entered on the Journal of each House respectively. If any Bill shall not be returned by the President within ten Days (Sundays excepted) after it shall have been presented to him, the Same shall be a Law, in like Manner as if he had signed it, unless the Congress by their Adjournment prevent its Return, in which Case it shall not be a Law.

Every Order, Resolution, or Vote to which the Concurrence of the Senate and House of Representatives may be necessary (except on a question of Adjournment) shall be presented to the President of the United States; and before the Same shall take Effect, shall be approved by him, or being disapproved by him, shall be repassed by two thirds of the Senate and House of Representatives, according to the Rules and Limitations prescribed in the Case of a Bill.

Section. 8.

The Congress shall have Power To lay and collect Taxes, Duties, Imposts and Excises, to pay the Debts and provide for the common Defence and general Welfare of the United States; but all Duties, Imposts and Excises shall be uniform throughout the United States;

To borrow Money on the credit of the United States;

To regulate Commerce with foreign Nations, and among the several States, and with the Indian Tribes;

To establish an uniform Rule of Naturalization, and uniform Laws on the subject of Bankruptcies throughout the United States;

To coin Money, regulate the Value thereof, and of foreign Coin, and fix the Standard of Weights and Measures;

To provide for the Punishment of counterfeiting the Securities and current Coin of the United States;

To establish Post Offices and post Roads;

To promote the Progress of Science and useful Arts, by securing for limited Times to Authors and Inventors the exclusive Right to their respective Writings and Discoveries;

To constitute Tribunals inferior to the supreme Court;

To define and punish Piracies and Felonies committed on the high Seas, and Offences against the Law of Nations;

To declare War, grant Letters of Marque and Reprisal, and make Rules concerning Captures on Land and Water;

To raise and support Armies, but no Appropriation of Money to that Use shall be for a longer Term than two Years;

To provide and maintain a Navy;

To make Rules for the Government and Regulation of the land and naval Forces;

To provide for calling forth the Militia to execute the Laws of the Union, suppress Insurrections and repel Invasions;

To provide for organizing, arming, and disciplining, the Militia, and for governing such Part of them as may be employed in the Service of the United States, reserving to the States respectively, the Appointment of the Officers, and the Authority of training the Militia according to the discipline prescribed by Congress;

To exercise exclusive Legislation in all Cases whatsoever, over such District (not exceeding ten Miles square) as may, by Cession of particular States, and the Acceptance of Congress, become the Seat of the Government of the United States, and to exercise like Authority over all Places purchased by the Consent of the Legislature of the State in which the Same shall be, for the Erection of Forts, Magazines, Arsenals, dock-Yards, and other needful Buildings;—And

To make all Laws which shall be necessary and proper for carrying into Execution the foregoing

Powers, and all other Powers vested by this Constitution in the Government of the United States, or in any Department or Officer thereof.

Section. 9.

The Migration or Importation of such Persons as any of the States now existing shall think proper to admit, shall not be prohibited by the Congress prior to the Year one thousand eight hundred and eight, but a Tax or duty may be imposed on such Importation, not exceeding ten dollars for each Person.

The Privilege of the Writ of Habeas Corpus shall not be suspended, unless when in Cases of Rebellion or Invasion the public Safety may require it.

No Bill of Attainder or ex post facto Law shall be passed.

No Capitation, or other direct, Tax shall be laid, unless in Proportion to the Census or enumeration herein before directed to be taken.

No Tax or Duty shall be laid on Articles exported from any State.

No Preference shall be given by any Regulation of Commerce or Revenue to the Ports of one State over those of another: nor shall Vessels bound to, or from, one State, be obliged to enter, clear, or pay Duties in another.

No Money shall be drawn from the Treasury, but in Consequence of Appropriations made by Law; and a regular Statement and Account of the Receipts and Expenditures of all public Money shall be published from time to time.

No Title of Nobility shall be granted by the United States: And no Person holding any Office of Profit or Trust under them, shall, without the Consent of the Congress, accept of any present, Emolument, Office, or Title, of any kind whatever, from any King, Prince, or foreign State.

Section. 10.

No State shall enter into any Treaty, Alliance, or Confederation; grant Letters of Marque and Reprisal; coin Money; emit Bills of Credit; make any Thing but gold and silver Coin a Tender in Payment of Debts; pass any Bill of Attainder, ex post facto Law, or Law impairing the Obligation of Contracts, or grant any Title of Nobility.

No State shall, without the Consent of the Congress, lay any Imposts or Duties on Imports or Exports, except what may be absolutely necessary for executing it's inspection Laws: and the net Produce of all Duties and Imposts, laid by any State on Imports or Exports, shall be for the Use of the Treasury of the United States; and all such Laws shall be subject to the Revision and Controul of the Congress.

No State shall, without the Consent of Congress, lay any Duty of Tonnage, keep Troops, or Ships of War in time of Peace, enter into any Agreement or Compact with another State, or with a foreign Power, or engage in War, unless actually invaded, or in such imminent Danger as will not admit of delay.

Article. II.

Section. 1.

The executive Power shall be vested in a President of the United States of America. He shall hold his Office during the Term of four Years, and, together with the Vice President, chosen for the same Term, be elected, as follows

Each State shall appoint, in such Manner as the Legislature thereof may direct, a Number of Electors, equal to the whole Number of Senators and Representatives to which the State may be entitled in the Congress: but no Senator or Representative, or Person holding an Office of Trust or Profit under the United States, shall be appointed an Elector.

The Electors shall meet in their respective States, and vote by Ballot for two Persons, of whom one at least shall not be an Inhabitant of the same State with themselves. And they shall make a List of all the Persons voted for, and of the Number of Votes for each; which List they shall sign and certify, and transmit sealed to the Seat of the Government of the United States, directed to the President of the Senate. The President of the Senate shall, in the Presence of the Senate and House of Representatives, open all the Certificates, and the Votes shall then be counted. The Person having the greatest Number of Votes shall be the President, if such Number be a Majority of the whole Number of Electors appointed; and if there be more than one who have such Majority, and have an equal Number of Votes, then the House of Representatives shall immediately chuse by Ballot one of them for President; and if no Person have a Majority, then from the five highest on the List the said House shall in like Manner chuse the President. But in chusing the President, the Votes shall be taken by States, the Representation from each State having one Vote; A quorum for this Purpose shall consist of a Member or Members from two thirds of the States, and a Majority of all the States shall be necessary to a Choice. In every Case, after the Choice of the President, the Person having the greatest Number of Votes of the Electors shall be the Vice President. But if there should remain two or more who have equal Votes, the Senate shall chuse from them by Ballot the Vice President.

The Congress may determine the Time of chusing the Electors, and the Day on which they shall give their Votes; which Day shall be the same throughout the United States.

No Person except a natural born Citizen, or a Citizen of the United States, at the time of the Adoption of this Constitution, shall be eligible to the Office of President; neither shall any Person be eligible to that Office who shall not have attained to the Age of thirty five Years, and been fourteen Years a Resident within the United States.

In Case of the Removal of the President from Office, or of his Death, Resignation, or Inability to discharge the Powers and Duties of the said Office, the Same shall devolve on the Vice President, and the Congress may by Law provide for the Case of Removal, Death, Resignation or Inability, both of the President and Vice President, declaring what Officer shall then act as President, and such Officer shall act accordingly, until the Disability be removed, or a President shall be elected.

The President shall, at stated Times, receive for his Services, a Compensation, which shall neither be encreased nor diminished during the Period for which he shall have been elected, and he shall not receive within that Period any other Emolument from the United States, or any of them.

Before he enter on the Execution of his Office, he shall take the following Oath or Affirmation:—"I do solemnly swear (or affirm) that I will faithfully execute the Office of President of the United States, and will to the best of my Ability, preserve, protect and defend the Constitution of the United States."

Section. 2.

The President shall be Commander in Chief of the Army and Navy of the United States, and of the Militia of the several States, when called into the actual Service of the United States; he may require the Opinion, in writing, of the principal Officer in each of the executive Departments, upon any Subject relating to the Duties of their respective Offices, and he shall have Power to grant Reprieves and Pardons for Offences against the United States, except in Cases of Impeachment.

He shall have Power, by and with the Advice and Consent of the Senate, to make Treaties, provided two thirds of the Senators present concur; and he shall nominate, and by and with the Advice and Consent of the Senate, shall appoint Ambassadors, other public Ministers and Consuls, Judges of the supreme Court, and all other Officers of the United States, whose Appointments are not herein otherwise provided for, and which shall be established by Law: but the Congress may by Law vest the Appointment of such inferior Officers, as they think proper, in the President alone, in the Courts of Law, or in the Heads of Departments.

The President shall have Power to fill up all Vacancies that may happen during the Recess of the Senate, by granting Commissions which shall expire at the End of their next Session.

Section. 3.

He shall from time to time give to the Congress Information of the State of the Union, and recommend to their Consideration such Measures as he shall judge necessary and expedient; he may, on extraordinary Occasions, convene both Houses, or either of them, and in Case of Disagreement between them, with Respect to the Time of Adjournment, he may adjourn them to such Time as he shall think proper; he shall receive Ambassadors and other public Ministers; he shall take Care that the Laws be faithfully executed, and shall Commission all the Officers of the United States.

Section. 4.

The President, Vice President and all civil Officers of the United States, shall be removed from Office on Impeachment for, and Conviction of, Treason, Bribery, or other high Crimes and Misdemeanors.

Article. III.

Section. 1.

The judicial Power of the United States, shall be vested in one supreme Court, and in such inferior Courts as the Congress may from time to time ordain and establish. The Judges, both of the supreme and inferior Courts, shall hold their Offices during good Behaviour, and shall, at stated Times, receive for their Services, a Compensation, which shall not be diminished during their Continuance in Office.

Section. 2.

The judicial Power shall extend to all Cases, in Law and Equity, arising under this Constitution, the Laws of the United States, and Treaties made, or which shall be made, under their Authority;—to all Cases affecting Ambassadors, other public Ministers and Consuls;—to all Cases of admiralty and maritime Jurisdiction;—to Controversies to which the United States shall be a Party;—to Controversies between two or more States;—between a State and Citizens of another State,—between Citizens of different States,—between Citizens of the same State claiming Lands under Grants of different States, and between a State, or the Citizens thereof, and foreign States, Citizens or Subjects.

In all Cases affecting Ambassadors, other public Ministers and Consuls, and those in which a State shall be Party, the supreme Court shall have original Jurisdiction. In all the other Cases before mentioned, the supreme Court shall have appellate Jurisdiction, both as to Law and Fact, with such Exceptions, and under such Regulations as the Congress shall make.

The Trial of all Crimes, except in Cases of Impeachment, shall be by Jury; and such Trial shall be held in the State where the said Crimes shall have been committed; but when not committed within any State, the Trial shall be at such Place or Places as the Congress may by Law have directed.

Section. 3.

Treason against the United States, shall consist only in levying War against them, or in adhering to their Enemies, giving them Aid and Comfort. No Person shall be convicted of Treason unless on the Testimony of two Witnesses to the same overt Act, or on Confession in open Court.

The Congress shall have Power to declare the Punishment of Treason, but no Attainder of Treason shall work Corruption of Blood, or Forfeiture except during the Life of the Person attainted.

Article. IV.

Section. 1.

Full Faith and Credit shall be given in each State to the public Acts, Records, and judicial Proceedings of every other State. And the Congress may by general Laws prescribe the Manner in which such Acts, Records and Proceedings shall be proved, and the Effect thereof.

Section. 2.

The Citizens of each State shall be entitled to all Privileges and Immunities of Citizens in the several States.

A Person charged in any State with Treason, Felony, or other Crime, who shall flee from Justice, and be found in another State, shall on Demand of the executive Authority of the State from which he fled, be delivered up, to be removed to the State having Jurisdiction of the Crime.

No Person held to Service or Labour in one State, under the Laws thereof, escaping into another, shall, in Consequence of any Law or Regulation therein, be discharged from such Service or Labour, but shall be delivered up on Claim of the Party to whom such Service or Labour may be due.

Section. 3.

New States may be admitted by the Congress into this Union; but no new State shall be formed or erected within the Jurisdiction of any other State; nor any State be formed by the Junction of two or more States, or Parts of States, without the Consent of the Legislatures of the States concerned as well as of the Congress.

The Congress shall have Power to dispose of and make all needful Rules and Regulations respecting the Territory or other Property belonging to the United States; and nothing in this Constitution shall be so construed as to Prejudice any Claims of the United States, or of any particular State.

Section. 4.

The United States shall guarantee to every State in this Union a Republican Form of Government, and shall protect each of them against Invasion; and on Application of the Legislature, or of the Executive (when the Legislature cannot be convened) against domestic Violence.

Article. V.

The Congress, whenever two thirds of both Houses shall deem it necessary, shall propose Amendments to this Constitution, or, on the Application of the Legislatures of two thirds of the several States, shall call a Convention for proposing Amendments, which, in either Case, shall be valid to all Intents and Purposes, as Part of this Constitution, when ratified by the Legislatures of three fourths of the several States, or by Conventions in three fourths thereof, as the one or the other Mode of Ratification may be proposed by the Congress; Provided that no Amendment which may be made prior to the Year One thousand eight hundred and eight shall in any Manner affect the first and fourth Clauses in the Ninth Section of the first Article; and that no State, without its Consent, shall be deprived of its equal Suffrage in the Senate.

Article. VI.

All Debts contracted and Engagements entered into, before the Adoption of this Constitution, shall be as valid against the United States under this Constitution, as under the Confederation.

This Constitution, and the Laws of the United States which shall be made in Pursuance thereof; and all Treaties made, or which shall be made, under the Authority of the United States, shall be the supreme Law of the Land; and the Judges in every State shall be bound thereby, any Thing in the Constitution or Laws of any State to the Contrary notwithstanding.

The Senators and Representatives before mentioned, and the Members of the several State Legislatures, and all executive and judicial Officers, both of the United States and of the several States, shall be bound by Oath or Affirmation, to support this Constitution; but no religious Test shall ever be required as a Qualification to any Office or public Trust under the United States.

Article. VII.

The Ratification of the Conventions of nine States, shall be sufficient for the Establishment of this Constitution between the States so ratifying the Same.

The Word, "the," being interlined between the seventh and eighth Lines of the first Page, The Word "Thirty" being partly written on an Erazure in the fifteenth Line of the first Page, The Words "is tried" being interlined between the thirty second and thirty third Lines of the first Page and the Word "the" being interlined between the forty third and forty fourth Lines of the second Page.

Attest William Jackson Secretary

done in Convention by the Unanimous Consent of the States present the Seventeenth Day of September in the Year of our Lord one thousand seven hundred and Eighty seven and of the Independance of the United States of America the Twelfth In witness whereof We have hereunto subscribed our Names,

G. Washington

President and deputy from Virginia

Delaware

George Read
Gunning Bedford, Jr.
John Dickinson
Richard Bassett
Jacob Broom

Maryland

James McHenry
Daniel of St. Thomas Jenifer
Daniel Carroll

Virginia

John Blair
James Madison, Jr.

North Carolina

William Blount
Richard Dobbs Spaight
Hugh Williamson

South Carolina

John Rutledge
Charles Cotesworth Pinckney
Charles Pinckney
Pierce Butler

Georgia

William Few
Abraham Baldwin

New Hampshire

John Langdon
Nicholas Gilman

Massachusetts

Nathaniel Gorham
Rufus King

Connecticut

William Samuel Johnson
Roger Sherman

New York

Alexander Hamilton

New Jersey

William Livingston
David Brearley
William Paterson
Jonathon Dayton

Pennsylvania

Benjamin Franklin
Thomas Mifflin
Robert Morris
George Clymer
Thomas FitzSimons

Jared Ingersoll
James Wilson
Gouverneur Morris

Appendix B

The Constitution: Amendments 11–27

Amendments 11-27," The Constitution of the United States of America, 1992.

AMENDMENT XI

Passed by Congress March 4, 1794. Ratified February 7, 1795.

Note: Article III, section 2, of the Constitution was modified by amendment 11. The Judicial power of the United States shall not be construed to extend to any suit in law or equity, commenced or prosecuted against one of the United States by Citizens of another State, or by Citizens or Subjects of any Foreign State.

AMENDMENT XII

Passed by Congress December 9, 1803. Ratified June 15, 1804.

Note: A portion of Article II, section 1 of the Constitution was superseded by the 12th amendment. The Electors shall meet in their respective states and vote by ballot for President and Vice-President, one of whom, at least, shall not be an inhabitant of the same state with themselves; they shall name in their ballots the person voted for as President, and in distinct ballots the person voted for as Vice-President, and they shall make distinct lists of all persons voted for as President, and of all persons voted for as Vice-President, and of the number of votes for each, which lists they shall sign and certify, and transmit sealed to the seat of the government of the United States, directed to the President of the Senate; — the President of the Senate shall, in the presence of the Senate and House of Representatives, open all the certificates and the votes shall then be counted; — The person having the greatest number of votes for President, shall be the President, if such number be a majority of the whole number of Electors appointed; and if no person have such majority, then from the persons having the highest numbers not exceeding three on the list of those voted for as President, the House of Representatives shall choose immediately, by ballot, the President. But in choosing the President, the votes shall be taken by states, the representation from each state having one vote; a quorum for this purpose shall consist of a member or members from two-thirds of the states, and a majority of all the states shall be necessary to a choice. [And if the House of Representatives shall not choose a President whenever the right of choice shall devolve upon them, before the fourth day of March next following, then the Vice-President shall act as President, as in case of the death or other constitutional disability of the President. —]* The person having the greatest number of votes as Vice-President, shall be the Vice-President, if such number be a majority of the whole number of Electors appointed, and if no person have a majority, then from the two highest numbers on the list, the Senate shall choose the Vice-President; a quorum for the purpose shall consist of two-thirds of the whole number of Senators, and a majority of the whole number shall be necessary to a choice. But no person constitutionally ineligible to the office of President shall be eligible to that of Vice-President of the United States. *Superseded by section 3 of the 20th amendment.

AMENDMENT XIII

Passed by Congress January 31, 1865. Ratified December 6, 1865.

Note: A portion of Article IV, section 2, of the Constitution was superseded by the 13th amendment.

Section 1.

Neither slavery nor involuntary servitude, except as a punishment for crime whereof the party shall have been duly convicted, shall exist within the United States, or any place subject to their jurisdiction.

Section 2.

Congress shall have power to enforce this article by appropriate legislation.

AMENDMENT XIV

Passed by Congress June 13, 1866. Ratified July 9, 1868.

Note: Article I, section 2, of the Constitution was modified by section 2 of the 14th amendment.

Section 1.

All persons born or naturalized in the United States, and subject to the jurisdiction thereof, are citizens of the United States and of the State wherein they reside. No State shall make or enforce any law which shall abridge the privileges or immunities of citizens of the United States; nor shall any State deprive any person of life, liberty, or property, without due process of law; nor deny to any person within its jurisdiction the equal protection of the laws.

Section 2.

Representatives shall be apportioned among the several States according to their respective numbers, counting the whole number of persons in each State, excluding Indians not taxed. But when the right to vote at any election for the choice of electors for President and Vice-President of the United States, Representatives in Congress, the Executive and Judicial officers of a State, or the members of the Legislature thereof, is denied to any of the male inhabitants of such State, being twenty-one years of age,* and citizens of the United States, or in any way abridged, except for participation in rebellion, or other crime, the basis of representation therein shall be reduced in the proportion which the number of such male citizens shall bear to the whole number of male citizens twenty-one years of age in such State.

Section 3.

No person shall be a Senator or Representative in Congress, or elector of President and Vice-President, or hold any office, civil or military, under the United States, or under any State, who, having previously taken an oath, as a member of Congress, or as an officer of the United States, or as a member of any State legislature, or as an executive or judicial officer of any State, to support the Constitution of the United States, shall have engaged in insurrection or rebellion against the same, or given aid or comfort to the enemies thereof. But Congress may by a vote of two-thirds of each House, remove such disability.

Section 4.

The validity of the public debt of the United States, authorized by law, including debts incurred for payment of pensions and bounties for services in suppressing insurrection or rebellion, shall not be questioned. But neither the United States nor any State shall assume or pay any debt or obligation incurred in aid of insurrection or rebellion against the United States, or any claim for the loss or emancipation of any slave; but all such debts, obligations and claims shall be held illegal and void.

Section 5.

The Congress shall have the power to enforce, by appropriate legislation, the provisions of this article.

**Changed by section 1 of the 26th amendment.*

AMENDMENT XV

Passed by Congress February 26, 1869. Ratified February 3, 1870.

Section 1.

The right of citizens of the United States to vote shall not be denied or abridged by the United States or by any State on account of race, color, or previous condition of servitude—

Section 2.

The Congress shall have the power to enforce this article by appropriate legislation.

AMENDMENT XVI

Passed by Congress July 2, 1909. Ratified February 3, 1913.

Note: Article I, section 9, of the Constitution was modified by amendment 16.

The Congress shall have power to lay and collect taxes on incomes, from whatever source derived, without apportionment among the several States, and without regard to any census or enumeration.

AMENDMENT XVII

Passed by Congress May 13, 1912. Ratified April 8, 1913.

Note: Article I, section 3, of the Constitution was modified by the 17th amendment.

The Senate of the United States shall be composed of two Senators from each State, elected by the people thereof, for six years; and each Senator shall have one vote. The electors in each State shall have the qualifications requisite for electors of the most numerous branch of the State legislatures.

When vacancies happen in the representation of any State in the Senate, the executive authority of such State shall issue writs of election to fill such vacancies: Provided, That the legislature of any State may empower the executive thereof to make temporary appointments until the people fill the vacancies by election as the legislature may direct.

This amendment shall not be so construed as to affect the election or term of any Senator chosen before it becomes valid as part of the Constitution.

AMENDMENT XVIII

Passed by Congress December 18, 1917. Ratified January 16, 1919. Repealed by amendment 21.

Section 1.

After one year from the ratification of this article the manufacture, sale, or transportation of intoxicating liquors within, the importation thereof into, or the exportation thereof from the United States and all territory subject to the jurisdiction thereof for beverage purposes is hereby prohibited.

Section 2.

The Congress and the several States shall have concurrent power to enforce this article by appropriate legislation.

Section 3.

This article shall be inoperative unless it shall have been ratified as an amendment to the Constitution by the legislatures of the several States, as provided in the Constitution, within seven years from the date of the submission hereof to the States by the Congress.

AMENDMENT XIX

Passed by Congress June 4, 1919. Ratified August 18, 1920.

The right of citizens of the United States to vote shall not be denied or abridged by the United States or by any State on account of sex.

Congress shall have power to enforce this article by appropriate legislation.

AMENDMENT XX

Passed by Congress March 2, 1932. Ratified January 23, 1933.

Note: Article I, section 4, of the Constitution was modified by section 2 of this amendment. In addition, a portion of the 12th amendment was superseded by section 3.

Section 1.

The terms of the President and the Vice President shall end at noon on the 20th day of January, and the terms of Senators and Representatives at noon on the 3d day of January, of the years in which such terms would have ended if this article had not been ratified; and the terms of their successors shall then begin.

Section 2.

The Congress shall assemble at least once in every year, and such meeting shall begin at noon on the 3d day of January, unless they shall by law appoint a different day.

Section 3.

If, at the time fixed for the beginning of the term of the President, the President elect shall have died, the Vice President elect shall become President. If a President shall not have been chosen before the time fixed for the beginning of his term, or if the President elect shall have failed to qualify, then the Vice President elect shall act as President until a President shall have qualified; and the Congress may by law provide for the case wherein neither a President elect nor a Vice President elect shall have qualified, declaring who shall then act as President, or the manner in which one who is to act shall be selected, and such person shall act accordingly until a President or Vice President shall have qualified.

Section 4.

The Congress may by law provide for the case of the death of any of the persons from whom the House of Representatives may choose a President whenever the right of choice shall have devolved upon them, and for the case of the death of any of the persons from whom the Senate may choose a Vice President whenever the right of choice shall have devolved upon them.

Section 5.

Sections 1 and 2 shall take effect on the 15th day of October following the ratification of this article.

Section 6.

This article shall be inoperative unless it shall have been ratified as an amendment to the Constitution by the legislatures of three-fourths of the several States within seven years from the date of its submission.

AMENDMENT XXI

Passed by Congress February 20, 1933. Ratified December 5, 1933.

Section 1.

The eighteenth article of amendment to the Constitution of the United States is hereby repealed.

Section 2.

The transportation or importation into any State, Territory, or possession of the United States for delivery or use therein of intoxicating liquors, in violation of the laws thereof, is hereby prohibited.

Section 3.

This article shall be inoperative unless it shall have been ratified as an amendment to the Constitution by conventions in the several States, as provided in the Constitution, within seven years from the date of the submission hereof to the States by the Congress.

AMENDMENT XXII

Passed by Congress March 21, 1947. Ratified February 27, 1951.

Section 1.

No person shall be elected to the office of the President more than twice, and no person who has held the office of President, or acted as President, for more than two years of a term to which some other person was elected President shall be elected to the office of the President more than once. But this Article shall not apply to any person holding the office of President when this Article was proposed by the Congress, and shall not prevent any person who may be holding the office of President, or acting as President, during the term within which this Article becomes operative from holding the office of President or acting as President during the remainder of such term.

Section 2.

This article shall be inoperative unless it shall have been ratified as an amendment to the Constitution by the legislatures of three-fourths of the several States within seven years from the date of its submission to the States by the Congress.

AMENDMENT XXIII

Passed by Congress June 16, 1960. Ratified March 29, 1961.

Section 1.

The District constituting the seat of Government of the United States shall appoint in such manner as the Congress may direct:

A number of electors of President and Vice President equal to the whole number of Senators and Representatives in Congress to which the District would be entitled if it were a State, but in no event more than the least populous State; they shall be in addition to those appointed by the States, but they shall be considered, for the purposes of the election of President and Vice President, to be electors appointed by a State; and they shall meet in the District and perform such duties as provided by the twelfth article of amendment.

Section 2.

The Congress shall have power to enforce this article by appropriate legislation.

AMENDMENT XXIV

Passed by Congress August 27, 1962. Ratified January 23, 1964.

Section 1.

The right of citizens of the United States to vote in any primary or other election for President or Vice President, for electors for President or Vice President, or for Senator or Representative in Congress, shall not be denied or abridged by the United States or any State by reason of failure to pay any poll tax or other tax.

Section 2.

The Congress shall have power to enforce this article by appropriate legislation.

AMENDMENT XXV

Passed by Congress July 6, 1965. Ratified February 10, 1967.

Note: Article II, section 1, of the Constitution was affected by the 25th amendment.

Section 1.

In case of the removal of the President from office or of his death or resignation, the Vice President shall become President.

Section 2.

Whenever there is a vacancy in the office of the Vice President, the President shall nominate a Vice President who shall take office upon confirmation by a majority vote of both Houses of Congress.

Section 3.

Whenever the President transmits to the President pro tempore of the Senate and the Speaker of the House of Representatives his written declaration that he is unable to discharge the powers and duties of his office, and until he transmits to them a written declaration to the contrary, such powers and duties shall be discharged by the Vice President as Acting President.

Section 4.

Whenever the Vice President and a majority of either the principal officers of the executive departments or of such other body as Congress may by law provide, transmit to the President pro tempore of the Senate and the Speaker of the House of Representatives their written declaration that the President is unable to discharge the powers and duties of his office, the Vice President shall immediately assume the powers and duties of the office as Acting President.

Thereafter, when the President transmits to the President pro tempore of the Senate and the Speaker of the House of Representatives his written declaration that no inability exists, he shall resume the powers and duties of his office unless the Vice President and a majority of either the principal officers of the executive department or of such other body as Congress may by law provide, transmit within four days to the President pro tempore of the Senate and the Speaker of the House of Representatives their written declaration that the President is unable to discharge the powers and duties of his office. Thereupon Congress shall decide the issue, assembling within forty-eight hours for that purpose if not in session. If the Congress, within twenty-one days after receipt of the latter written declaration, or, if Congress is not in session, within twenty-one days after Congress is required to assemble, determines by two-thirds vote of both Houses that the President is unable to discharge the powers and duties of his office, the Vice President shall continue to discharge the same as Acting President; otherwise, the President shall resume the powers and duties of his office.

AMENDMENT XXVI

Passed by Congress March 23, 1971. Ratified July 1, 1971.

Note: Amendment 14, section 2, of the Constitution was modified by section 1 of the 26th amendment.

Section 1.

The right of citizens of the United States, who are eighteen years of age or older, to vote shall not be denied or abridged by the United States or by any State on account of age.

Section 2.

The Congress shall have power to enforce this article by appropriate legislation.

AMENDMENT XXVII

Originally proposed Sept. 25, 1789. Ratified May 7, 1992.

No law, varying the compensation for the services of the Senators and Representatives, shall take effect, until an election of Representatives shall have intervened.

Appendix C

The Bill of Rights: A Transcription

"The Bill of Rights," The Constitution of the United States of America, 1789.

On September 25, 1789, the First Congress of the United States proposed 12 amendments to the Constitution. The 1789 Joint Resolution of Congress proposing the amendments is on display in the Rotunda in the National Archives Museum. Ten of the proposed 12 amendments were ratified by three-fourths of the state legislatures on December 15, 1791. The ratified Articles (Articles 3–12) constitute the first 10 amendments of the Constitution, or the U.S. Bill of Rights. In 1992, 203 years after it was proposed, Article 2 was ratified as the 27th Amendment to the Constitution. Article 1 was never ratified.

Transcription of the 1789 Joint Resolution of Congress Proposing 12 Amendments to the U.S. Constitution

Congress of the United States begun and held at the City of New-York, on Wednesday the fourth of March, one thousand seven hundred and eighty nine.

THE Conventions of a number of the States, having at the time of their adopting the Constitution, expressed a desire, in order to prevent misconstruction or abuse of its powers, that further declaratory and restrictive clauses should be added: And as extending the ground of public confidence in the Government, will best ensure the beneficent ends of its institution.

RESOLVED by the Senate and House of Representatives of the United States of America, in Congress assembled, two thirds of both Houses concurring, that the following Articles be proposed to the Legislatures of the several States, as amendments to the Constitution of the United States, all, or any of which Articles, when ratified by three fourths of the said Legislatures, to be valid to all intents and purposes, as part of the said Constitution; viz.

ARTICLES in addition to, and Amendment of the Constitution of the United States of America, proposed by Congress, and ratified by the Legislatures of the several States, pursuant to the fifth Article of the original Constitution.

Article the first ... After the first enumeration required by the first article of the

Constitution, there shall be one Representative for every thirty thousand, until the number shall amount to one hundred, after which the proportion shall be so regulated by Congress, that there shall be not less than one hundred Representatives, nor less than one Representative for every forty thousand persons, until the number of Representatives shall amount to two hundred; after which the proportion shall be so regulated by Congress, that there shall not be less than two hundred Representatives, nor more than one Representative for every fifty thousand persons.

Article the second ... No law, varying the compensation for the services of the Senators and Representatives, shall take effect, until an election of Representatives shall have intervened.

Article the third ... Congress shall make no law respecting an establishment of religion, or prohibiting the free exercise thereof; or abridging the freedom of speech, or of the press; or the right of the people peaceably to assemble, and to petition the Government for a redress of grievances.

Article the fourth ... A well regulated Militia, being necessary to the security of a free State, the right of the people to keep and bear Arms, shall not be infringed.

Article the fifth ... No Soldier shall, in time of peace be quartered in any house, without the consent of the Owner, nor in time of war, but in a manner to be prescribed by law.

Article the sixth ... The right of the people to be secure in their persons, houses, papers, and effects, against unreasonable searches and seizures, shall not be violated, and no Warrants shall issue, but upon probable cause, supported by Oath or affirmation, and particularly describing the place to be searched, and the persons or things to be seized.

Article the seventh ... No person shall be held to answer for a capital, or otherwise infamous crime, unless on a presentment or indictment of a Grand Jury, except in cases arising in the land or naval forces, or in the Militia, when in actual service in time of War or public danger; nor shall any person be subject for the same offence to be twice put in jeopardy of life or limb; nor shall be compelled in any criminal case to be a witness against himself, nor be deprived of life, liberty, or property, without due process of law; nor shall private property be taken for public use, without just compensation.

Article the eighth ... In all criminal prosecutions, the accused shall enjoy the right to a speedy and public trial, by an impartial jury of the State and district wherein the crime shall have been committed, which district shall have been previously ascertained by law, and to be informed of the nature and cause of the accusation; to be confronted with the witnesses against him; to have compulsory process for obtaining witnesses in his favor, and to have the Assistance of Counsel for his defence.

Article the ninth ... In suits at common law, where the value in controversy shall exceed twenty dollars, the right of trial by jury shall be preserved, and no fact tried by a jury, shall be otherwise re-examined in any Court of the United States, than according to the rules of the common law.

Article the tenth ... Excessive bail shall not be required, nor excessive fines imposed, nor cruel and unusual punishments inflicted.

Article the eleventh ... The enumeration in the Constitution, of certain rights, shall not be construed to deny or disparage others retained by the people.

Article the twelfth ... The powers not delegated to the United States by the Constitution, nor prohibited by it to the States, are reserved to the States respectively, or to the people.

ATTEST,

Frederick Augustus Muhlenberg, Speaker of the House of Representatives

John Adams, Vice-President of the United States, and President of the Senate

John Beckley, Clerk of the House of Representatives.

Sam. A Otis Secretary of the Senate

The U.S. Bill of Rights

Note: The following text is a transcription of the first ten amendments to the Constitution in their original form. These amendments were ratified December 15, 1791, and form what is known as the "Bill of Rights."

Amendment I

Congress shall make no law respecting an establishment of religion, or prohibiting the free exercise thereof; or abridging the freedom of speech, or of the press; or the right of the people peaceably to assemble, and to petition the Government for a redress of grievances.

Amendment II

A well regulated Militia, being necessary to the security of a free State, the right of the people to keep and bear Arms, shall not be infringed.

Amendment III

No Soldier shall, in time of peace be quartered in any house, without the consent of the Owner, nor in time of war, but in a manner to be prescribed by law.

Amendment IV

The right of the people to be secure in their persons, houses, papers, and effects, against unreasonable searches and seizures, shall not be violated, and no Warrants shall issue, but upon probable cause, supported by Oath or affirmation, and particularly describing the place to be searched, and the persons or things to be seized.

Amendment V

No person shall be held to answer for a capital, or otherwise infamous crime, unless on a presentment or indictment of a Grand Jury, except in cases arising in the land or naval forces, or in the Militia, when in actual service in time of War or public danger; nor shall any person be subject for the same offence to be twice put in jeopardy of life or limb; nor shall be compelled in any criminal case to be a witness against himself, nor be deprived of life, liberty, or property, without due process of law; nor shall private property be taken for public use, without just compensation.

Amendment VI

In all criminal prosecutions, the accused shall enjoy the right to a speedy and public trial, by an impartial jury of the State and district wherein the crime shall have been committed, which district shall have been previously ascertained by law, and to be informed of the nature and cause of the accusation; to be confronted with the witnesses against him; to have compulsory process for obtaining witnesses in his favor, and to have the Assistance of Counsel for his defence.

Amendment VII

In Suits at common law, where the value in controversy shall exceed twenty dollars, the right of trial by jury shall be preserved, and no fact tried by a jury, shall be otherwise re-examined in any Court of the United States, than according to the rules of the common law.

Amendment VIII

Excessive bail shall not be required, nor excessive fines imposed, nor cruel and unusual punishments inflicted.

Amendment IX

The enumeration in the Constitution, of certain rights, shall not be construed to deny or disparage others retained by the people.

Amendment X

The powers not delegated to the United States by the Constitution, nor prohibited by it to the States, are reserved to the States respectively, or to the people.

www.ingramcontent.com/pod-product-compliance
Ingram Content Group UK Ltd.
Pitfield, Milton Keynes, MK11 3LW, UK
UKHW051453290926
15471UKWH00008B/1173

9 781793 551504